Images of Modern America

AROUND BINGHAMTON

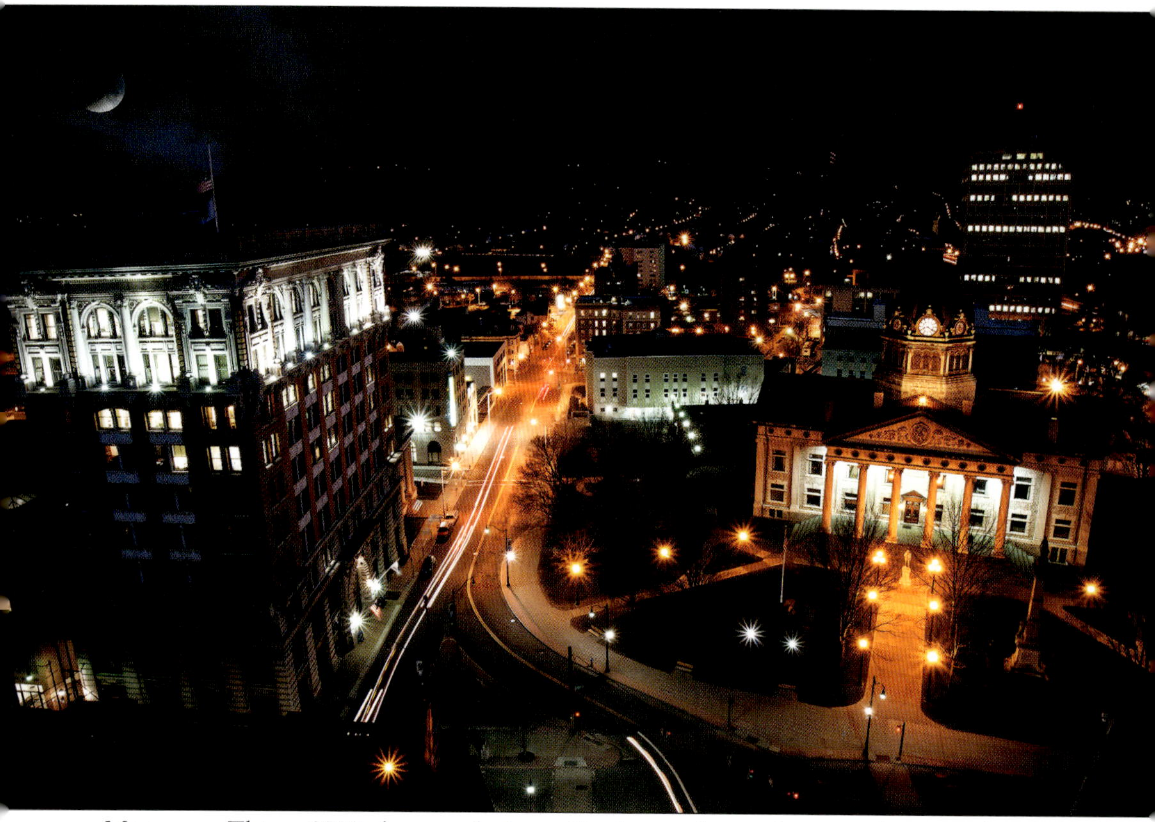

MOONRISE. This c. 2008 photograph shows Binghamton's courthouse and surrounding streets as the moon rises over the Security Mutual Insurance Building. This view is similar to the one Kevin Anderson, playing the role of Nick Kaminsky, has from his hotel room in the 1991 movie *Liebestraum*, which was shot in Binghamton. (Courtesy of Michael Ricciardi.)

ON THE FRONT COVER: Competitive cyclist Mark McCormack turns the corner of Henry and State Streets as part of the Chris Thater Memorial Races, around 1988, when McCormack competed in the junior division. In the background is the restaurant Burger Mondays. (Courtesy of Kirk Van Zanbergen.)

ON THE UPPER BACK COVER: This is a ground-level view of the annual Spiedie Fest and Balloon Rally. (Courtesy of Binghamton University.)

ON THE LOWER BACK COVER: (from left to right) Binghamton Mets manager Rick Sweet conducts a baseball clinic as part of Knothole Gang activities in 1996 (Courtesy of Binghamton Mets); cartoonist Johnny Hart and his family pose with golfer Lee Trevino in the early days of the B.C. Open (Courtesy of Michael McCann and the Alex Alexander Collection, Broome County Historical Society); Tony Lo Bianco portrays New York City Mayor Fiorello H. La Guardia in his one-man show, *The Little Flower*, a performance sponsored by the Goodwill Theatre Performing Arts Complex and Professional Training Academy in Johnson City (Courtesy of Tony Lo Bianco and the Goodwill Theatre).

Images of Modern America

AROUND BINGHAMTON

Jim Maggiore

ARCADIA PUBLISHING

ISBN 978-1-4671-2445-4

Published by Arcadia Publishing
Charleston, South Carolina

Printed in the United States of America

Library of Congress Control Number: 2016943662

For all general information, please contact Arcadia Publishing:
Telephone 843-853-2070
Fax 843-853-0044
E-mail sales@arcadiapublishing.com
For customer service and orders:
Toll-Free 1-888-313-2665

Visit us on the Internet at www.arcadiapublishing.com

This work is dedicated to the memory of Chris Thater. A Long Island native, Thater was killed by a drunk driver while cycling on a country road in Broome County in October 1983. He had graduated from Binghamton University only a few months earlier.

Contents

ACKNOWLEDGMENTS

This work owes its completion to the efforts of many: Sharon Ball, retired executive director of the Broome County Arts Council (BCAC); Laurie Bowen, director of the Levene Gouldin & Thompson Tennis Challenger Tournament; Yvonne Deligato, archivist at Binghamton University; Eric Eckman at the Bundy Museum of History and Art (BMHA); Gary George (GG), whose work was the foundation for the car racing material; Margaret Hadsell, town of Vestal historian; John Karedes, director of the Dick's Sporting Goods Open; Naima Kradijan, CEO of the Goodwill Theatre Performing Arts Complex and Professional Training Academy; Peg Johnston of the Cooperative Gallery; Suzanne Meredith, historian for the town of Union; Dave Pessagno from Broome County Community Charities; Michael Pipher, Rod Serling volunteer archivist and historian at the BMHA; Anthony Quagliata, founder of the Greater Binghamton Sports Hall of Fame; Jeff Smith, president of the Endwell Rotary Club; Michael Starke, director of the Binghamton Tennis Center; and Ryan Yarosh, director of media and public relations for Binghamton University. Last but not least, thanks go to all at the Endicott Visitor Center, including Colleen Becker and Jacqueline Tedesco; a wonderful copy editor, my daughter Alice Maggiore; and to the editors at Arcadia, Liz Gurley and Tim Sumerel.

All photographs are from my collection, unless otherwise noted. Sources are identified with the respective abbreviation: Binghamton University (BU), the Broome County Historical Society (BCHS), Binghamton Tennis Challenger Tournament (BTC), Chris Thater Races (CTR), Endicott Visitor Center (EVC), Goodwill Theatre (GT), Endicott History and Heritage Center (EHHC), Owego Historical Society (OHS), Rod Serling Archive at the Bundy Museum of History and Art (RSA @ BMHA), Spiedie Fest and Balloon Rally archives (SF), Town of Union Historical Society (UHS), Town of Kirkwood Historical Society (KHS), Town of Vestal History Center (VHC), and the private collections of David Burch (DB), Gert Byers (GB), Joe Donahue Jr (JD), Gary George (GG), Michael McCann (MM), Michael Pipher (MP), and Michael Ricciardi (MR). Thanks also go to the area Binghamton photographers whose work appears here: Justin Cohen (JC, photographer for Binghamton University); Kirk Van Zanbergen (KVZ, photographer for Chris Thater Races); Stephen J. Appel (SJA, photographer for Binghamton's Tennis Challenger Tournament); and Tom Ryder (TR, photographer for the Binghamton Senators and the Greater Binghamton Sports Hall of Fame [GBSHOF]).

And finally, thanks go to the University Archives, Special Collections, Binghamton University Libraries, Binghamton University, State University of New York (BU Special Collections) for giving me access to the archives; and to the Rod Serling Video Festival, the Rod Serling School of the Arts at Binghamton City Schools, and the Rod Serling Memorial Foundation for sponsoring the "Twilight Zone at 50" celebration, where Michael Ricciardi was one of the photographers.

INTRODUCTION

When people think of Binghamton and the surrounding area, ancillary discussions of it being a thriving community are not the norm. The Greater Binghamton Area, located in the Southern Tier of New York State, is often seen as being an area in decline, owing to its reliance on employment from manufacturers that have severely shrunken their area footprint or have become extinct. Today's area denizens remember all too well when the industrial behemoths Endicott-Johnson, IBM, and Link Aviation dominated the business news.

Recently, however, Greater Binghamton has started to rebound. Binghamton University and SUNY Broome continue to expand, and Binghamton has been named as one of the top 20 college towns in America by *the America Institute for Economic Research* and *Business Insider*. National corporations such as British Aerospace Marconi Electronic Systems (BAE), IBM, Lockheed Martin, and McIntosh continue to have a community presence while the number of active Rotary and booster clubs are prolific. Organizations such as the Southern Tier Young Professionals and the Broome County Arts Council promote a rich plate of cultural activities.

In 2015 Binghamton was selected as the 13th-best minor-league city in the nation, according to the *Sports Business Journal*. In December 2015, New York State's Southern Tier region (which stretches from Hancock to the east, Elmira to the west, Cortland to the north, and the Pennsylvania border to the south) won over $500 million in state aid to be distributed in $100 million increments over the next five years as part of the state's Urban Revitalization Initiative program. In the fall of 2015, the Tioga Downs "racino" received authority from the state to be developed into a full-fledged casino. Starting in 2017, the Floyd L. Maines Veterans Memorial Arena will host the annual New York State High School Basketball Championship Tournament.

The resurgent activity can be traced to the area's inherent resiliency, and while other photographic books discuss Greater Binghamton—Arcadia itself has published eight titles—no previous book captures the area's spirit of resiliency. This work focuses on the Greater Binghamton Area through its arts and sports, for in exploring these two areas, we learn about the commitment to community that permeates the lives of area denizens.

In the first chapter, "From Cigars to College Town and Beyond," we provide a short "then and now" depiction of Binghamton, while also capturing significant milestones in its development. In Chapter 2, we show how the arts community thrives. Whether it is the production of a mainstream movie set in the Southern Tier or a music video set in a local park, the Greater Binghamton Area has made its mark in films. The development of serious television drama owes a bit to Greater Binghamton as well, and the city's legacy includes being the hometown of *Twilight Zone* creator Rod Serling. Greater Binghamton also has the luxury of housing numerous venues for both its local and visiting talent; groups such as the Binghamton Philharmonic, Broadway in Binghamton, the Tri-Cities Opera, and various regional and collegiate theaters have made Binghamton a beacon for entertainment. Whether it is through exhibits at the Cooperative Gallery, the scheduling of classes and workshops at the Windsor Whip Works Art Center, or participation in international art festivals by the Anthony Brunelli Fine Arts Gallery, the arts community is a vibrant presence in Binghamton. This chapter also recognizes the individuals who have given the area a firm foothold in the arts, by discussing Binghamton's Walk of Fame.

Chapter 3, "Sports Mecca," discusses the heritage of baseball and hockey in the community, as an area's history in minor-league sports was one of the key criteria the *Sports Business Journal* used to rank America's minor-league cities. The area is one of the few in America that has hosted professional baseball for over 100 years and this history includes sending over 760 players to the majors. Among local sports fans, the area is sometimes referred to as "the Core of Big Apple Baseball." Entering 2016, the Binghamton area team has been either a Yankees' or a Mets' affiliate for 58 years—no other area in the nation has sent so many players to the Big Apple. Hockey has entertained fans since 1973 and during the hockey stoppage of 2004–2005, the area was home to a score of NHL players. The inaugural season of professional golf in the area was in 1971, as Endicott hosted its first golf tournament at the En-Joie Golf Club.

The area's diamonds, rinks, and links are not the only showcases for athletic talent, however. Tennis greats Billie Jean King, Andy Murray, Fred Stolle, and Rod Laver are just a few of the titans who have competed in locally sponsored tennis tournaments. Today, Binghamton's Recreation Park hosts the annual Levene Gouldin and Thomson Challenger Tennis Tournament, while Binghamton's downtown streets serve as the course for the annual Chris Thater Memorial Races. Finally, Binghamton is the home of two marathons a year, and for those who love speed, neighboring Kirkwood and Owego have a rich legacy of sports car racing, while Tioga Downs, in Nichols, New York, provides harness racing.

Interweaved throughout these chapters are tales of some of the famous events and protagonists of Greater Binghamton. As you turn these pages, you will be entertained, informed, and surprised, but keep in mind that whether it is supplying players for a World Series winner or introducing advancements in technology, the Greater Binghamton Area continues to add to its rich legacy, though pausing for some ignominious interludes as well.

One

From Cigars to College Town and Beyond

The city of Binghamton has had a meandering and undulating economic path, with steady growth populating the region until the latter part of the 20th century. For the past quarter century, the area has seen a steady decline, but now, riding on the coattails of the arts, higher education, and sports, the area shows signs of rebirth.

The area's forests, along with the opening of the Chenango Canal in 1847 and the arrival of the Erie Railroad in 1848, served as a foundation for the growth of Greater Binghamton. As the city became a transportation hub, it also became a manufacturing center for cigars, furniture, and lumber. Ornate mansions were built in downtown Binghamton, complete with sitting rooms, giving it an early appellation of "the Parlor City."

In the early 1900s, the development of the Endicott-Johnson Shoe Company drew thousands of immigrants from Eastern Europe. "Which way EJ?" was a common refrain of those arriving in the area, and the villages of Johnson City and Endicott grew dramatically. At the same time, IBM also was dramatically increasing its footprint in Endicott, giving the village the monikers of "the Magic City" and "the Valley of Opportunity." Back in Binghamton, in the same building that once housed the CTR (Computing Time Recording) company, which would later become IBM, Ed Link created a "blue box" flight simulator in the basement of his father's piano company. The simulation grew to become an internationally known company: Link Aviation.

Since the 1970s, manufacturing companies steadily left the area or, in the case of IBM, dramatically decreased its footprint. Through all the years, however, the undulating terrain of Binghamton has echoed the resiliency of its residents. The city, located at the confluence of the Chenango and Susquehanna Rivers, has seen major flooding in 1935, 1936, 1973, 2006, and 2011. To protect against future floods, structures such as the Endicott Girls and Boys Club and MacArthur Elementary School now reside on industrial stilts. Binghamton University and SUNY Broome, coming into existence shortly after World War II, have steadily grown and are major economic forces in the area. Binghamton University has extended into the city's downtown streets, serving as a catalyst for growth.

This opening chapter provides a sketch of Binghamton's history and its neighboring towns, laying the groundwork for a closer look at its culture in the ensuing chapters.

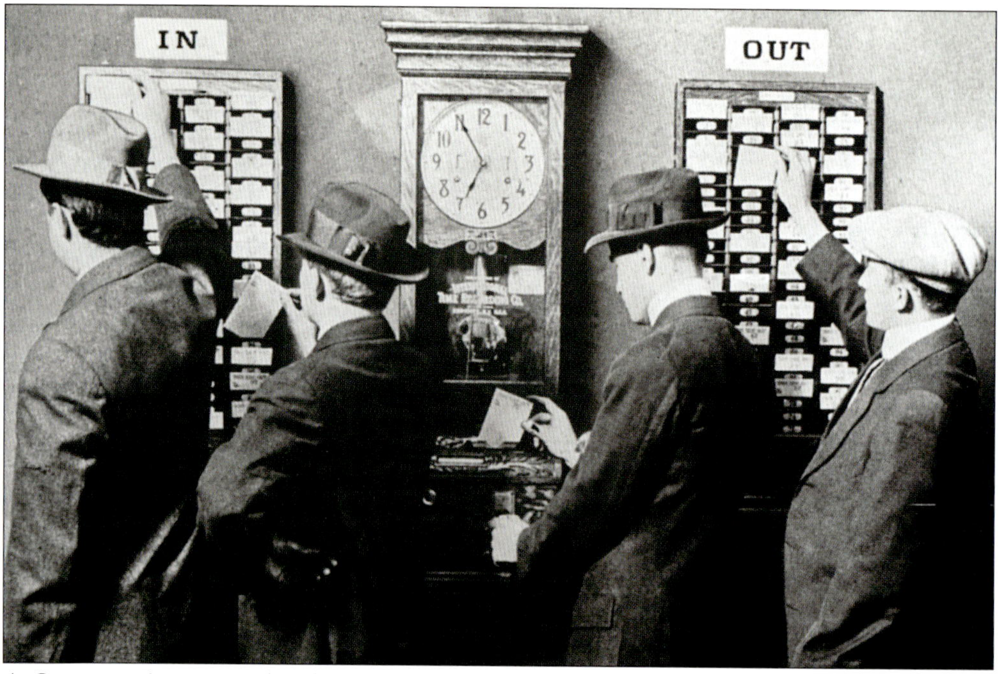

A CENTURY APART. In the above photograph, workers use the time clocks produced by the International Time Recording Company (ITR) to "punch" into work. Today, a wall mural in the Water Street Parking Ramp depicts this same photograph and is shown in the below image. In the early 1900s, the site of the Water Street Parking Ramp in downtown Binghamton housed one of the original buildings that manufactured these time clocks. ITR was one of the companies that merged to create the Computing Time Recording (CTR) in 1914, which changed its name to International Business Machines Corporation (IBM) on February 14, 1924. Besides its link to IBM in its nascent stage, the site of the parking ramp has also served as a home to the Link Piano Company, as well as the location where the Link flight simulator was first developed. Today, a series of colorful murals, painted by Binghamton's Department of Public Art, fill the Water Street Parking Ramp that pay tribute to the businesses that used to operate there. (Above, courtesy of EVC.)

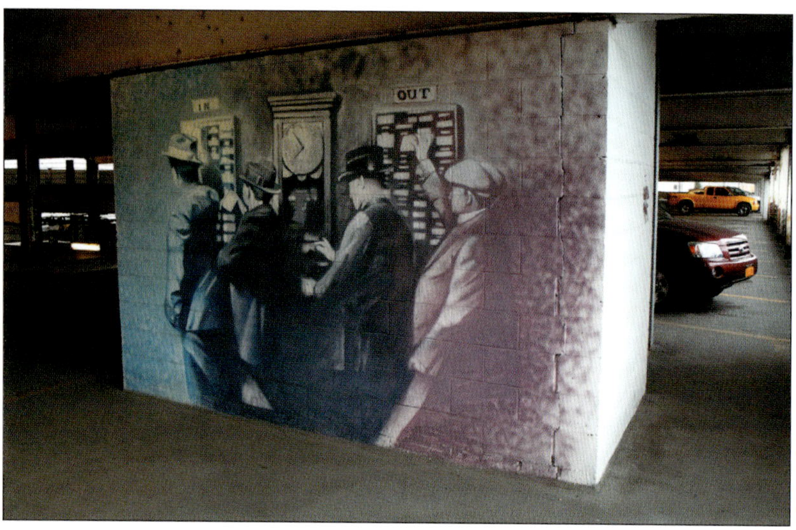

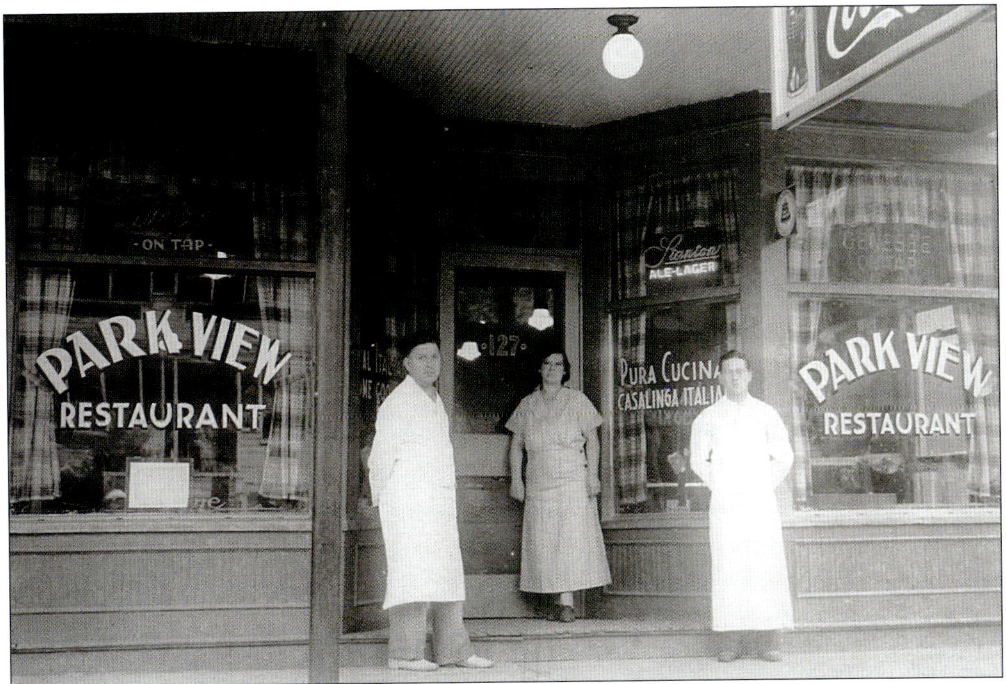

Spiedies Started Here. Above is a view of the Parkview Restaurant at 127 Oak Street in Endicott. According to documents stored in the Endicott Visitor Center, the Parkview was the first place in the area to sell spiedie sandwiches. Newspaper stories credit Camillo Iacovelli and his wife, Josephine, with bringing spiedies to the area. Josephine brought the recipe with her from Italy when she and Camillo came to America in 1921. Spiedies are small pieces of marinated meat (lamb, chicken, pork or beef) that can be skewered and then grilled; the name comes from the Italian words *spiedo* or *spiedini*, referring to meat cooked on a skewer. Below, some spiedies are on the grill at a recent Spiedie Fest and Balloon Rally at Binghamton's Otsiningo Park. After all these years, the delectable is still cooked over the grill. (Above, courtesy of EVC; below, courtesy of SF.)

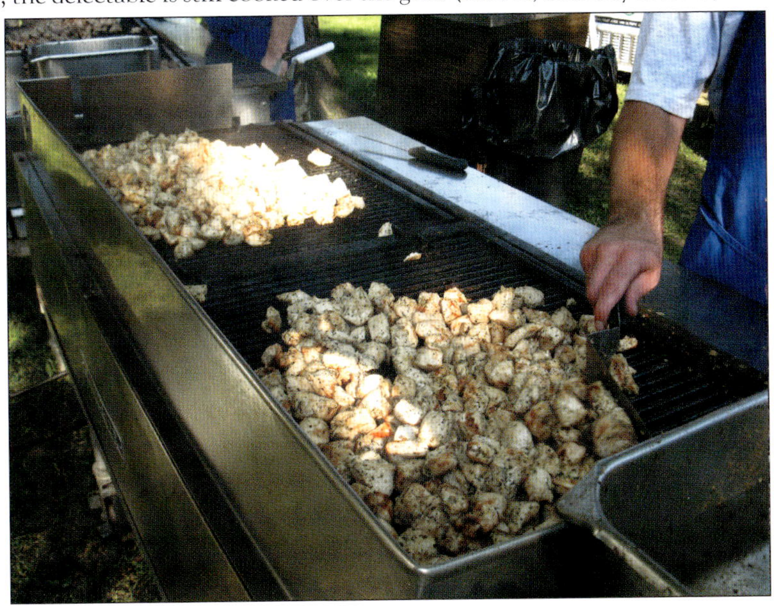

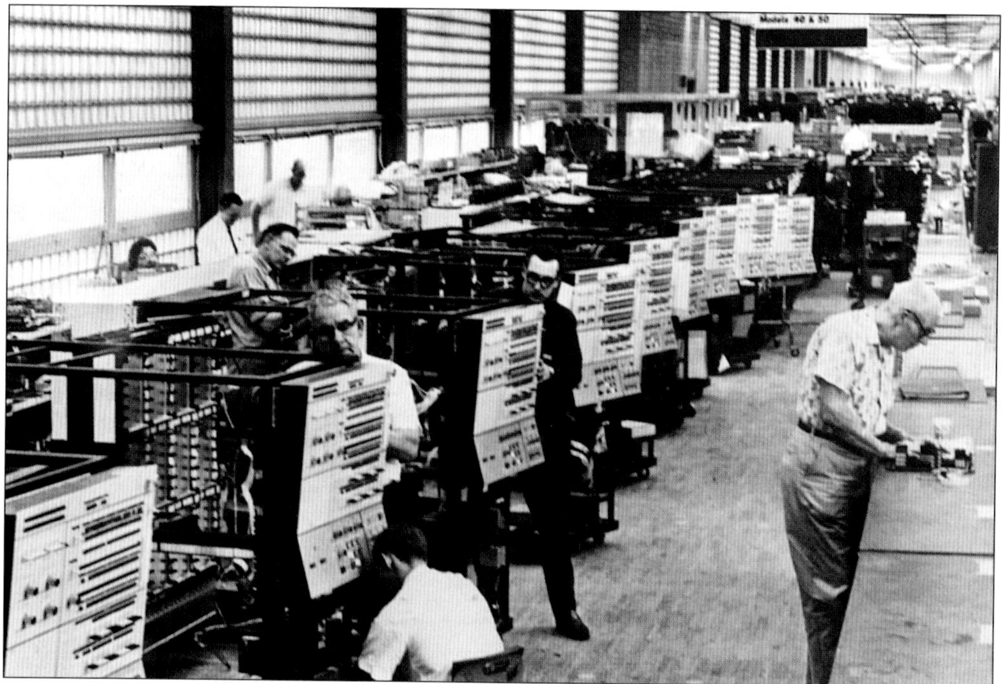

Banking on the 360. Above, IBM employees build computers that are part of the System/360 architecture in the 1960s. Developing this new line of computers was a dramatic step for IBM and fueled growth for the next few decades, as this architecture did not require businesses to rewrite their software when they upgraded computers. One of the reasons for IBM predecessor CTR expanding its business in Endicott in the early 1900s was the willingness of George F. Johnson to sell land in Endicott to the company. In the early 20th century, Thomas J. Watson was the CEO of CTR/IBM, and he and Johnson often shared ideas on leadership, with both firmly believing that workers were a company's most valuable asset. CTR officially changed its name to IBM in 1924. (Courtesy of EHHC.)

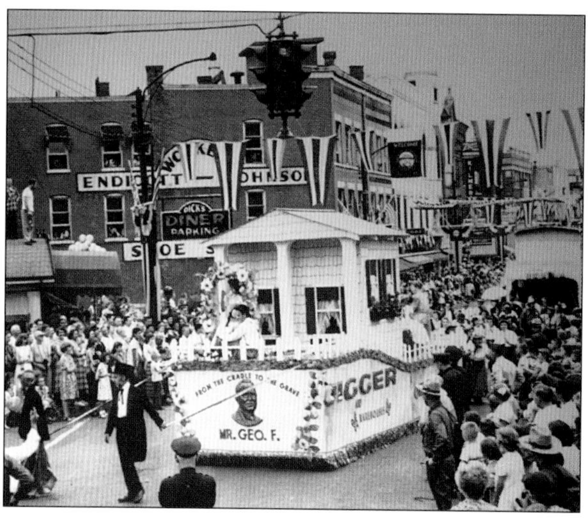

Everyone Loves a Parade. Seen here is a view of a parade down Main Street in Johnson City, with an Endicott-Johnson float in the foreground. In the early 1900s, the Endicott-Johnson Company was the biggest employer in the area, and EJ, as it became known, subsidized the building of homes for its employees. It was a wonderful life in Johnson City back then, and George F. Johnson was the "George Bailey" of the town. Perhaps it is not a coincidence the "EJ Homes," as they were called, did not have garages—better for people to walk and wear out their shoes. (Courtesy of EVC.)

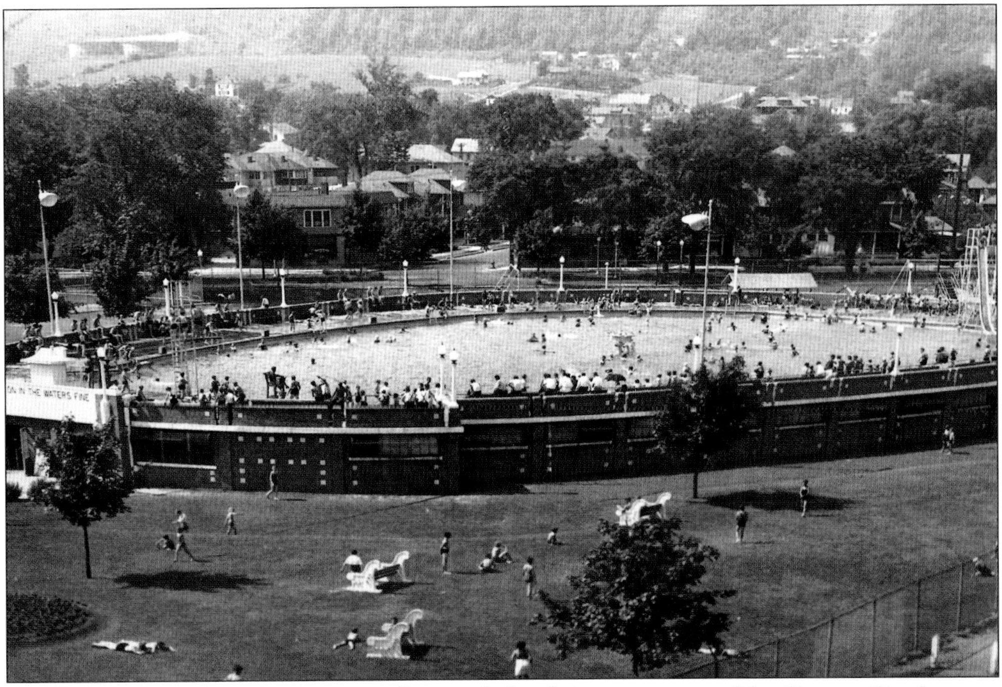

Iconic Pleasures. Two of the icons that symbolized the prosperity of the Greater Binghamton area in the 1950s are shown on this page. The above photograph shows the huge pool that was a popular attraction at Charles F. Johnson Park in Johnson City. The photograph below shows the IBM Country Club, which not only provided golf courses for use by its employees, but also provided billiards, bowling, and Ping-Pong in its game room, as well as a gym and numerous athletic fields. Bing Crosby was among the celebrities who golfed there. Today, the club is nonexistent and the area is in disrepair, ravaged by the September 2011 flood. (Both, courtesy of EVC.)

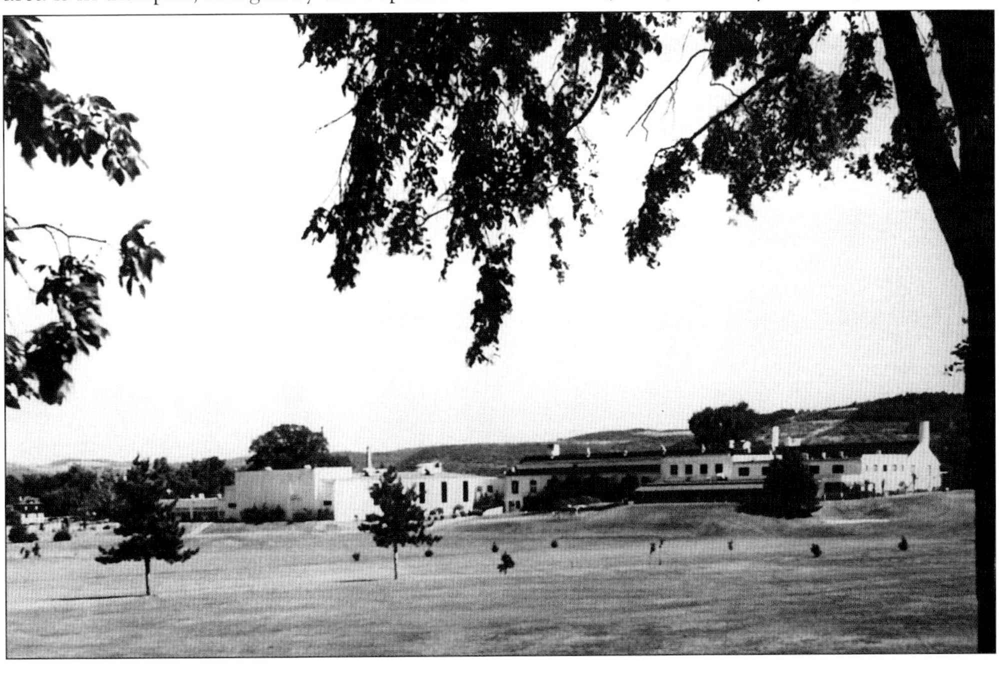

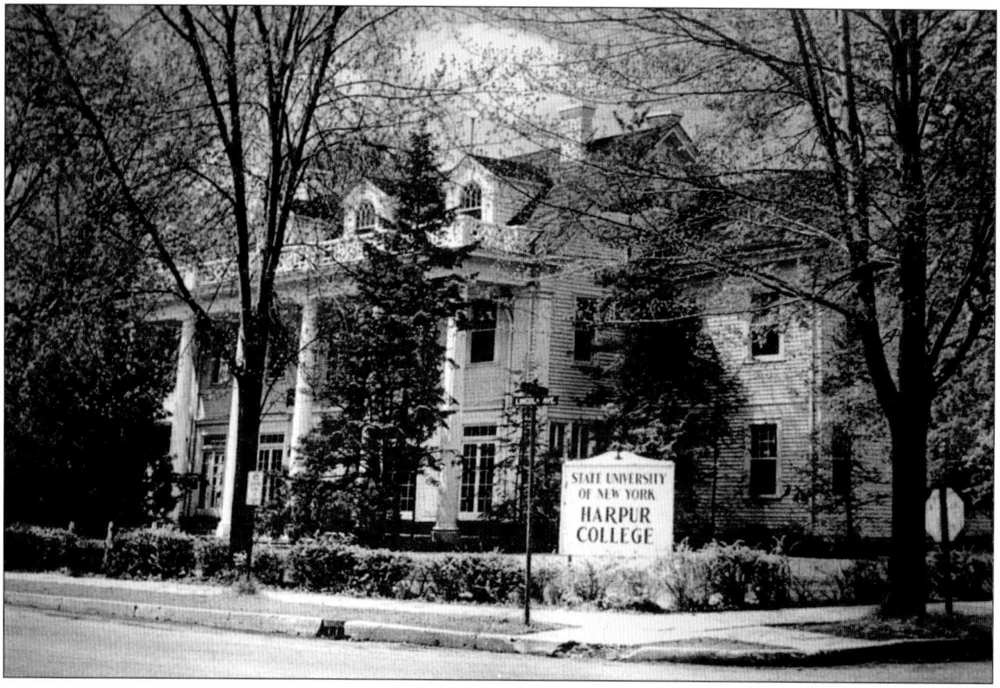

HOUSE OF ERUDITION. The building where Binghamton University began as a branch of Syracuse University in 1947 is shown in this photograph. Originally known as Triple Cities College, in recognition of the neighboring towns of Binghamton, Endicott, and Johnson City, the university is now seen as a growth engine of the region. The building pictured was known as Colonial Hall, and not coincidentally, the college's sports teams became known as the Colonials. Today, this building serves as the Endicott Visitor Center. (Courtesy of BU, Special Collections.)

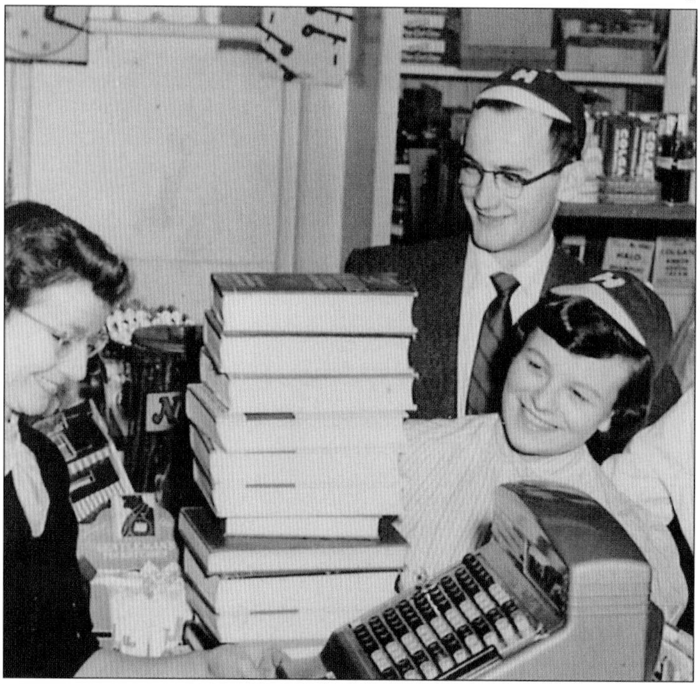

LEISURE TIME. In this image, students gather inside the Triple Cities College bookstore in 1954. The bookstore served as a center of campus activity in the early stages of the college. Today, leisure time is often taken up with Division 1 basketball at the university's Events Center, which opened its doors on January 31, 2004, when the men's basketball team defeated the University of Hartford, 75-68, in front of 4,660 fans. The university's sports teams are now known as the Bearcats. (Courtesy of BU, Special Collections.)

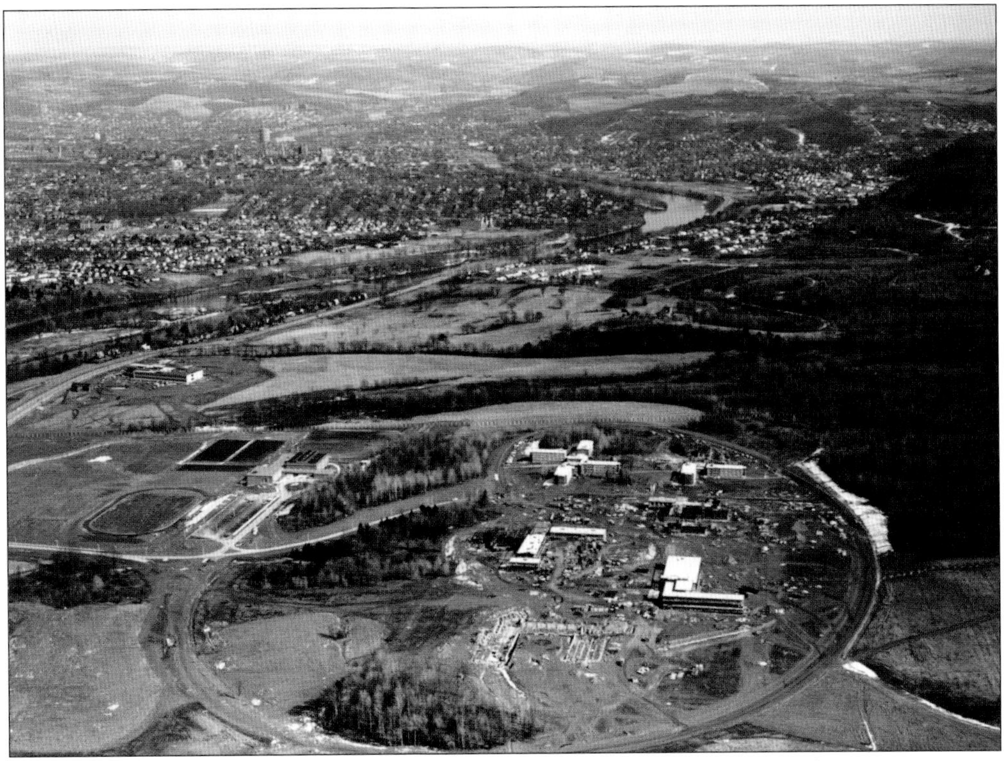

A Growth Engine. The above photograph shows a 1959 aerial view of the Binghamton University campus, looking east. Though known as Binghamton University, the campus is actually in the town of Vestal, across the Susquehanna River from Johnson City. In the picture below, the aerial view looks west in 1967. The huge growth of the university in the 1960s can be seen in the increased number of buildings that fill the campus in the image below. Vestal Parkway is the road that runs from top to bottom below; the parkway runs parallel with State Highway 17 (soon to be Interstate 86). (Both, courtesy of BU, Special Collections.)

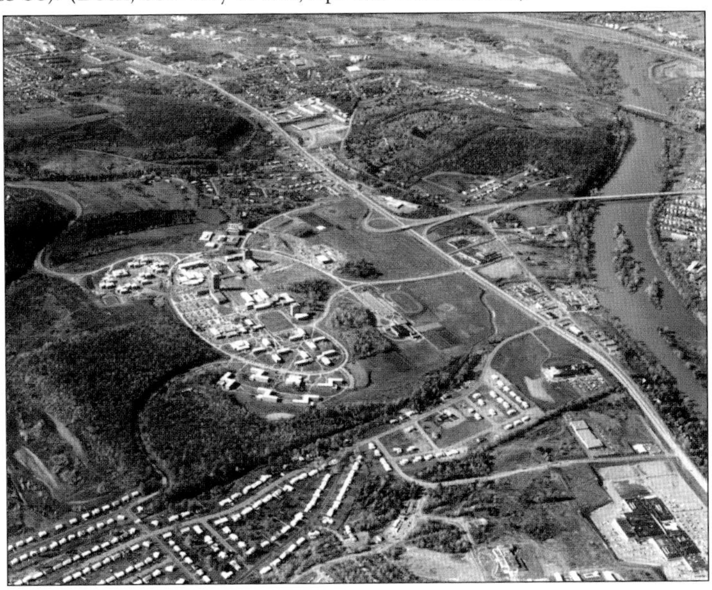

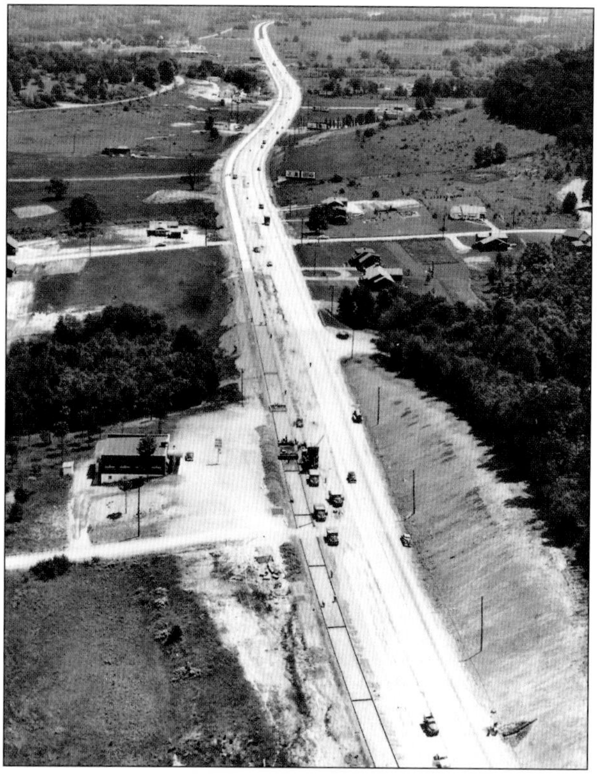

Crossroads of Vestal and Endicott. The picture at left, with a view looking east, shows the Vestal Parkway in 1951. Today, the parkway has become a four-lane highway that connects Binghamton to Owego. It has become the major thoroughfare of the Binghamton-Vestal area and houses numerous hotels, restaurants, shopping malls, and a Cineplex. Pictured below is an aerial view of the IBM Endicott campus around 1970. The 1970s were booming years for Endicott and IBM, as IBM's S/360 line of computers fueled the company's growth. The Glendale development lab, a research and development complex, was located in Glendale, about seven miles to the west of the Endicott campus. (Left, courtesy of VHS; below, courtesy of UHS.)

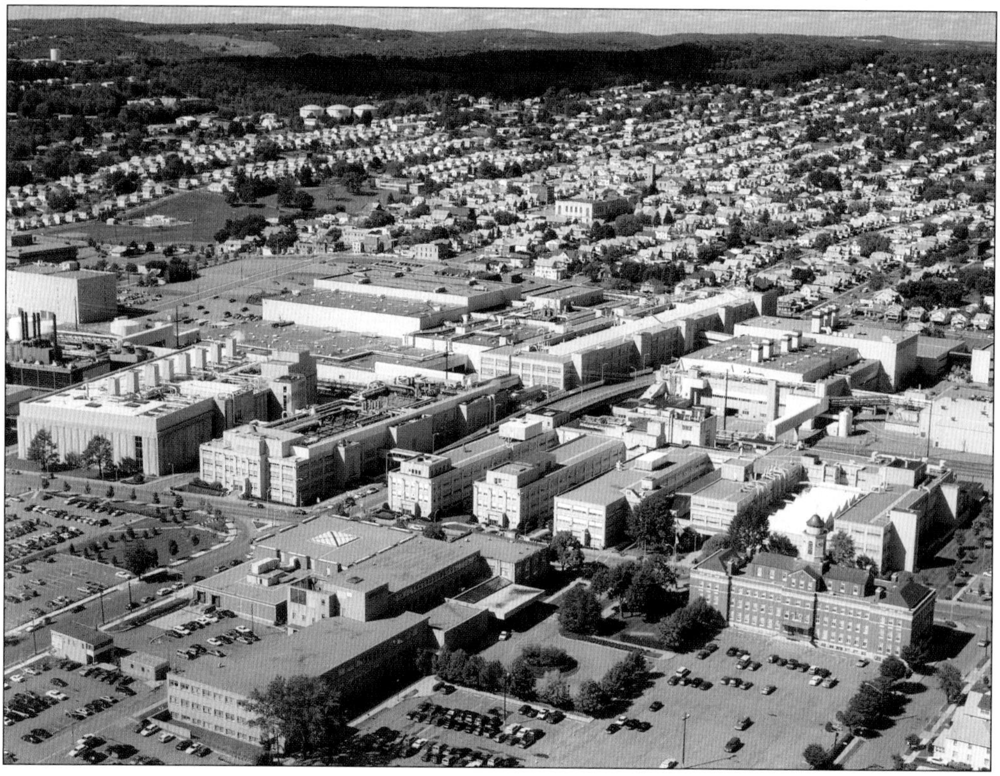

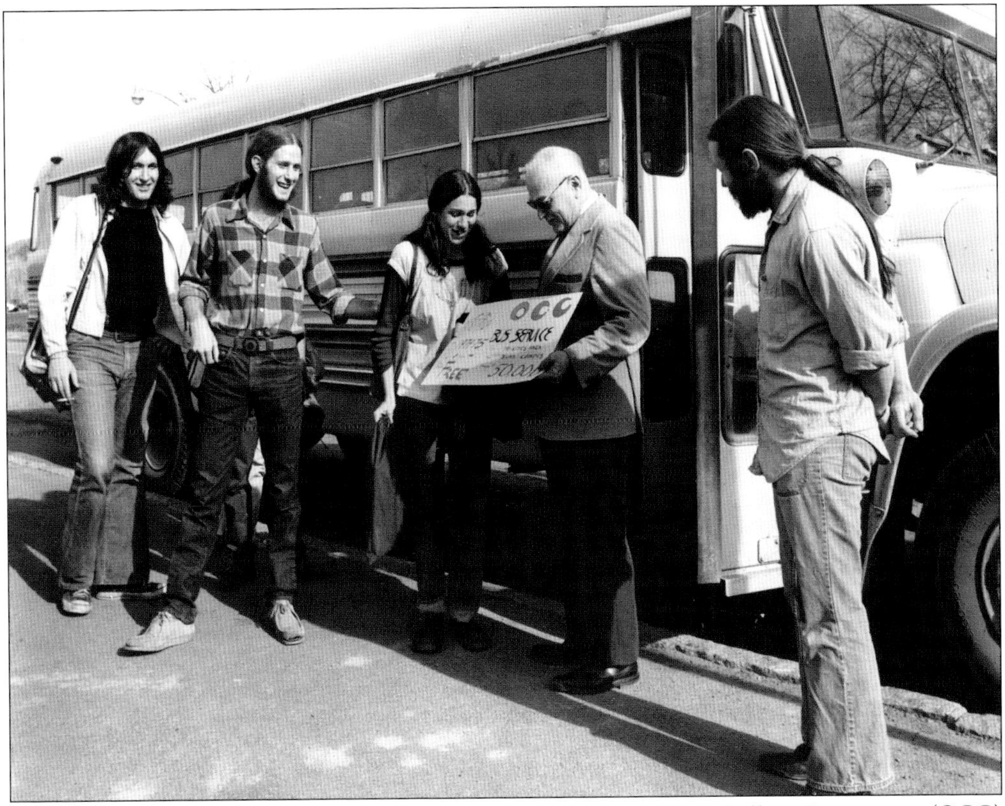

BEGINNINGS OF A COLLEGE TOWN. With the advent of the Off Campus College Community (OCC) bus service, Binghamton University took a major step in integrating itself into its surrounding community. Today, this symbiotic relationship has culminated in a downtown university center that has spurred much downtown development along the streets of Binghamton. (Courtesy of BU, Special Collections.)

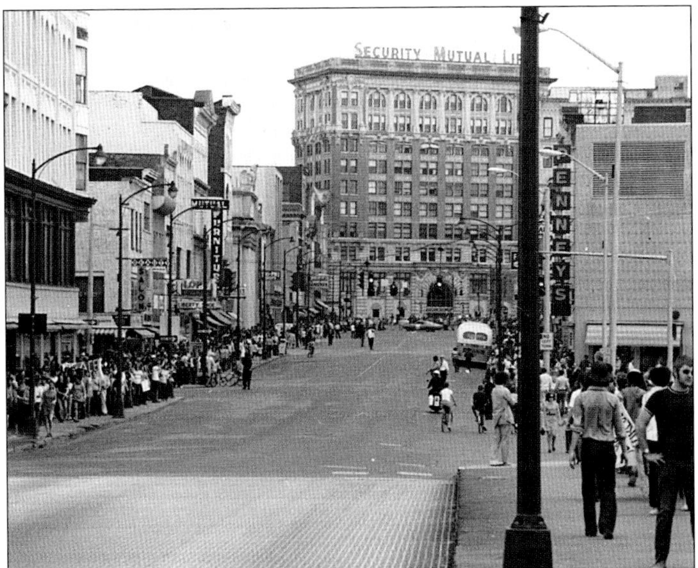

A MARCH FOR PEACE. Pictured here are thousands of Binghamton University students and local residents who filled the streets of downtown Binghamton on May 6, 1970, two days after the tragic shootings of four students at Kent State. The photograph shows a view of Court Street looking east, with the Security Mutual Insurance Building dominating the background. (Courtesy of BU, Special Collections.)

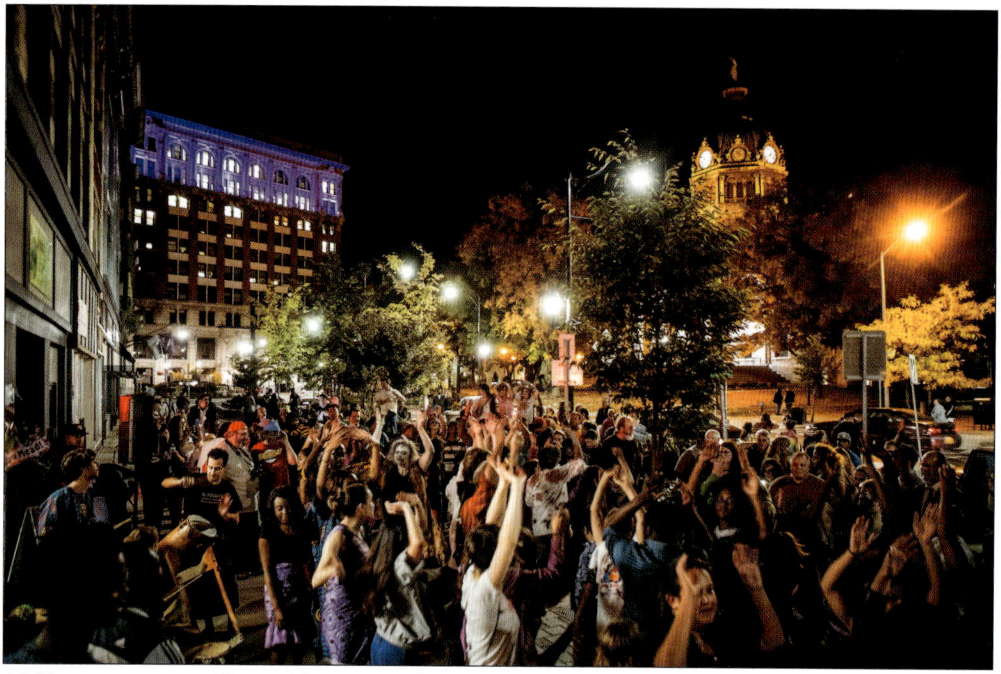

40 Years after the Peace March. In the image above, the Security Mutual Insurance Building is in the background once again, with the courthouse to the right. This c. 2010 photograph shows college students in happier times as they participate in a dance festival held by the university's Nukporfe African Dance and Drumming Ensemble. Perched across from the city's courthouse, the Security Mutual Insurance Building, housing the headquarters for the insurance company, was completed in 1905. Its lobby is one of the grandest in the area, complete with a two-story marble staircase and colorful murals depicting the history of the city. Below, pedestrians line State Street to see the back of the Forum Theater become a giant movie screen during the city's LUMA Festival in September 2015. (Both, courtesy of BU.)

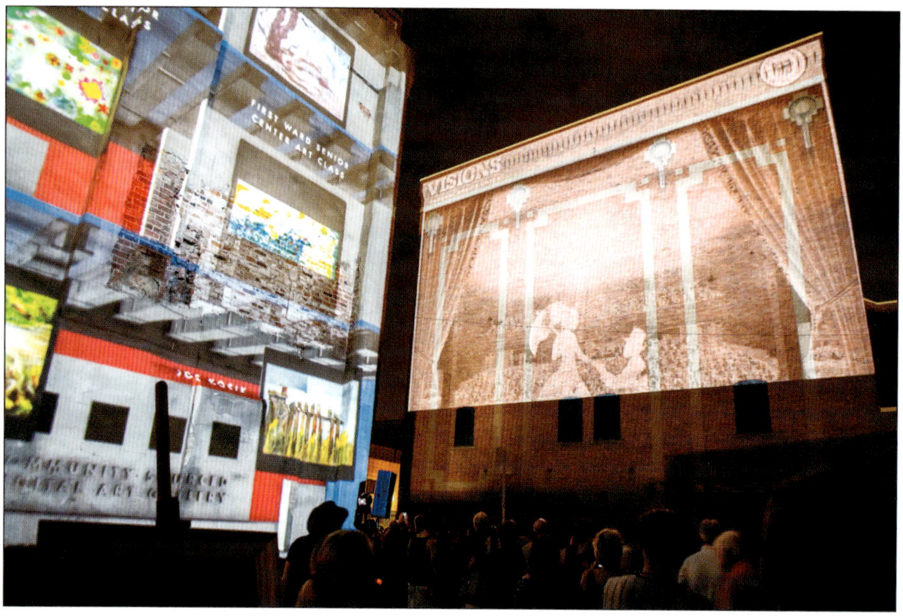

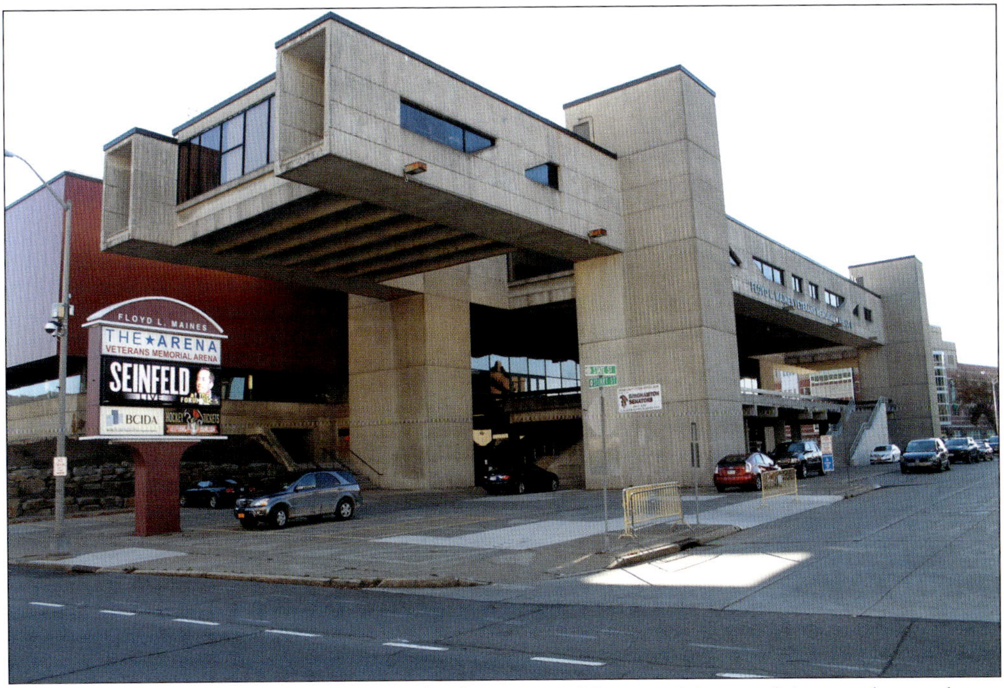

Indoor and Outdoor Beacons. The Floyd L. Maines Veterans Memorial Arena, shown above, opened its doors in 1973 and was originally known as the Broome County Veterans Memorial Arena. Besides hosting professional hockey and high school basketball games, the arena has also hosted such national entertainment figures as Bob Dylan, Dolly Parton, Elvis Presley, and Kenny Rogers. Jerry Seinfeld performed at the arena in December 2014; the marquee in the above photograph advertises his appearance. In the below picture, the facade of NYSEG (New York State Electric and Gas) Stadium has served as beacon for downtown Binghamton since its opening in 1992 as Binghamton Municipal Stadium.

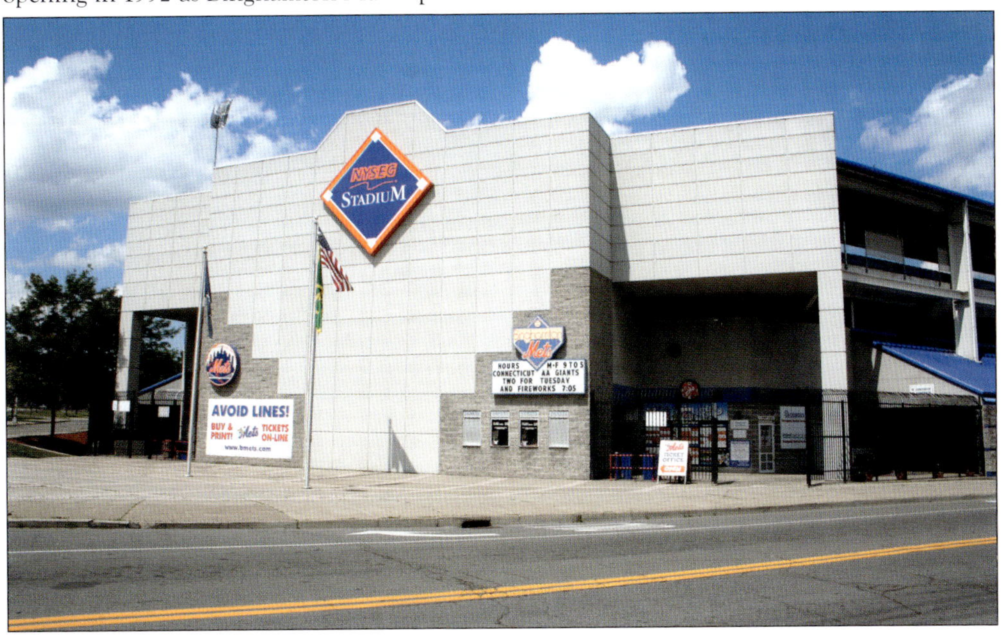

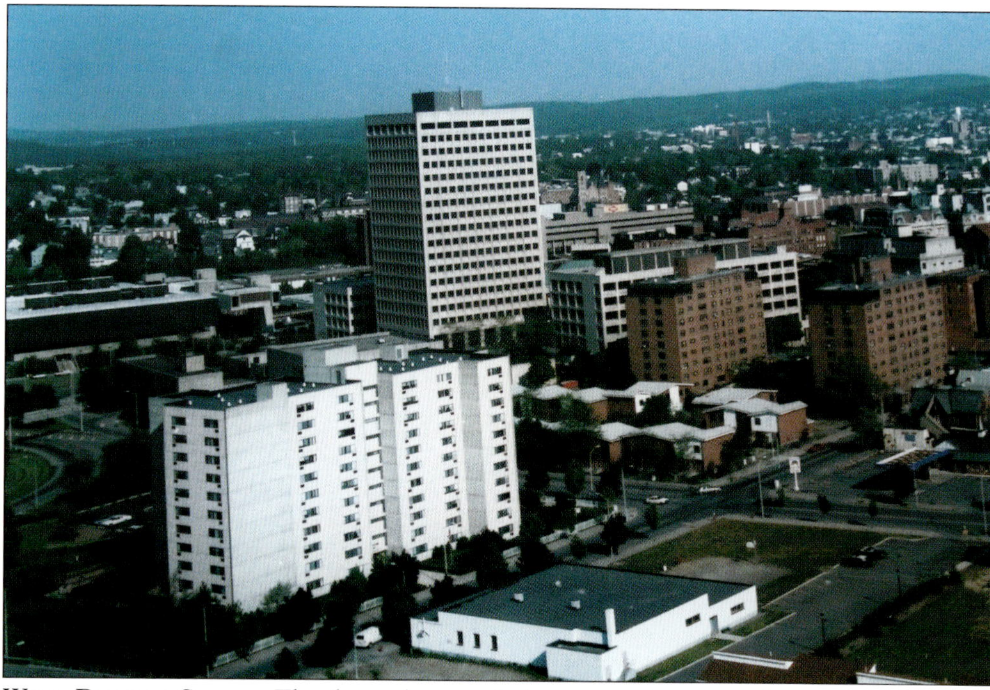

When Disaster Strikes. The above photograph shows a northwest aerial view of Binghamton, with its State Office Building dominating the skyline. On February 5, 1981, a fire in the basement's transformer released polychlorinated biphenyls (PCBs), along with dioxin and dibenzofurans—deadly toxins. In March of that year, then-governor Hugh Carey offered to visit Binghamton and drink a glass of PCBs. By April, Carey apologized, stating, "I did not intend in any way intend to minimize the danger of PCB contamination." The below photograph shows the athletic fields adjoining MacArthur Elementary School at dusk the night of September 8, 2011, after they filled with water from the Susquehanna River. (Above, courtesy of KVG for CTR.)

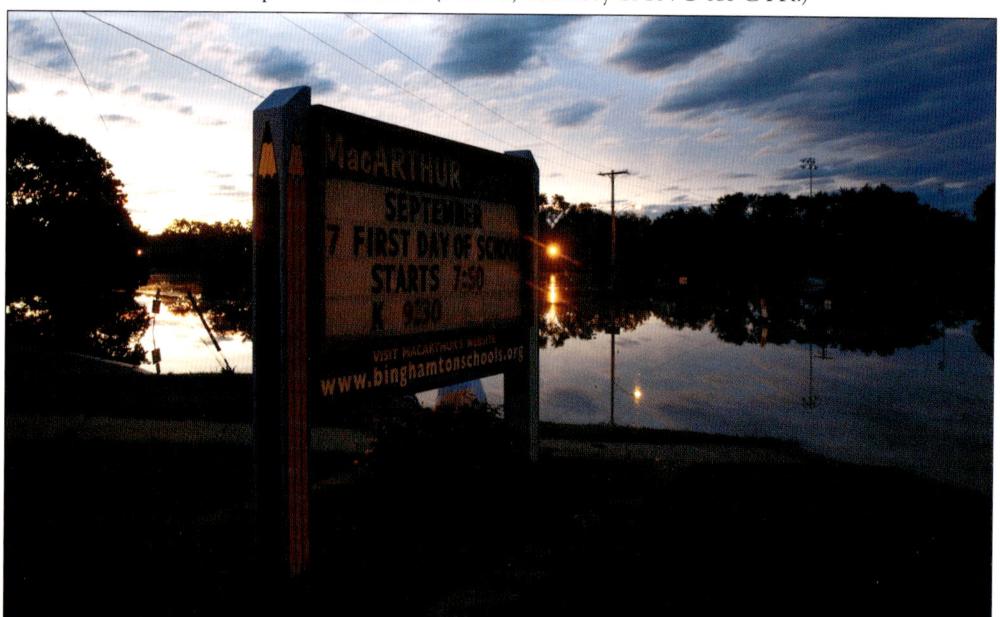

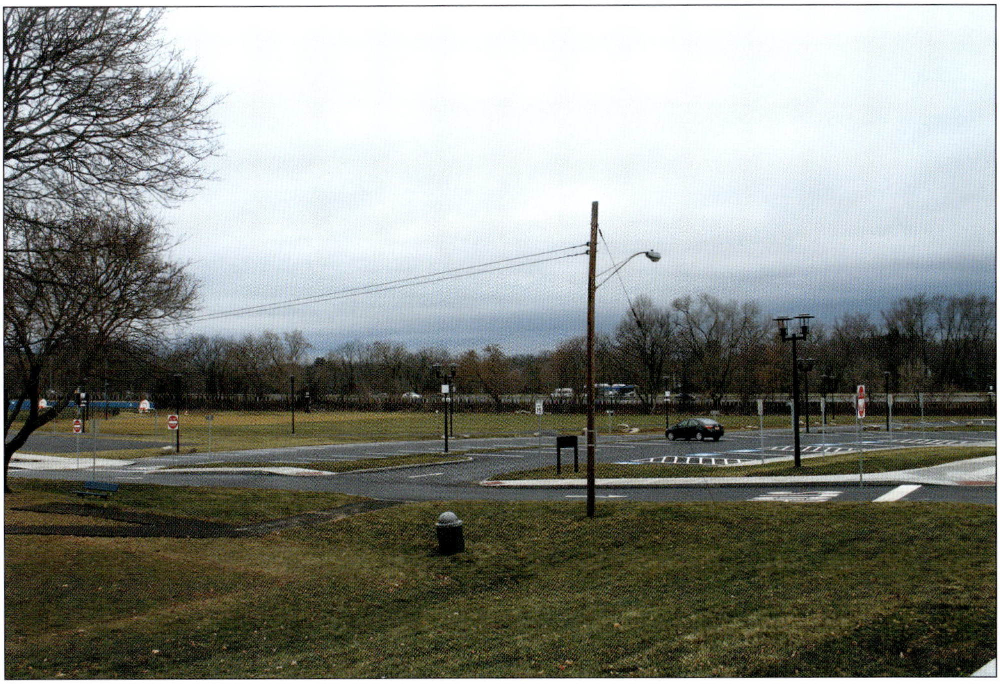

Rebuilding Commences. This is a view of the athletic fields at MacArthur Park today from approximately the same spot as the photograph on the preceding page. The "lake" of floodwaters is gone, and as part of the rebuilding of the elementary school and its grounds, a parking lot, walking trail, and baseball field are now present. Directly across from the terrain pictured above is the elementary school, which is shown below. Note how the school is now on stilts; a children's playground coexists with the stilts.

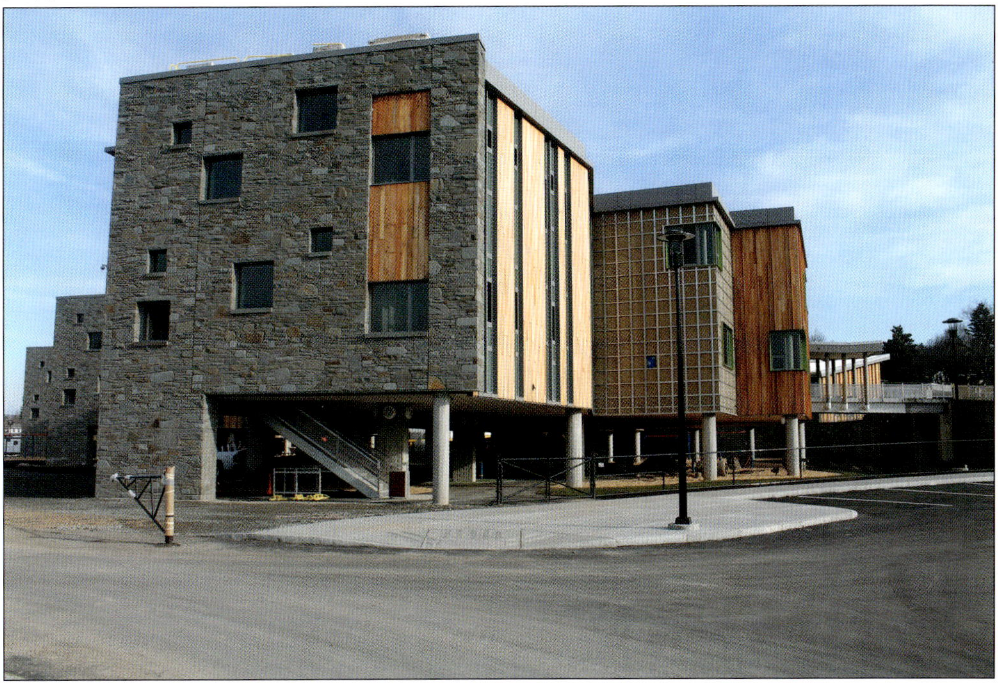

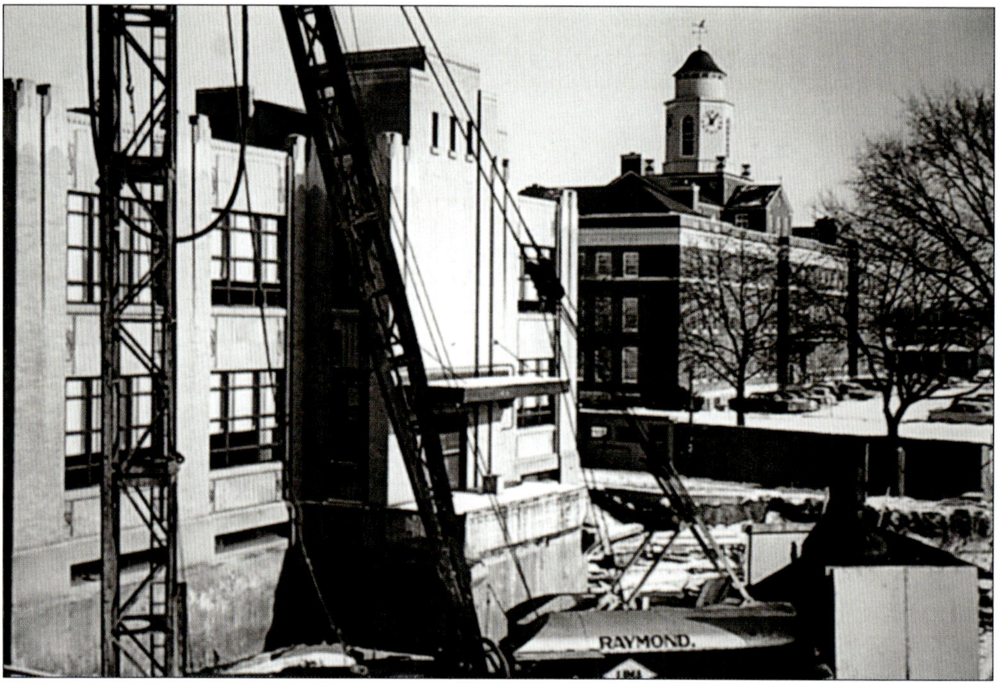

Heavy Equipment, Great Sounds. Above, a building goes up across from IBM's iconic clock tower in Endicott around 1957. In the foreground is equipment manufactured by the Raymond Corporation, the industrial forklift manufacturing company that has its headquarters in Greene, just outside of Binghamton. Below, Lady Antebellum performs on the McIntosh Soundstage at the Dick's Sporting Goods Open in 2015. McIntosh, the world-renowned producer of high-end music speakers, has been in Binghamton since 1960. (Above, courtesy of UHS.)

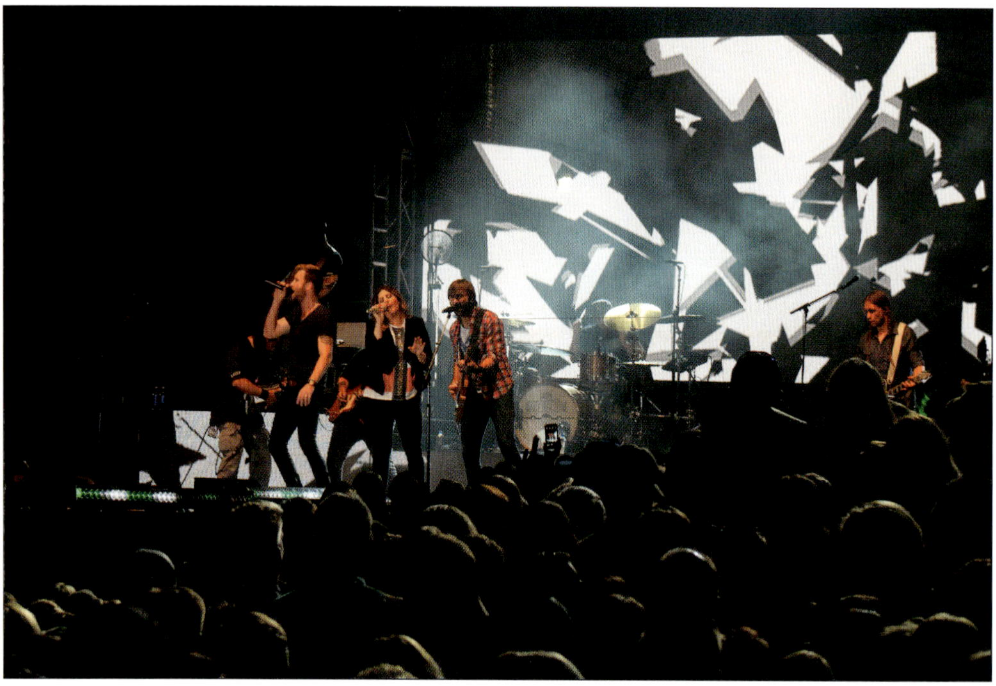

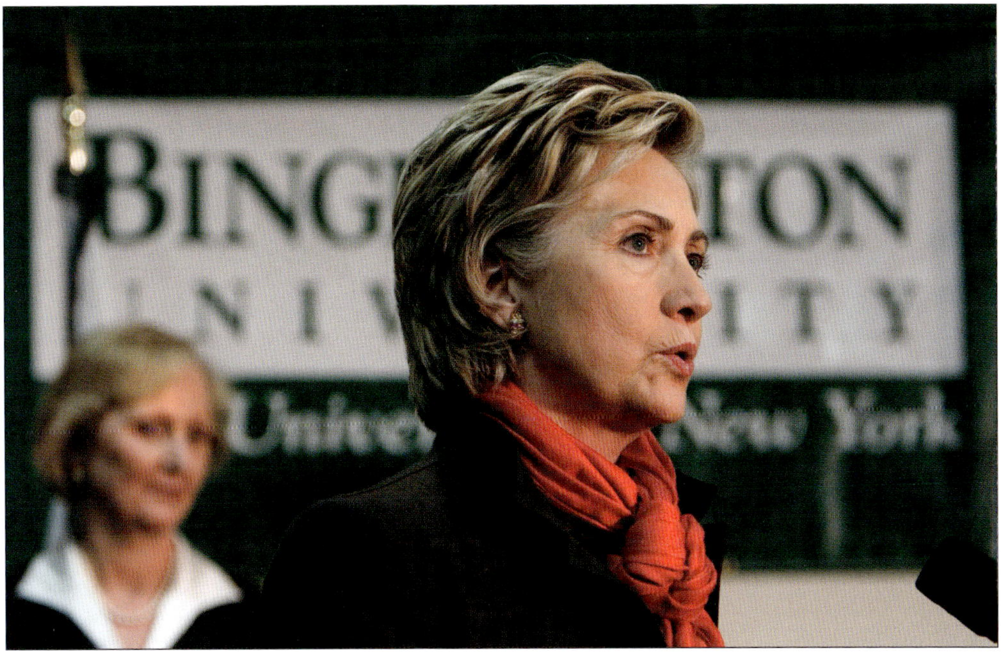

Political Stomping Grounds. Binghamton University is not only one of the area's largest employers, but it is also a draw from visits from national figures. On July 16, 2007, Hillary Clinton visited the campus and addressed students from the Decker School of Nursing. Lois DeFleur, then chancellor of the university, is in the background. In the below photograph, Pres. Barack Obama conducts a town hall meeting on the Binghamton University campus on August 23, 2014. During his visit, Obama not only listened to questions from area students and residents, but also had members of his entourage pick up some spiedies for lunch. (Both, courtesy of BU.)

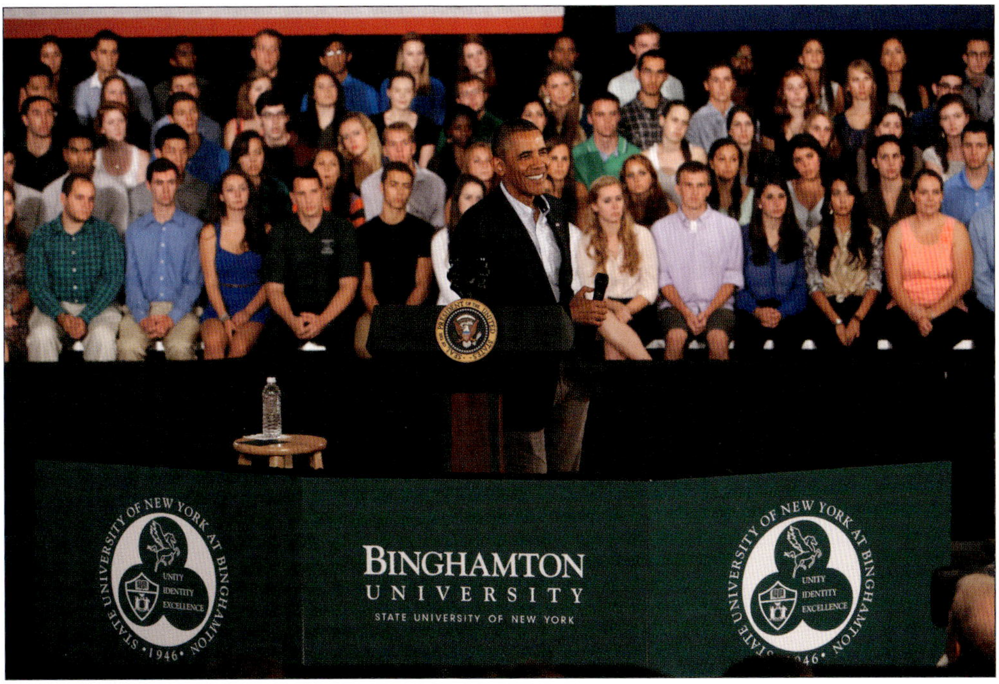

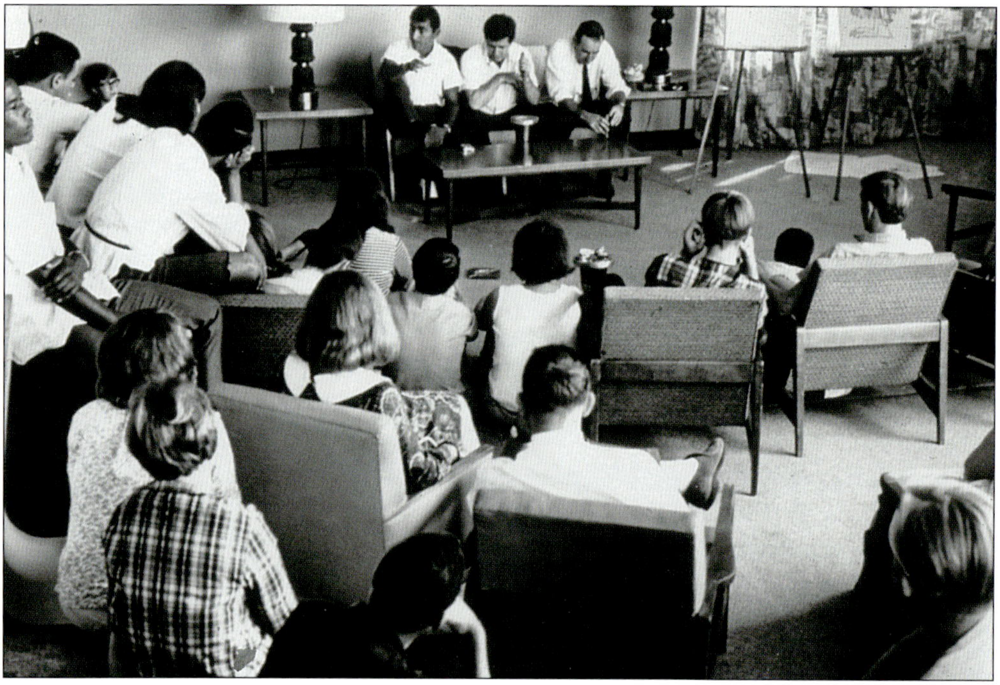

Hometown Luminaries. The above photograph shows Rod Serling, Johnny Hart, and Brant Parker (back, from left to right) speaking to college students at what was then Broome Community College (now SUNY Broome) in 1973. Serling had a home in nearby Interlaken, New York, and was a frequent visitor to Binghamton. Hart lived in neighboring Nineveh and was a graduate of Union-Endicott High School. Parker migrated to the area to work for a local newspaper. Hart and Parker would go on to create *The Wizard of Id* comic strip. Ironically, Hart and Parker passed away within eight days of one another in 2007; Hart passed on April 7, and Parker on April 15. In the photograph below, Tom Tull, founder of Legendary Entertainment (which produced such feature films as *42*, *Batman Begins*, and *The Hangover I, II*, and *III*) is interviewed by Roger Neel of WNBF radio. Through the years, Tull has donated millions of dollars to the Maine-Endwell Little League and Maine-Endwell athletic fields. Tull cherishes his time as a high school athlete and Little Leaguer in the area. (Above, photograph by *Binghamton Press*, courtesy of RSA @ BMHA.)

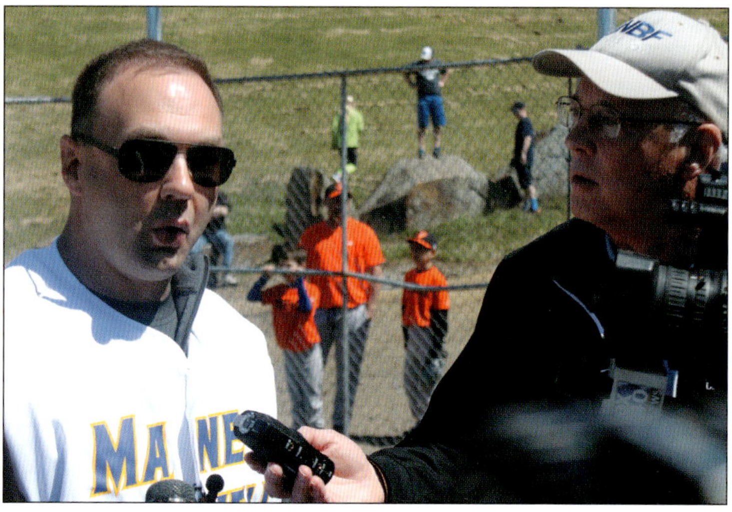

Two

Fun, Films, Festivals, and Hometown Performers

The streets of Greater Binghamton, as with any community, are a backlot of life; one can argue that Binghamton's streets have provided as much drama and entertainment as its numerous regional theaters and the large-scale movies filmed here. Many statues and sculptures date back well over a hundred years, beginning with Binghamton's courthouse, where a statue honoring statesman Daniel Dickinson greets all who climb its steps, and a Civil War Monument marks its southwestern corner. Street markers and monuments document the city's history.

This chapter starts with community celebrations through the years, moving from Halloween to First Friday Art Walk activities to a carousel restoration. It then discusses two feature movies filmed in Binghamton that use the city as a major character in the story line. The chapter discusses the area's strong regional theater offerings, showing a scene from the annual *Spirits of Binghamton's Past Downtown Walking Tour*, which is provided by the Preservation Association of the Southern Tier (PAST). From there, it moves on to a performance from the Schorr Family Firehouse Stage, which is part of the Goodwill Theatre Performing Arts Academy in Johnson City. The scene from the *Little Flower* is representative of the abundance of performing arts venues in the area, including such locales as the Broome County Forum, Cider Mill Playhouse, Chenango River Theatre, Endicott Performing Arts Center, Know Theatre; Ti-Ahwaga Playhouse, and the Tri-Cities Opera.

Today, as the weather warms up, the city of Binghamton becomes a stage for several festivals—the city has hosted Mural Fest, which draws mural artists from all over the Northeast. During July Fest, artists annually take over the streets of downtown Binghamton. The annual Spiedie Fest and Balloon Rally follows in August, with hot-air balloons and food and craft vendors filling Binghamton's Otsiningo Park. In the fall, LUMA Festival illuminates Binghamton, serving as a beacon for projection art enthusiasts, as well as returning students.

The closing pages focus on hometown performers. Notable thespians who have called the Greater Binghamton Area their home include Richard Deacon and Anthony George. Noted writers who grew up in the area include brothers Robert and Rod Serling and cartoonist Johnny Hart. Area professors and instructors have included writer John Gardner and film director Nicholas Ray, among others.

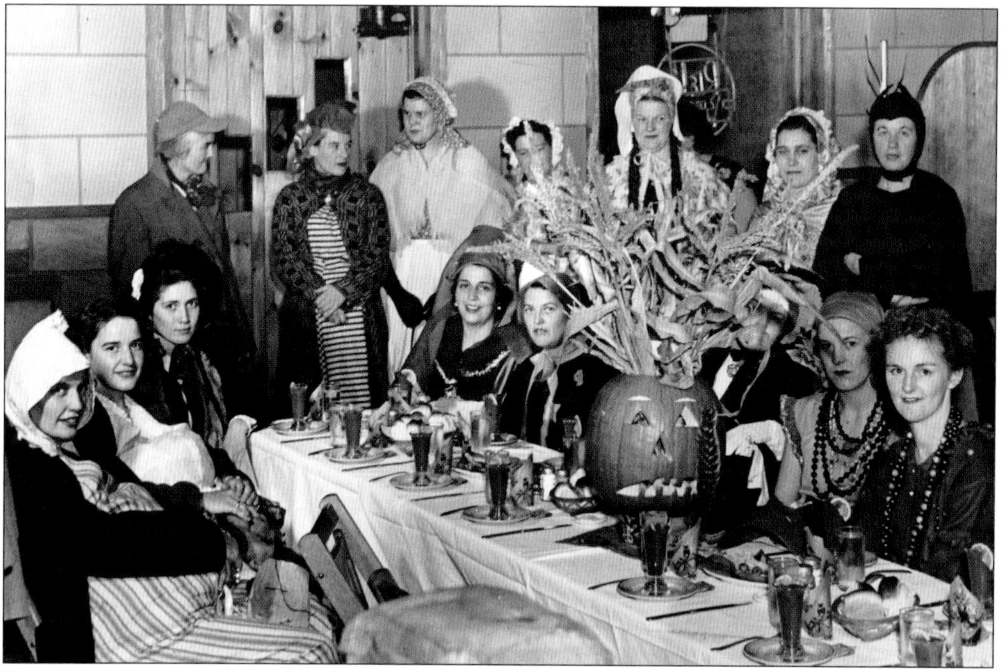

Halloween, c. 1945. In the above image, workers at the Endicott-Johnson Shoe Company pose for a Halloween memory. The below photograph shows the workers keeping their same positions, only this time, masks cover their faces. By the middle of the 20th century, the Greater Binghamton Area was a thriving example of corporate America, with a large presence from EJ, IBM, Link Aviation, Raymond Corporation, and various photographic companies. Living in the area was likened to living in a cocoon, protected from the world's ills. During the 1930s, while America was in the midst of the Depression, IBM and EJ served as beacons for workers, avoiding laying off any employees. (Both, courtesy of GB.)

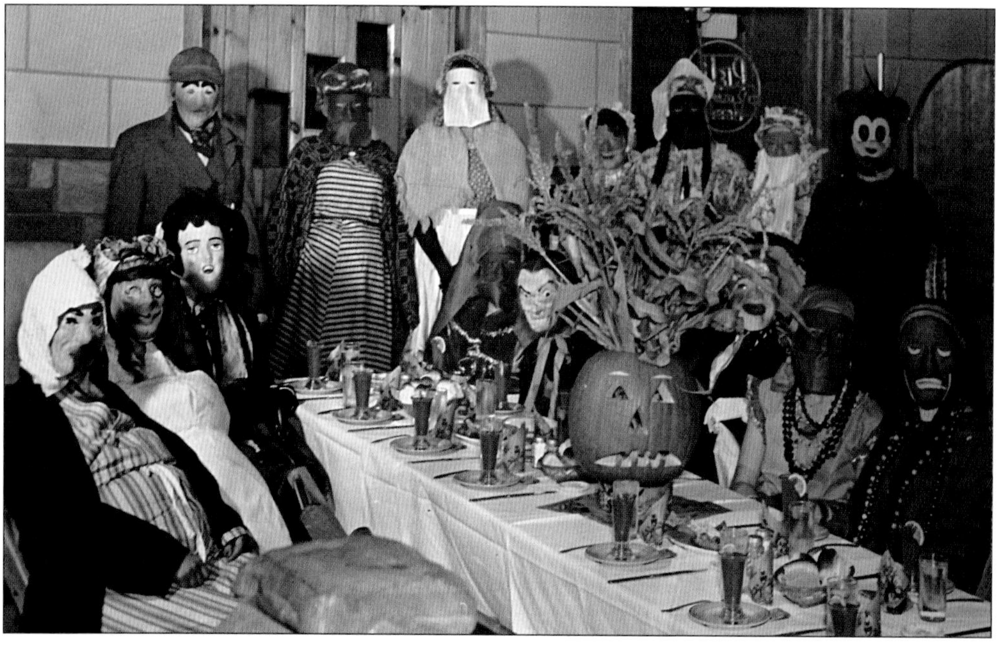

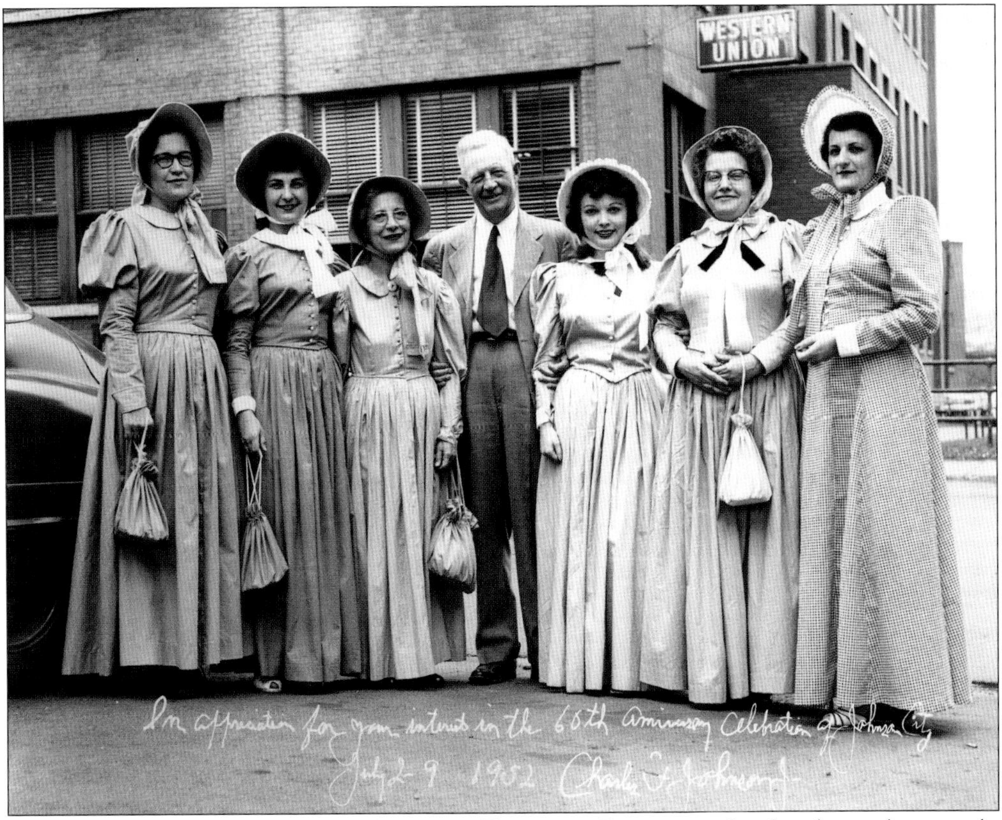

60TH ANNIVERSARY OF JOHNSON CITY AND ENDICOTT EXPANSION. In the above photograph, Charles F. Johnson, George's brother, poses with a group of women helping to celebrate the 60th anniversary of Johnson City in July 1952. From left to right are Jennie Wallace, Lena De Angelo, Genevieve Dugi, unidentified, Bernadine Macko, Regina Bishop, and Marion Kocak. The photograph below depicts windows being installed in a factory building for the Endicott-Johnson Corporation at the corner of North Street and Washington Avenue. In the background is Washington Avenue, the hub of shopping and restaurants in Endicott from 1950 through 2000. Thousands of EJ and IBM employees filled the streets of Washington Avenue during lunch hours during the second half of the 20th century. On the weekends, the avenue became a haven for shoppers. (Both, courtesy of UHS.)

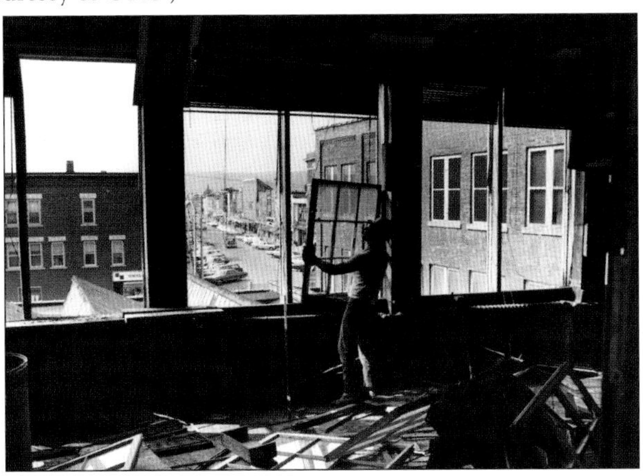

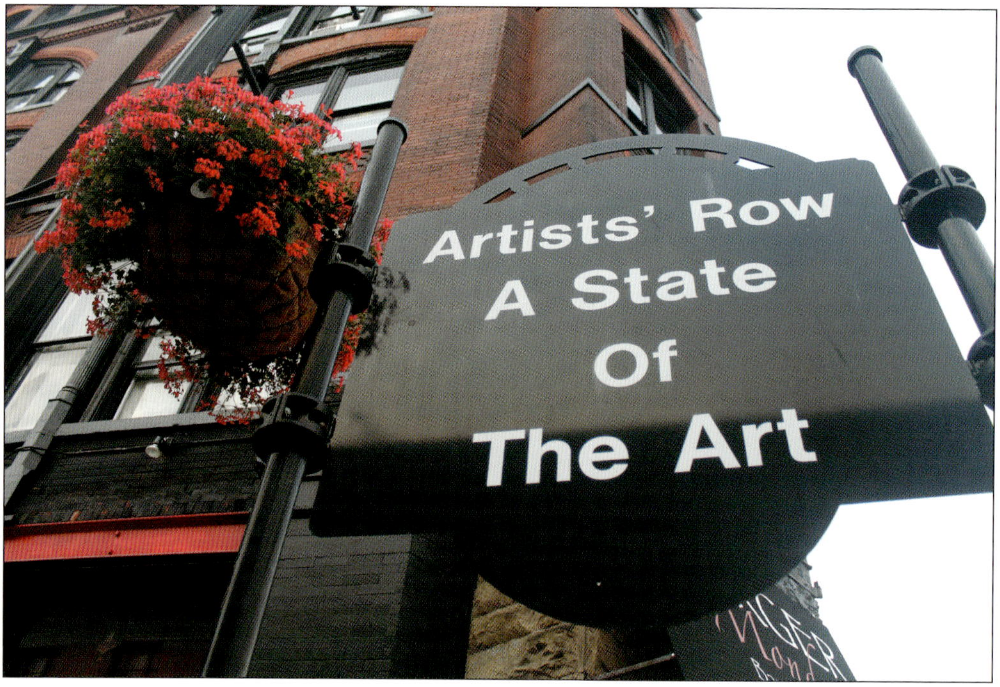

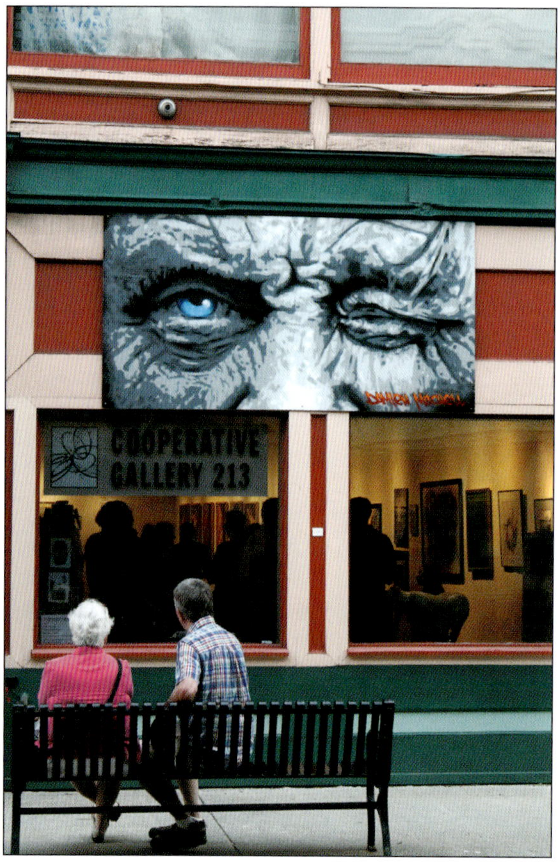

First Friday Fun. The above sign beckons pedestrians to stroll along Binghamton's State Street and stop in at its many art galleries. Among the many galleries on this street are the Cooperative Gallery, Anthony Brunelli Gallery, and the Orazio Salati Gallery, just to name a few. Brunelli was a proud sponsor of the work of Binghamton's Maria Olmstead, a child prodigy who was featured on *60 Minutes II* in 2005 and is the subject of the 2007 documentary *My Kid Could Paint That.* At left is a street view of the Cooperative Gallery; this gallery's founders were instrumental in establishing Binghamton's First Friday art walk. First Friday events extend beyond State Street, as various venues feature artists and entertainers every month.

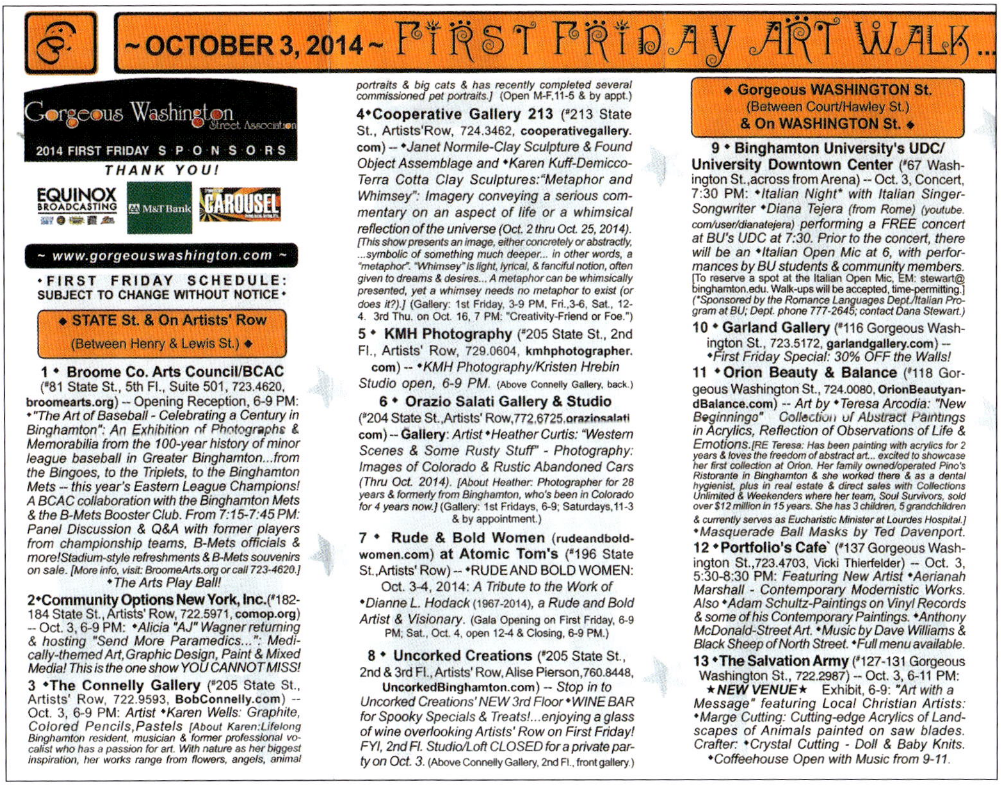

~ OCTOBER 3, 2014 ~ FIRST FRIDAY ART WALK...

Gorgeous Washington Street Association

2014 FIRST FRIDAY S·P·O·N·S·O·R·S

THANK YOU!

EQUINOX BROADCASTING · M&T Bank · CAROUSEL

~ www.gorgeouswashington.com ~

• FIRST FRIDAY SCHEDULE: SUBJECT TO CHANGE WITHOUT NOTICE •

◆ STATE St. & On Artists' Row (Between Henry & Lewis St.) ◆

1 • Broome Co. Arts Council/BCAC (#81 State St., 5th Fl., Suite 501, 723.4620, **broomearts.org**) -- Opening Reception, 6-9 PM: *•"The Art of Baseball - Celebrating a Century in Binghamton": An Exhibition of Photographs & Memorabilia from the 100-year history of minor league baseball in Greater Binghamton...from the Bingoes, to the Triplets, to the Binghamton Mets -- this year's Eastern League Champions! A BCAC collaboration with the Binghamton Mets & the B-Mets Booster Club. From 7:15-7:45 PM: Panel Discussion & Q&A with former players from championship teams, B-Mets officials & more! Stadium-style refreshments & B-Mets souvenirs on sale. [More info, visit: BroomeArts.org or call 723-4620.] •The Arts Play Ball!*

2•Community Options New York, Inc. (#182-184 State St., Artists' Row, 722.5971, **comop.org**) -- Oct. 3, 6-9 PM: *•Alicia "AJ" Wagner returning & hosting "Send More Paramedics...": Medically-themed Art, Graphic Design, Paint & Mixed Media! This is the one show YOU CANNOT MISS!*

3 •The Connelly Gallery (#205 State St., Artists' Row, 722.9593, **BobConnelly.com**) -- Oct. 3, 6-9 PM: *Artist •Karen Wells: Graphite, Colored Pencils, Pastels [About Karen: Lifelong Binghamton resident, musician & former professional vocalist who has a passion for art. With nature as her biggest inspiration, her works range from flowers, angels, animal portraits & big cats & has recently completed several commissioned pet portraits.]* (Open M-F, 11-5 & by appt.)

4•Cooperative Gallery 213 (#213 State St., Artists'Row, 724.3462, **cooperativegallery.com**) -- *•Janet Normile-Clay Sculpture & Found Object Assemblage and •Karen Kuff-Demicco-Terra Cotta Clay Sculptures: "Metaphor and Whimsey": Imagery conveying a serious commentary on an aspect of life or a whimsical reflection of the universe (Oct. 2 thru Oct. 25, 2014). [This show presents an image, either concretely or abstractly, ...symbolic of something much deeper... in other words, a "metaphor". "Whimsey" is light, lyrical, & fanciful notion, often given to dreams & desires... A metaphor can be whimsically presented, yet a whimsey needs no metaphor to exist (or does it?).]* (Gallery: 1st Friday, 3-9 PM, Fri., 3-6, Sat., 12-4. 3rd Thu. on Oct. 16, 7 PM: "Creativity-Friend or Foe.")

5 • KMH Photography (#205 State St., 2nd Fl., Artists' Row, 729.0604, **kmhphotographer.com**) -- *•KMH Photography/Kristen Hrebin Studio open, 6-9 PM.* (Above Connelly Gallery, back.)

6 • Orazio Salati Gallery & Studio (#204 State St., Artists' Row, 772.6725, **oraziosalati com**) -- **Gallery**: *Artist •Heather Curtis: "Western Scenes & Some Rusty Stuff" - Photography: Images of Colorado & Rustic Abandoned Cars (Thru Oct. 2014). [About Heather: Photographer for 28 years & formerly from Binghamton, who's been in Colorado for 4 years now.]* (Gallery: 1st Fridays, 6-9; Saturdays, 11-3 & by appointment.)

7 • Rude & Bold Women (**rudeandboldwomen.com**) **at Atomic Tom's** (#196 State St., Artists' Row) -- •RUDE AND BOLD WOMEN: Oct. 3-4, 2014: *A Tribute to the Work of •Dianne L. Hodack* (1967-2014), *a Rude and Bold Artist & Visionary.* (Gala Opening on First Friday, 6-9 PM; Sat., Oct. 4, open 12-4 & Closing, 6-9 PM.)

8 • Uncorked Creations (#205 State St., 2nd & 3rd Fl., Artists' Row, Alise Pierson, 760.8448, **UncorkedBinghamton.com**) -- *Stop in to Uncorked Creations' NEW 3rd Floor •WINE BAR for Spooky Specials & Treats!...enjoying a glass of wine overlooking Artists' Row on First Friday! FYI, 2nd Fl. Studio/Loft CLOSED for a private party on Oct. 3.* (Above Connelly Gallery, 2nd Fl., front gallery.)

◆ Gorgeous WASHINGTON St. (Between Court/Hawley St.) & On WASHINGTON St. ◆

9 • Binghamton University's UDC/ University Downtown Center (#67 Washington St., across from Arena) -- Oct. 3, Concert, 7:30 PM: *•Italian Night* with Italian Singer-Songwriter •Diana Tejera (from Rome) (youtube.com/user/dianatejera) performing a FREE concert at BU's UDC at 7:30. Prior to the concert, there will be an •Italian Open Mic at 6, with performances by BU students & community members.* [To reserve a spot at the Italian Open Mic, EM: stewart@binghamton.edu. Walk-ups will be accepted, time-permitting.] *(*Sponsored by the Romance Languages Dept./Italian Program at BU; Dept. phone 777-2645; contact Dana Stewart.)*

10 • Garland Gallery (#116 Gorgeous Washington St., 723.5172, **garlandgallery.com**) -- *•First Friday Special: 30% OFF the Walls!*

11 • Orion Beauty & Balance (#118 Gorgeous Washington St., 724.0080, **OrionBeautyandBalance.com**) -- *Art by •Teresa Arcodia: "New Beginnings" Collection of Abstract Paintings in Acrylics, Reflection of Observations of Life & Emotions. [RE Teresa: Has been painting with acrylics for 2 years & loves the freedom of abstract art... excited to showcase her first collection at Orion. Her family owned/operated Pino's Ristorante in Binghamton & she worked there & as a dental hygienist, plus in real estate & direct sales with Collections Unlimited & Weekenders where her team, Soul Survivors, sold over $12 million in 15 years. She has 3 children, 5 grandchildren & currently serves as Eucharistic Minister at Lourdes Hospital.] •Masquerade Ball Masks by Ted Davenport.*

12 •Portfolio's Cafe` (#137 Gorgeous Washington St., 723.4703, Vicki Thierfelder) -- Oct. 3, 5:30-8:30 PM: *Featuring New Artist •Aerianah Marshall - Contemporary Modernistic Works. Also •Adam Schultz-Paintings on Vinyl Records & some of his Contemporary Paintings. •Anthony McDonald-Street Art. •Music by Dave Williams & Black Sheep of North Street. •Full menu available.*

13 •The Salvation Army (#127-131 Gorgeous Washington St., 722.2987) -- Oct. 3, 6-11 PM: ★***NEW VENUE***★ Exhibit, 6-9: *"Art with a Message" featuring Local Christian Artists: •Marge Cutting: Cutting-edge Acrylics of Landscapes of Animals painted on saw blades. Crafter: •Crystal Cutting - Doll & Baby Knits. •Coffeehouse Open with Music from 9-11.*

Sample Menu for First Friday. On the First Friday of every month, the streets of Binghamton beckon all to explore galleries and other venues. The above image shows part of the flyer from October 3, 2014, that outlines the sundry events taking place, including exhibits of photography, paintings, and sculptures, complemented by a concert or two. Note that the first item listed is "The Art of Baseball—Celebrating a Century in Binghamton," which included a historical photograph display of baseball in Binghamton, as well as a baseball panel discussion. On this night in Binghamton, the featured speaker was the late Steve Kraly, a member of the 1953 world champion New York Yankees. Kraly settled in Johnson City after his playing days were done, as he and his wife, Irene, raised four children. In the below c. 1939 photograph, Sharon Ball, executive director of the BCAC, poses in front of a photograph showing, from left to right, Joe DiMaggio, George F. Johnson, and Lou Gehrig at Johnson Field.

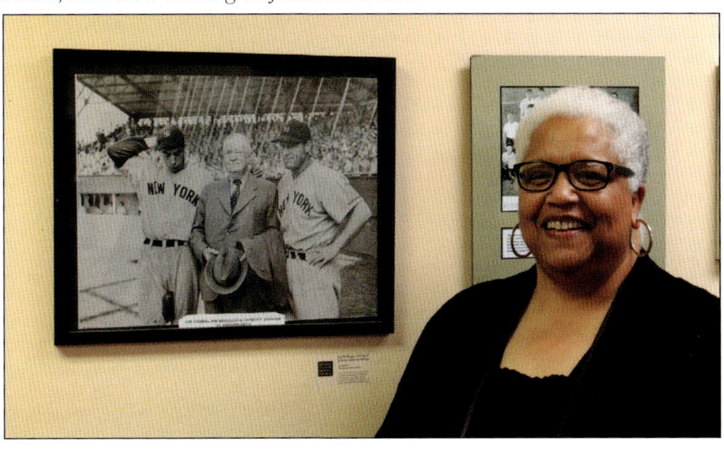

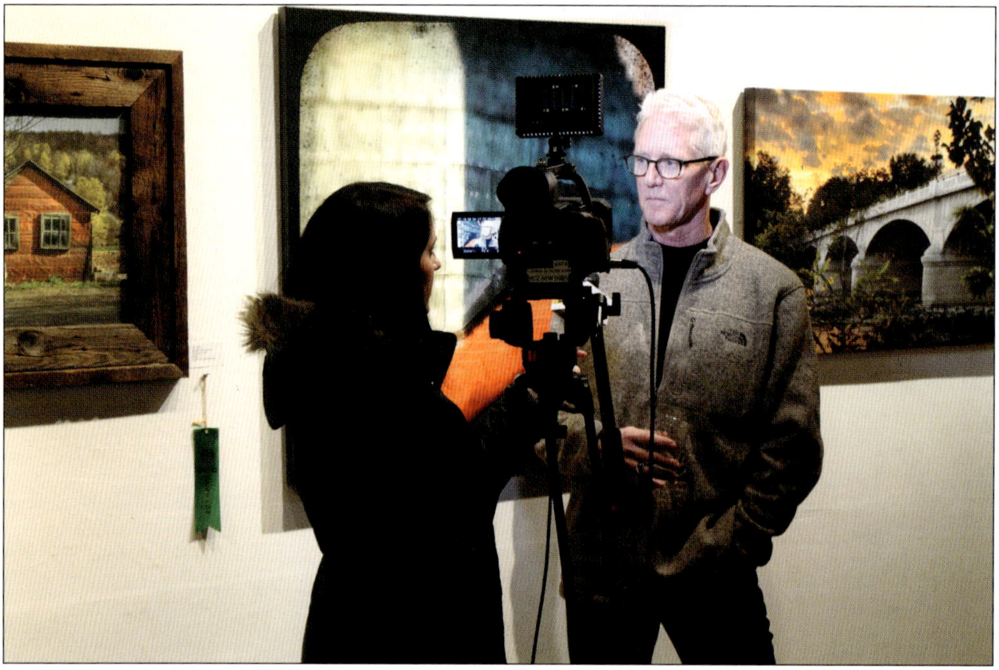

First Friday News. Above, Binghamton's WICZ reporter Emily Girsch interviews Kirk Van Zanbergen, whose digitally enhanced *Courthouse Detail* won first place in the Bob Johnston Regional Photography Competition in January 2016. The annual competition is sponsored by the Cooperative Gallery and the Two Rivers Photography Club and is named after Bob Johnston, a deceased lifelong photographer and gallery member who defined the successful photograph as "one in which both the abstract elements and the subject matter of the image reinforce each other to provide an emotional experience for the viewer." Below, Binghamton's Fox 40 reporter Faith Jesse feigns fear as she is surrounded by zombies at Binghamton's Confluence Park. The Zombie Walk occurs every First Friday in October to usher in October's haunting season.

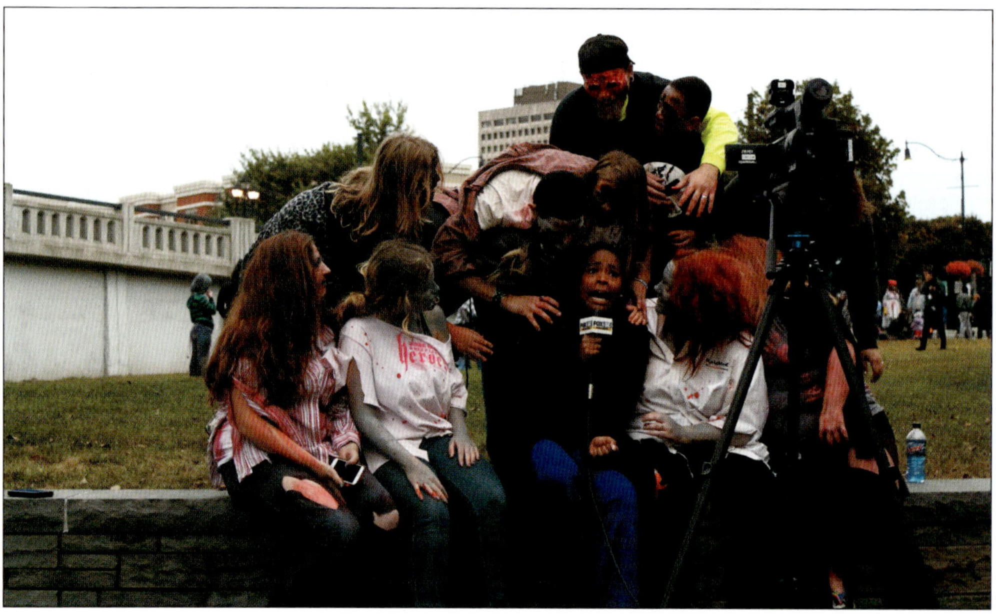

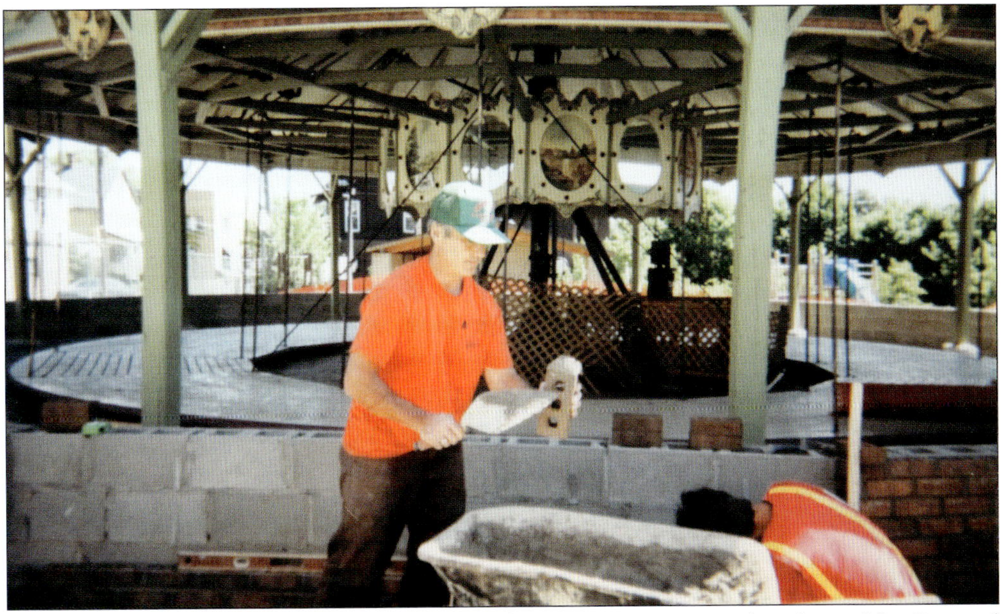

Carousel Capital of the World. Greater Binghamton is sometimes referred to as "the Carousel Capital of the World," due to its having six working carousels, all built by the Allan Herschell Company and donated to the community by the Johnson family. The above photograph shows Paul Polombaro laying a brick as part of the 1994 restoration of the carousel at George W. Johnson Park in West Endicott. The image below shows residents lining up for a carousel ride in celebration of its restoration. A fee has never been charged for a ride on any of the carousels; George F. Johnson felt strongly that no child should ever be deprived of a ride because of a lack of funds. Other area parks with working carousels include Binghamton's Ross Park Zoo, Recreation Park, Endwell's Highland Park, Endicott's West Endicott Park on Page Avenue, and Charles F. Johnson Park in Johnson City. (Both, courtesy of EVC.)

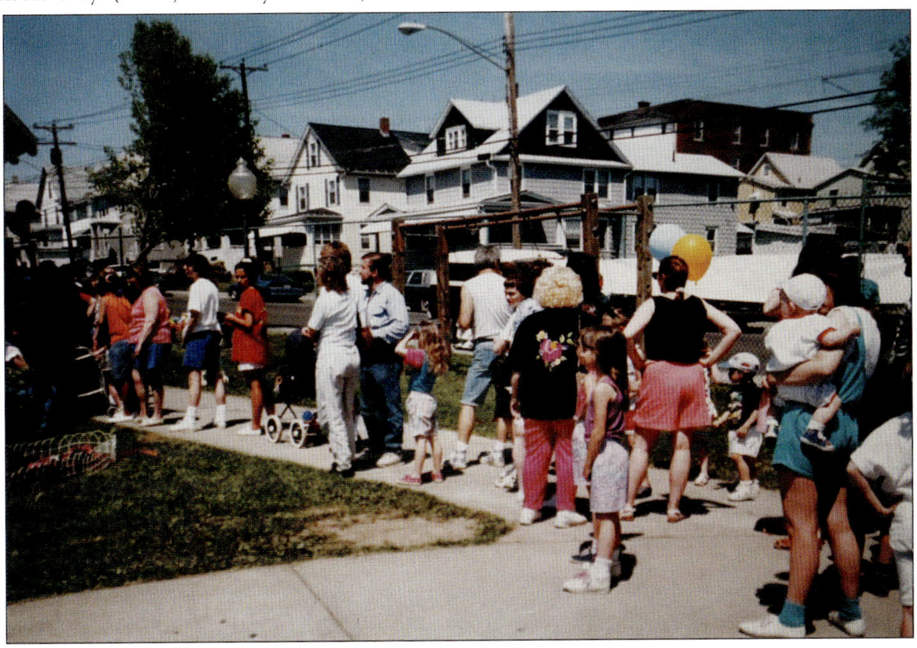

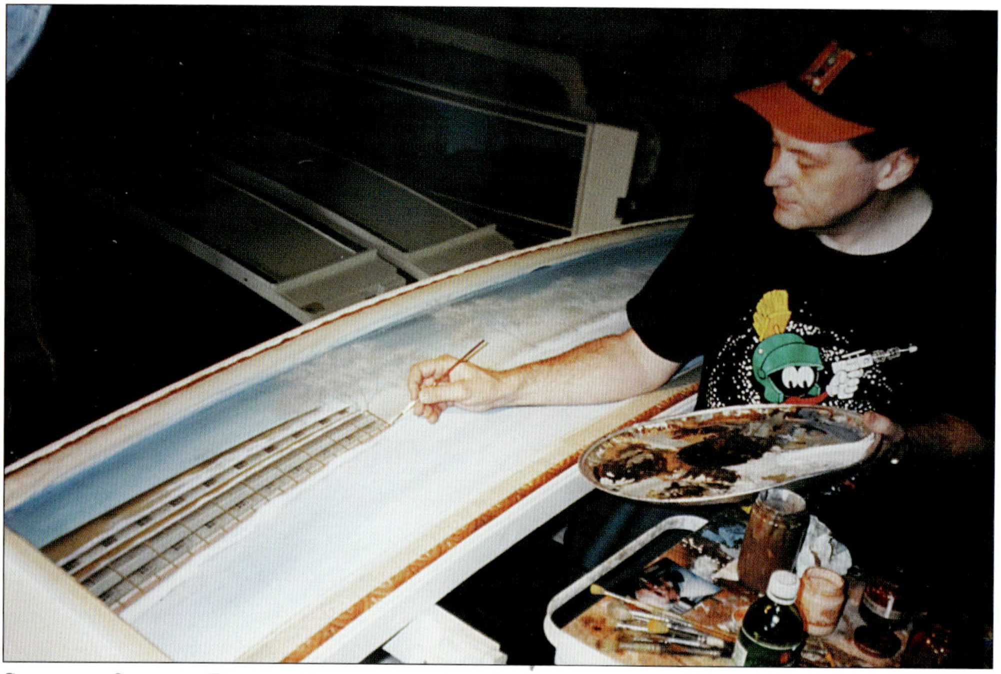

Stripped, Sanded, Primed, Painted. In the above image, artist Cortlandt Hull paints one of the rounding boards at the West Endicott Carousel, as part of the 1994 restoration. The below photograph shows the horses after they were stripped of their paint, but before they were sanded in preparation for a new coat. In addition to overhauling the carousel itself, the restoration included surrounding the carousel in a brick and glass enclosure, to protect it against the elements. Hull's skill in painting rounding boards is featured in the 2016 twelve-minute documentary *The Carousel*, which was shown at the 2016 Tribeca Film Festival. The documentary focuses on Hull's work on the carousel at Recreation Park. (Both, courtesy of EVC.)

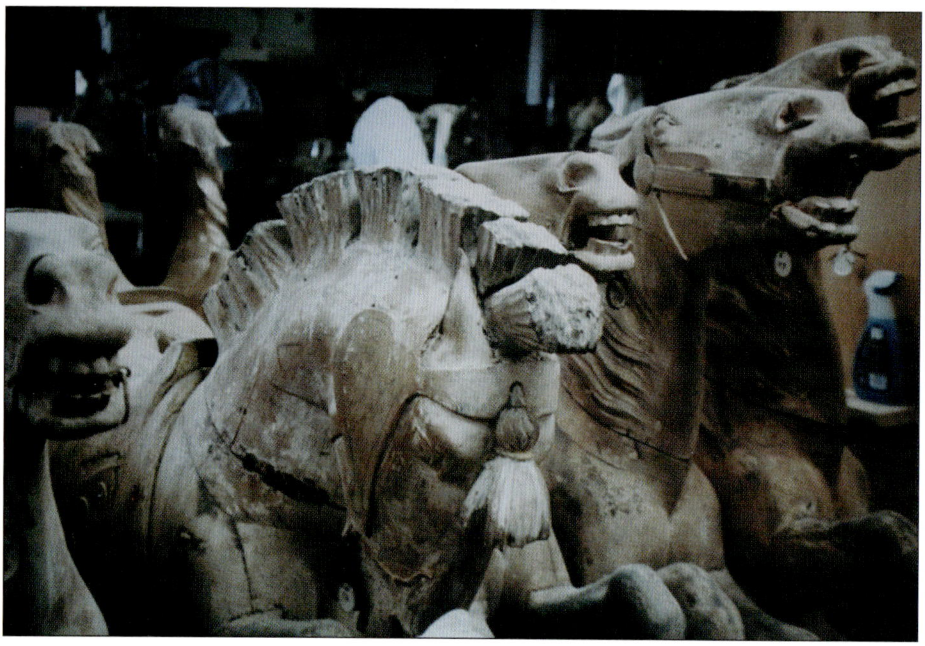

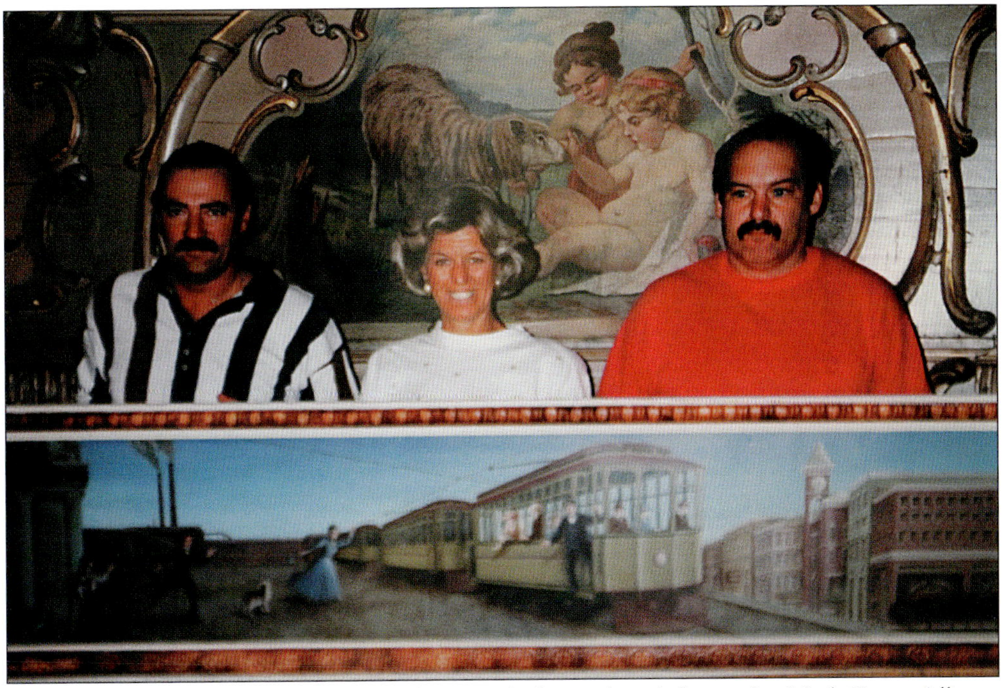

May 1994 Rededication. The above photograph shows, from left to right, Mark Carey, Alberta Giori-Gazda, and Jerry Mirra, who all posed for the rounding board painting that they are seen holding. Carey posed as the man running for the trolley while Giori-Gazda modeled for the woman beckoning the conductor; Mirra posed as the patient, but nervous conductor. Below, congressman Maurice Hinchey speaks at the dedication ceremony, and then-mayor David Archer is to his immediate left. Sandra Johnson, the granddaughter of George F. Johnson, is on the left, wearing a blue blazer. (Both, courtesy of EVC.)

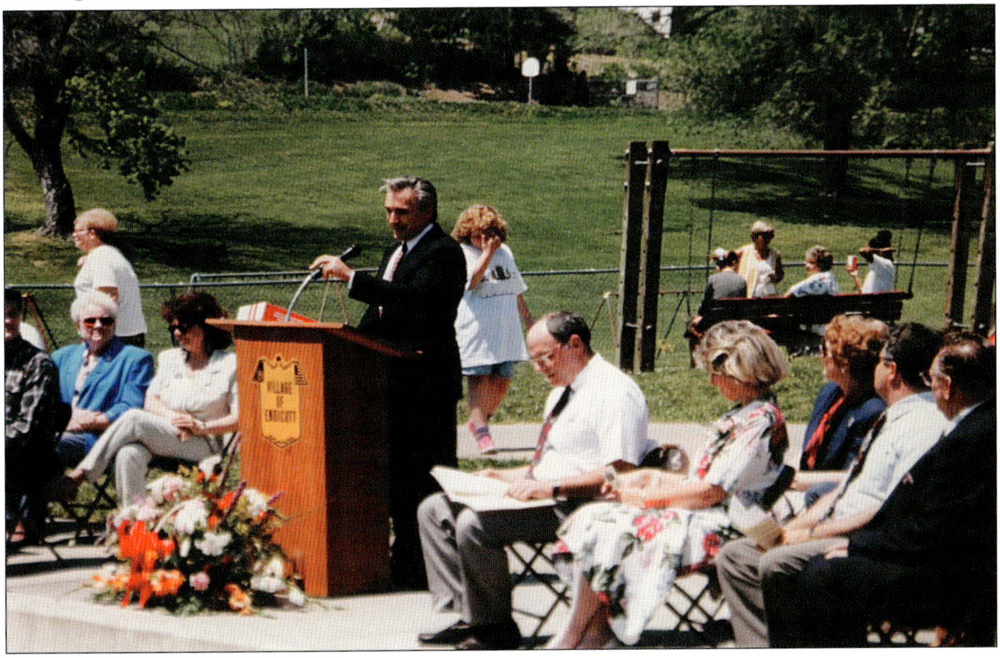

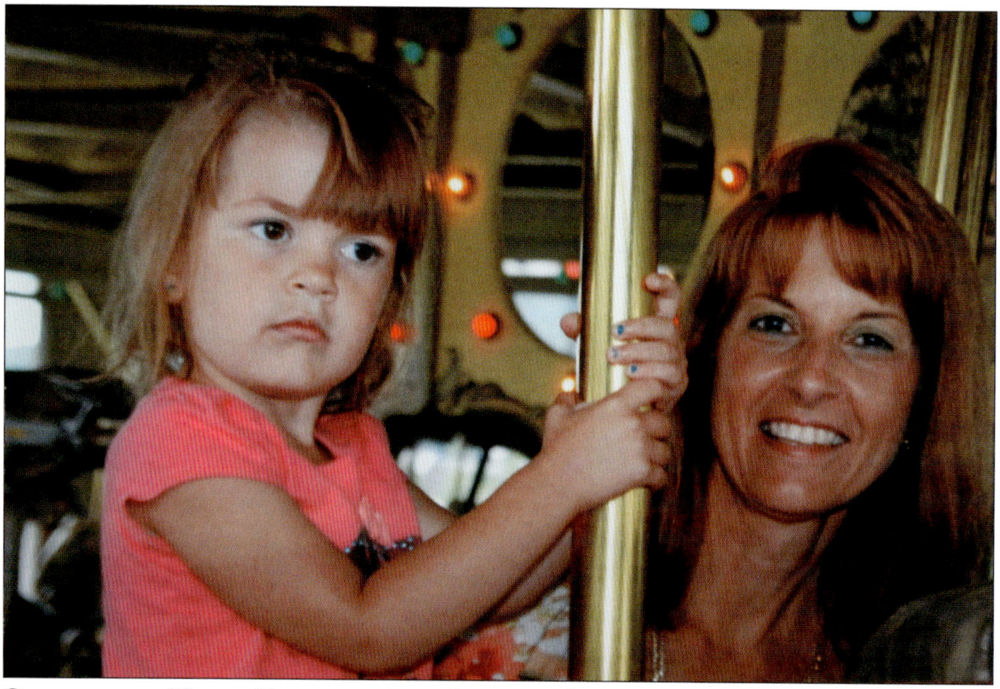

Generational Nexus. Two generations of women ride an area carousel in the above c. 1995 image. In the below photograph, note the rounding board where Rod Serling is in the foreground and the park's band shell is in the background. The park patrons resemble the denizens in *The Twilight Zone* episode "A Stop at Willoughby." The Serling family moved to Binghamton shortly after Rod's birth, and he stayed until he left to serve in World War II. One of the places the Serlings lived was on Bennett Avenue, only blocks from Recreation Park, where Rod spent many afternoons. The round boards of the Recreation Park carousel display scenes from episodes of *The Twilight Zone.* These scenes were painted by artist Cortlandt Hull as part of the carousel's 2011 restoration. The other episodes depicted include "One for the Angels," "Walking Distance," "Time Enough at Last," "The Howling Man," "It's a Good Life," "To Serve Man," "Nightmare at 20,000 Feet," and "A Living Doll." (Above, courtesy of EVC.)

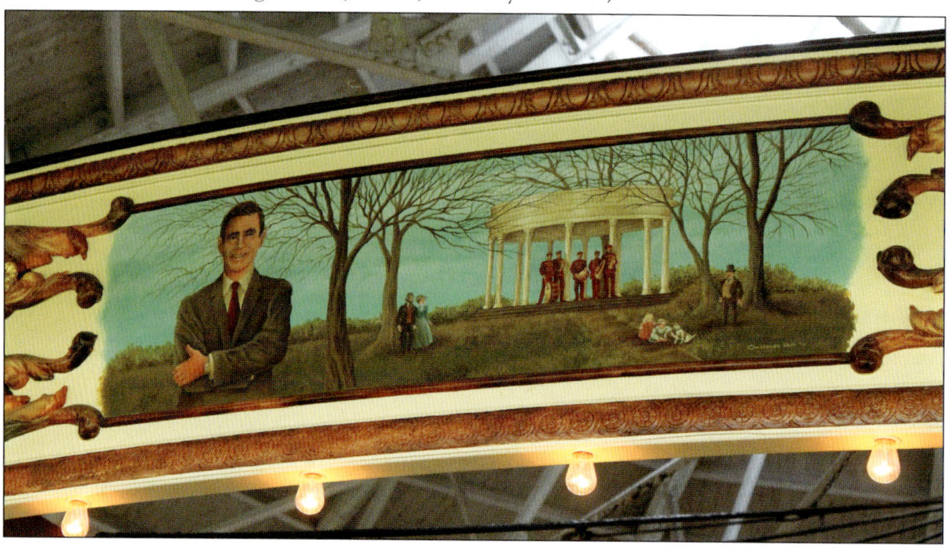

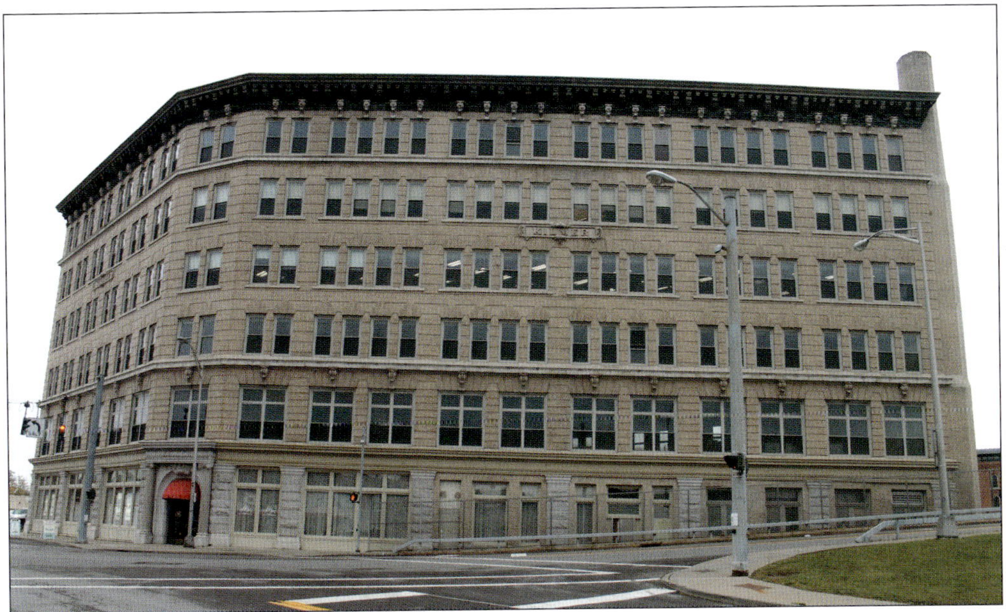

Lights, Camera, Action in Elderstown. The above photograph shows Binghamton's Kilmer Building, erected in 1903 on the corner of Lewis and Chenango Streets. The Kilmer Building was the manufacturing home of Dr. Kilmer's Swamp Root Liver, Bladder, and Kidney Cure. It now houses area businesses and Remlik's Oyster Bar and Grille. The Perry Building on Court Street is pictured below. The 1991 movie *Liebestraum*, which stars Kevin Anderson, Pamela Gidley, Bill Pullman, and the legendary Kim Novak, was primarily shot in Binghamton. (During her stay in Binghamton, Novak resided at the Hotel Deville in downtown Binghamton.) The cast-iron Perry Building is an integral part of the film, with its facade dominating many shots. Noted architect Isaac Perry designed the building, which has graced Court and Chenango Streets since 1876. As for the movie, *Liebestraum* is a dark and foreboding film that was generally panned by the critics. The isolated shots of these two buildings mirror the disconnection of the main characters of *Liebestraum*. In the movie, Binghamton takes on the name "Elderstown."

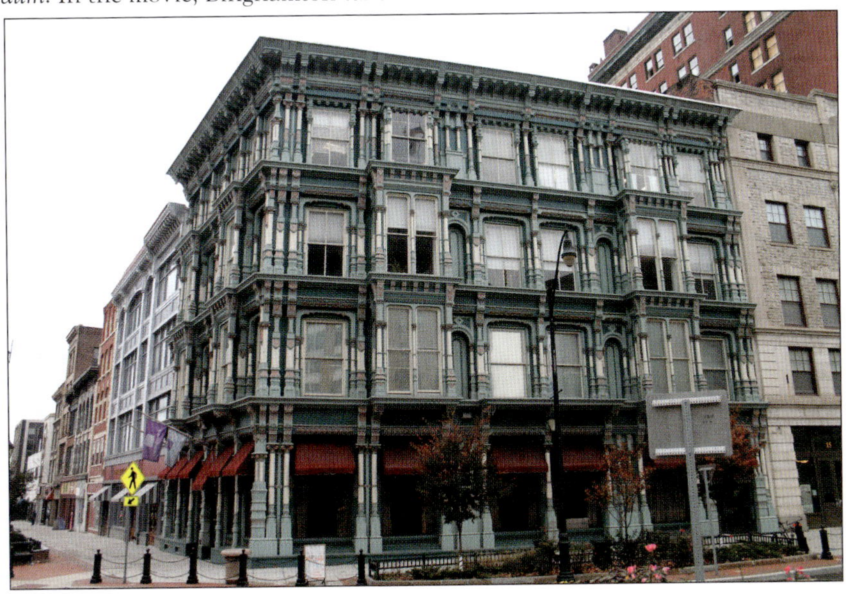

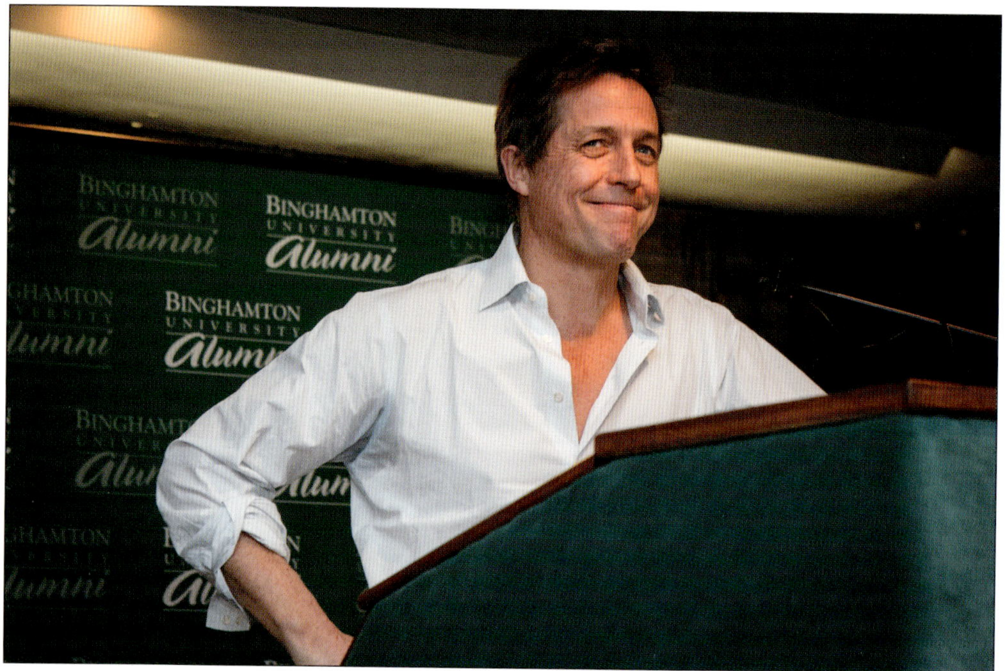

WHAT AM I DOING HERE? The first thoughts of faded Hollywood screenwriter Keith Michaels are ones of bewilderment in the 2015 movie *The Rewrite*. Ironically, by the movie's end, Michaels mewls to stay in town. Director, screenwriter, and Binghamton University graduate Marc Lawrence set the film in Binghamton. In the above photograph, Hugh Grant, who portrays Keith Michaels, addresses those attending the film's US premiere. Grant's costar Marisa Tomei, when asked by Lauren Le Vine of Refiner29.com if *The Rewrite* was shot in Binghamton, explained, "Yes, in the springtime. It was quite beautiful." Early in the movie, Michaels walks past the airport's Edwin A. Link exhibit, shown in the background below. The blue airplane-like device is the famous "blue box," the flight simulator that launched Link Aviation (first known as the Link Aeronautical Corporation). During World War II, over 10,000 simulators were in use to train pilots. (Above, courtesy of BU.)

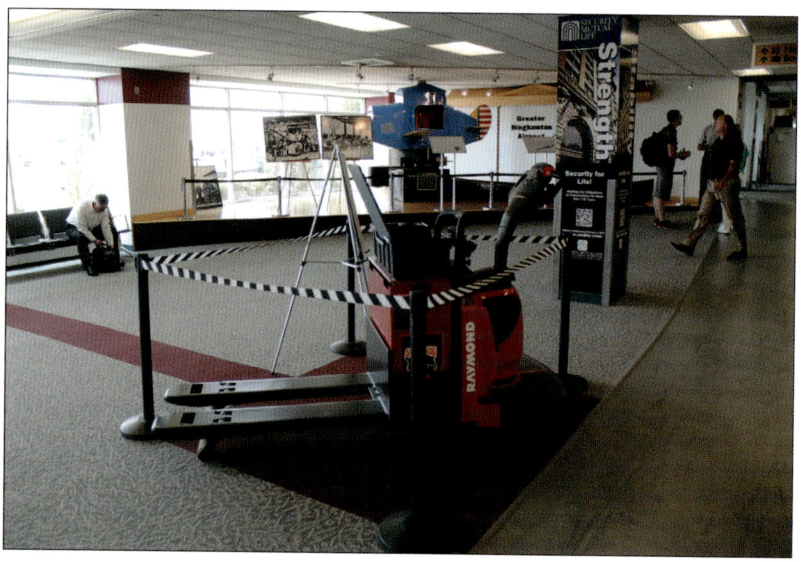

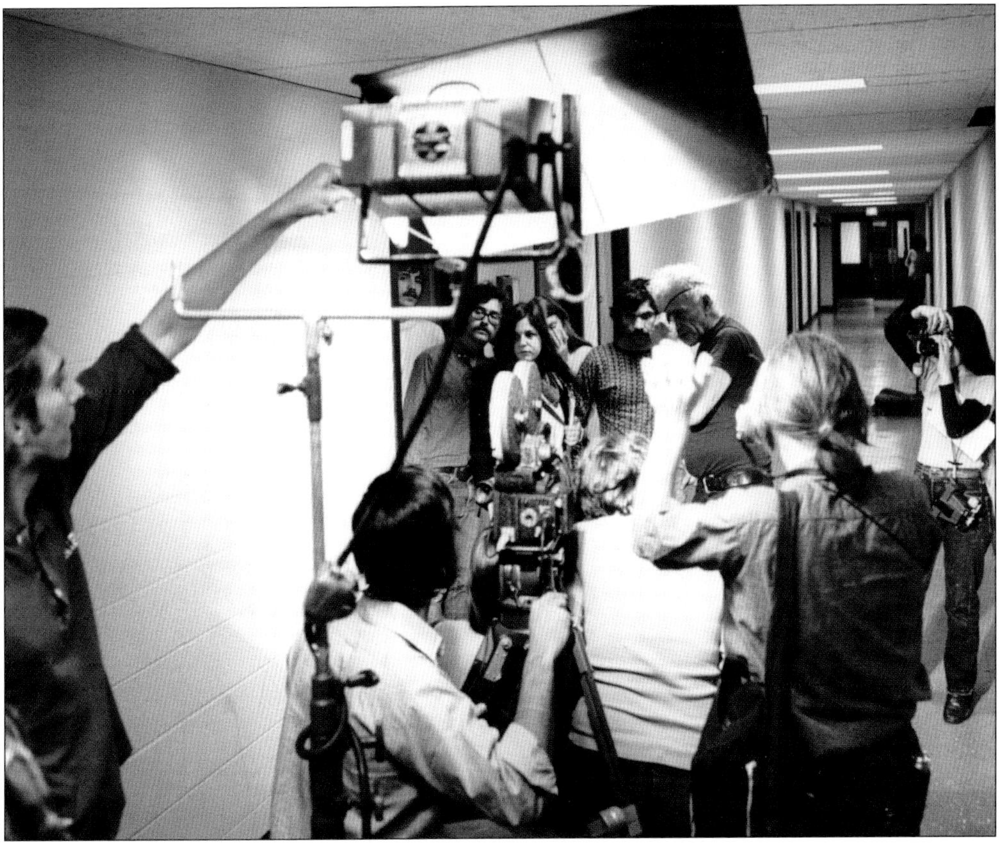

Echoes from the Past. Ironically, the career journey of the fictional Keith Michaels is similar to that of Nicholas Ray, who taught at Binghamton University (then known as State University of New York at Binghamton) in the early 1970s when he no longer could get work in Hollywood. In the two pictures on this page, Ray, easily identified by his eye patch, instructs Binghamton students on techniques of filmmaking. Ray's Hollywood career was at its zenith during the 1950s, when he directed such films as *In a Lonely Place* (starring Humphrey Bogart and Gloria Grahame), *Johnny Guitar* (starring Joan Crawford and Sterling Hayden), and *Rebel without a Cause* (starring James Dean, Sal Mineo, and Natalie Wood). (Both, courtesy of BU, Special Collections.)

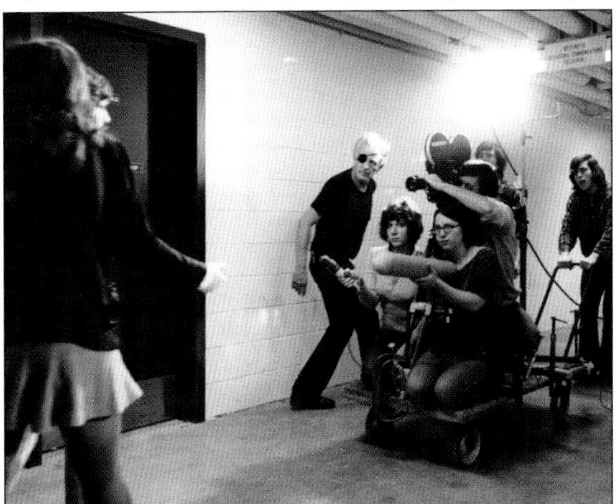

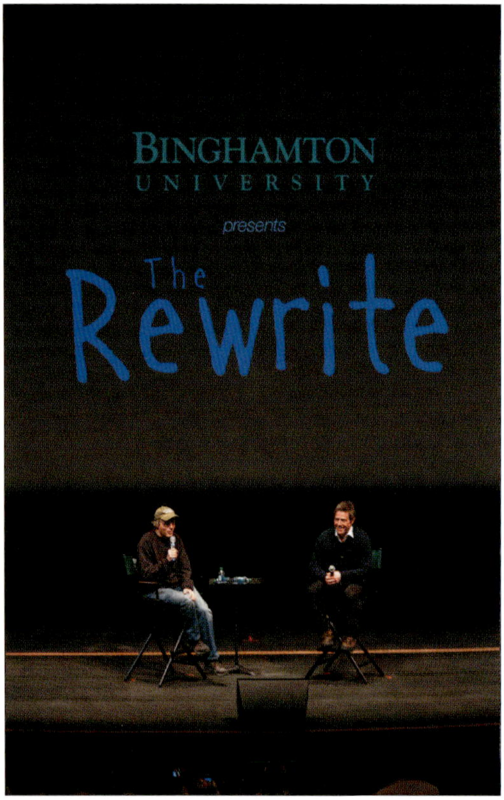

BINGHAMTON AS A PREMIERE HOST CITY. In the left photograph, Marc Lawrence and Hugh Grant field questions from the audience during the US premiere of *The Rewrite* at Binghamton University on February 8, 2015. Over 1,000 people attended the event, which took place in the Concert Theater in the university's Anderson Center. Over 30 years earlier, in the summer of 1983, Binghamton served as the host city for the world premiere of *Twilight Zone: The Movie*, which stars John Lithgow and Vic Morrow, among others. Pictured below is the flyer that announces Binghamton as the host of the world premiere, along with a movie ticket to the event. As the flyer indicates, special guests for the premiere included Richard Deacon (Binghamton actor), Helen Foley (Serling's middle school English teacher), Robert Serling (Rod Serling's brother), and Jodie Serling (Rod's daughter). The film premiered in the Crest Theater in Binghamton; a paint store now stands where the theater once was. (Left, courtesy of BU; below, courtesy of RSA @ BMHA.)

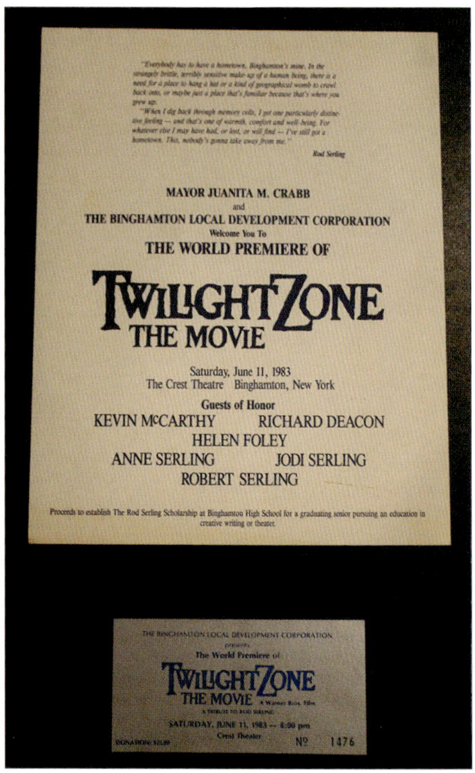

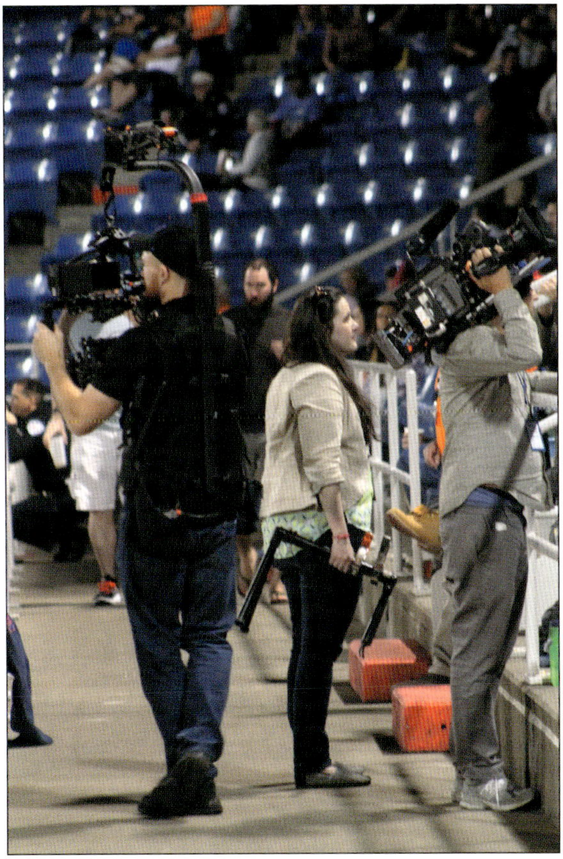

The Stadium as a Backlot. On April 21, 2015, the Entertainment and Sports Programming Network (ESPN) sent a three-person crew to NYSEG Stadium to gather material for an upcoming documentary on the rebranding of the hometown AA baseball team, the Binghamton Mets. This was the final day for fans to send in suggestions for the team's new moniker. Pictured is the three-person camera crew that spent some time interviewing fans on this night. Over 1,500 candidates were submitted for the new appellation for the team. In the below photograph, one of the cameramen poses for the author. Besides ESPN, Sports New York (SNY) has also been a frequent visitor to watch the Binghamton Mets, to gather footage for its New York Mets pregame and postgame shows.

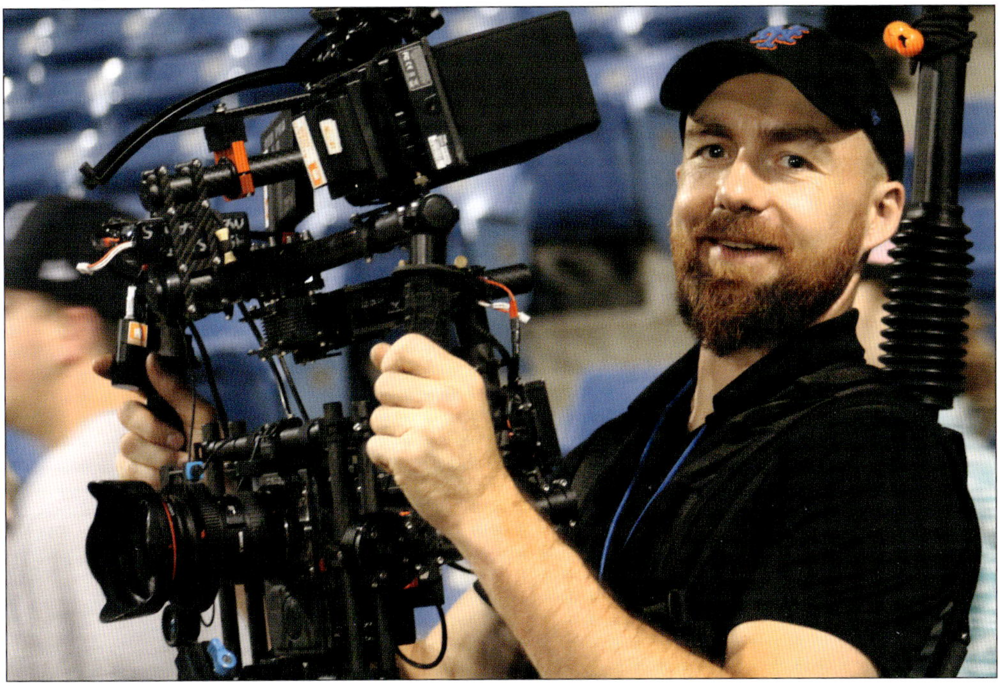

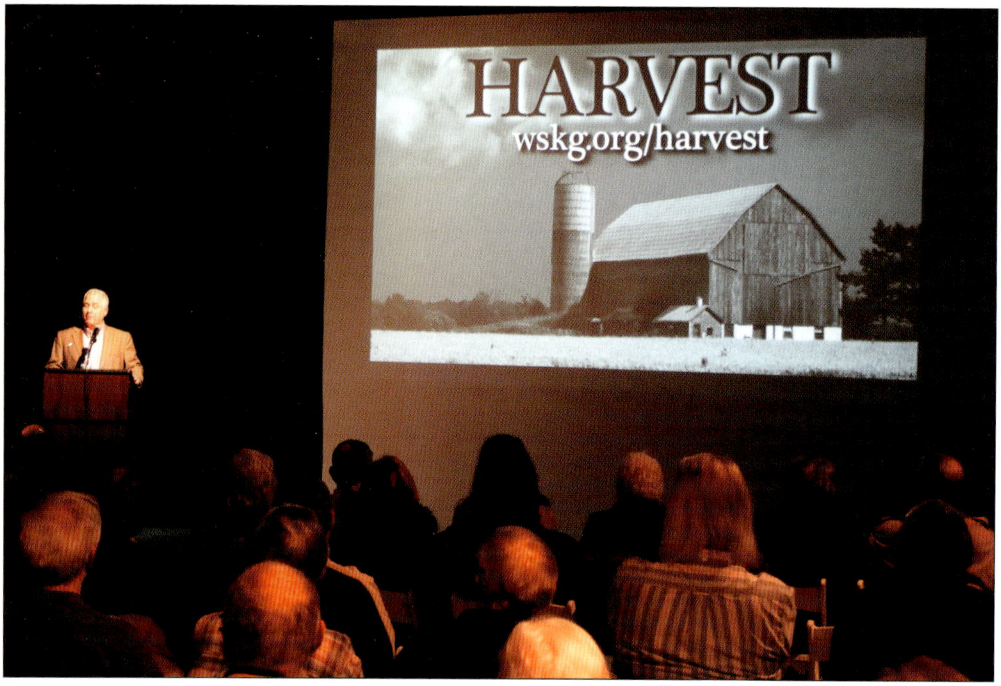

SHOWTIME FOR *HARVEST TIME*. Above, three-time Emmy Award–winning filmmaker Brian Frey, of television station WSKG in Binghamton, speaks to the Broome County Historical Society. He was showing segments from his most recent documentary for public television, *Harvest*, which aired in November 2015. Says Frey of his work, "I love to put music to images and that is part of the reason why I love what I do. I could never be a writer, because I couldn't find a way to weave sound into a book." Below, one of the opening shots of *Harvest* draws the audience into its story. Frey's work has centered on the area surrounding Binghamton, including the documentaries: *Johnson*, *Watson*, and *Cornell: Birth of the American University*. Concerning his interest in doing a documentary on agriculture, Frey explained, "I had previously done films on industry, but I've always felt farming has been just as much an integral part of the history of the area as well."

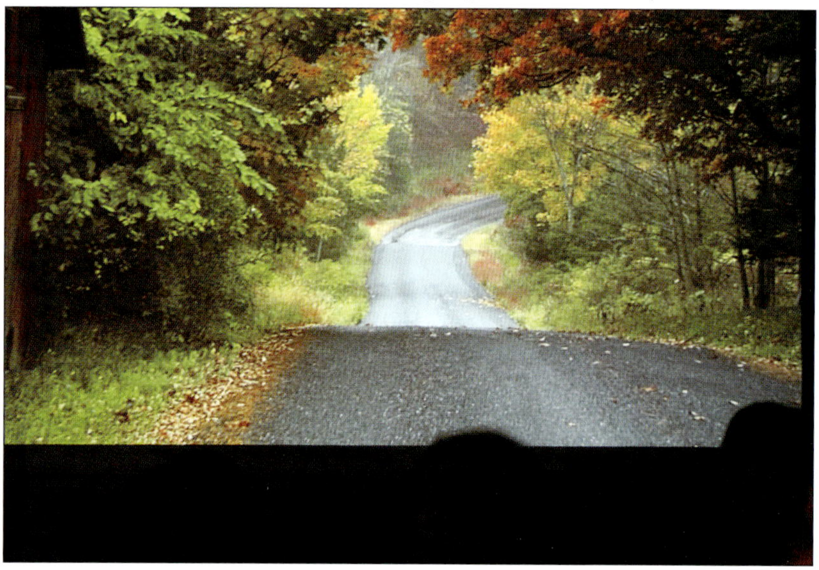

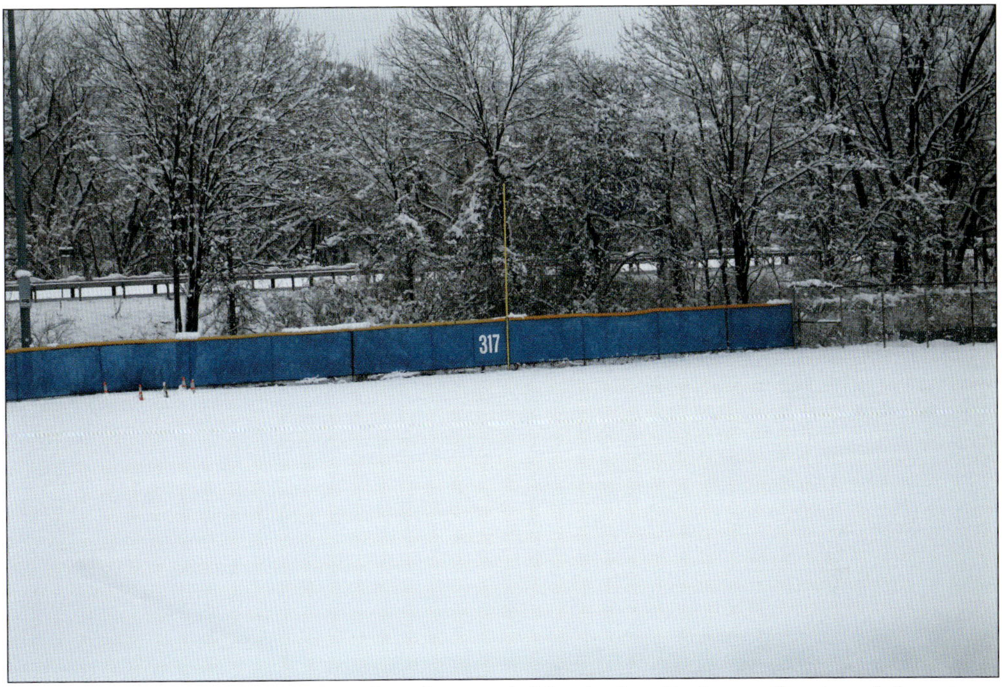

Singin' in the Snow and Sun. Binghamton's MacArthur Park was the site of the winter outdoor shots for Taylor Swift's 2011 music video, *Back to December.* The winter scene in the above photograph resembles part of the footage in the video. The loneliness and isolation of a snow-covered baseball field mirrors the music video's somber tone. Below, country singer LeAnn Rimes belts out a song at Binghamton's Annual Spiedie Fest and Balloon Rally in Otsiningo Park in August 2013.

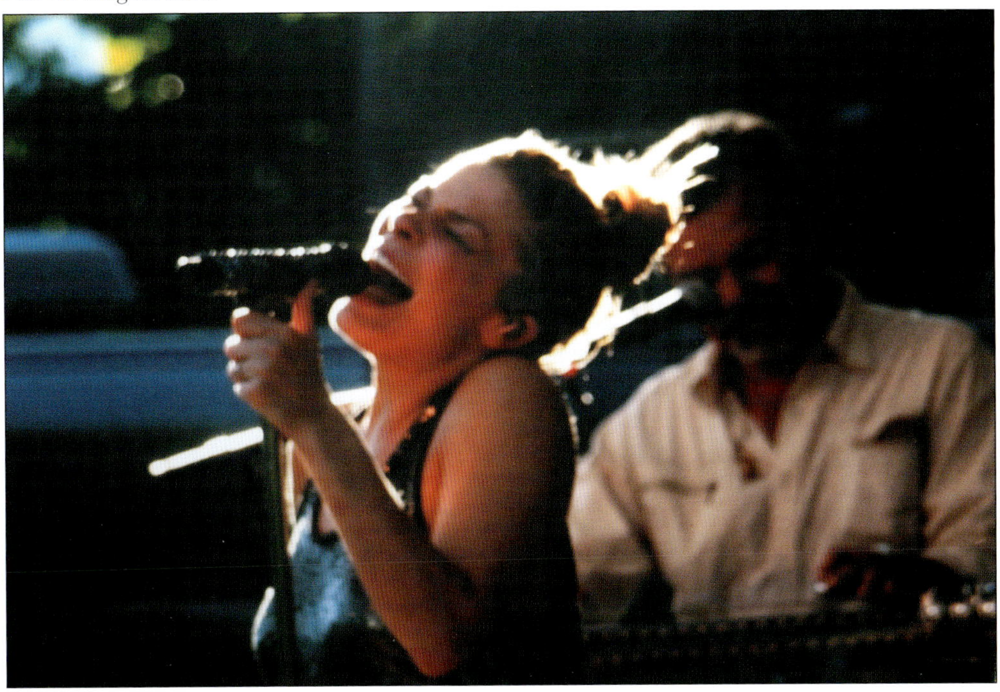

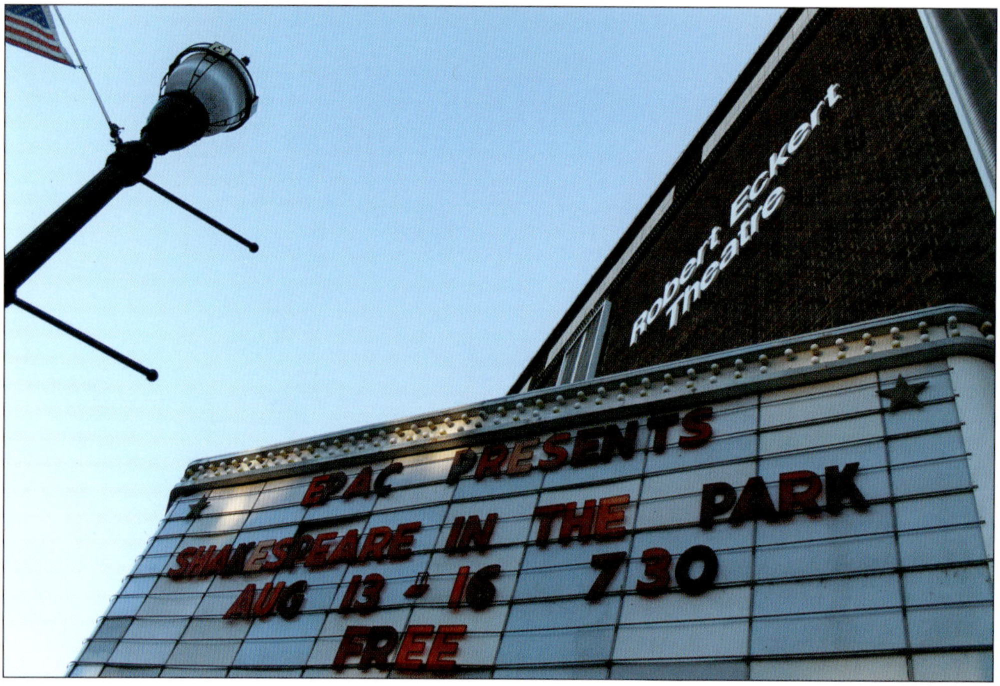

Strong Regional Theaters. The Endicott Performing Arts Center (EPAC) in Endicott houses numerous stage productions throughout the year in its Robert Eckert Theatre on Washington Avenue. Previously known as the Lyric and then the Towne movie theater, the building closed in 1993 before reopening as part of the performing arts center. Below, the Cider Mill Playhouse, approximately two miles from the Eckert Theatre, has hosted stage productions since 1971. Many Binghamton University professors and students have found their way to the Cider Mill stage.

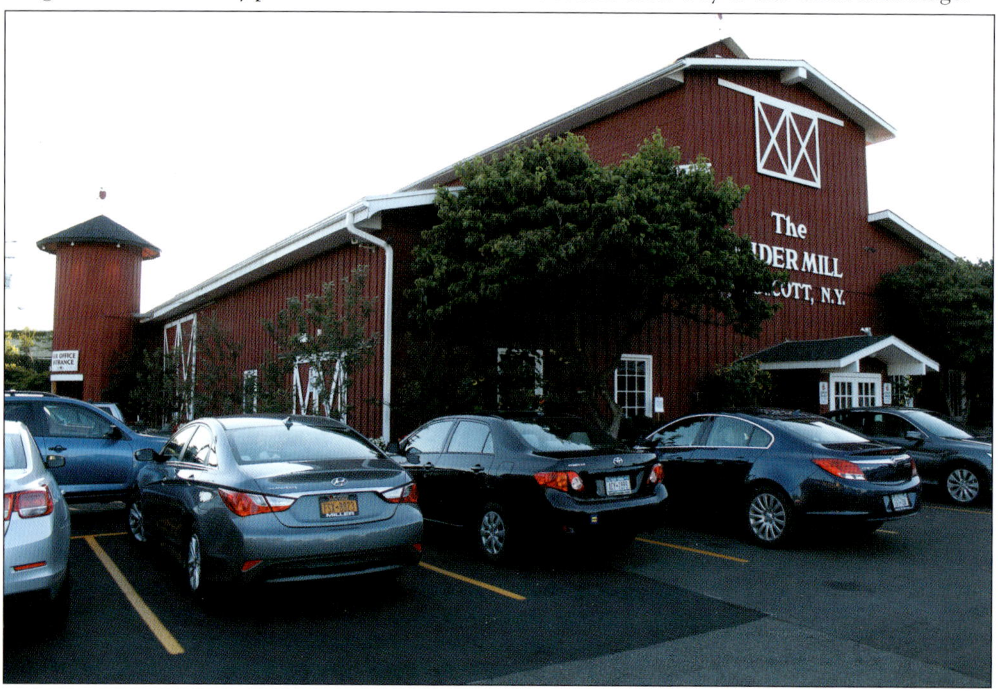

Before Achieving Fame, She was a Dame. Stephanie Courtney was a Binghamton University student when she played the role of Joan in the Cider Mill's production of *Dames at Sea* in July 1992. In the image to the right, the cover of the program bills the production as a "nostalgic Hollywood musical." The below image shows the musical productions from the show. Courtney displayed her singing and dancing talent throughout the show, something that she has not had to do as the ubiquitous Flo spokeswoman in the commercials for the Progressive Insurance Company. (Both, courtesy of BU, Special Collections, from the Cider Mill Playhouse.)

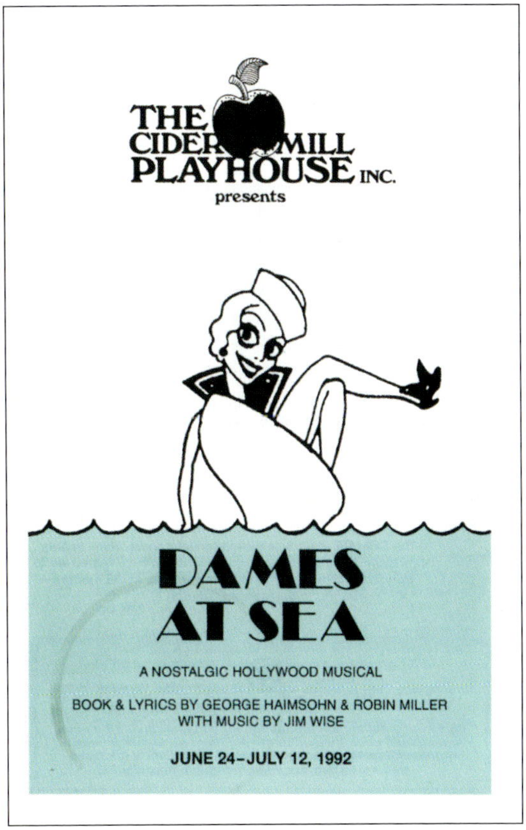

Dames at Sea

Cast

(in order of appearance)

Mona .... Joanne Borts*
Joan .... Stephanie Courtney
Hennesy .... Jack Lewis
Ruby .... Shannon Marie Roma
Dick .... Michael Polscer*
Lucky .... Jan DeAngelo
The Captain .... Jack Lewis
Jimmy. .... Scott Earle
Ginger .... Karen McMahon
Una. .... Lisa Raymond

**Appearing through the courtesy of Actors Equity Association.*

Musicians

Pianists .... Lisa DeSiro, Scherrill Van Horne
Percussionist .... Joe Roma
Rehearsal Pianist .... Scherrill Van Horne
Dance Captain .... Karen McMahon

Production Crew

Stage Manager .... David Sugarman
Scenic Artist .... John Lavarnway
Master Electrician .... Chris Ficke
Sound .... John T. Cotton
Set Crew .... Chris Carroll, David Kuhn, Kevin Simons
Properties .... Diana Ogas & Cheryl Thomas
Wardrobe .... L. Annette Short, Kathleen Rutkowski
Company Photographer .... Carol Paden

Dames at Sea

Time:

The early thirties.

Act One:

Any Forty Second Street Theater

Act Two:

On The Battleship

There will be a 15 minute intermission between acts.

Musical Numbers

Act One

Wall Street .... Mona
It's You .... Dick and Ruby
Broadway Baby .... Dick
That Mister Man of Mine .... Mona and Dick
Choo-Choo Honeymoon .... Joan and Lucky
*The Sailor of My Dreams .... Ruby
*Singapore Sue .... Lucky and Company
*Good Times are Here to Stay .... Joan & Company

Act Two

Dames at Sea .... Dick, Lucky, Captain, Joan, Ruby & Mona
The Beguine .... Mona and Captain
Raining in My Heart .... Ruby, Mona, Joan, Ginger and Una
There's Something About You .... Dick and Ruby
Raining in My Heart (Reprise) .... Ruby
*The Echo Waltz .... Mona, Joan, Ruby and Company
Star Tar .... Ruby, Joan, Ginger, Una, Dick, Lucky and Jimmy
Let's Have a Simple Wedding .... Dick and Ruby, Lucky and Joan, Captain and Mona

**Lyrics by George Haimsohn*

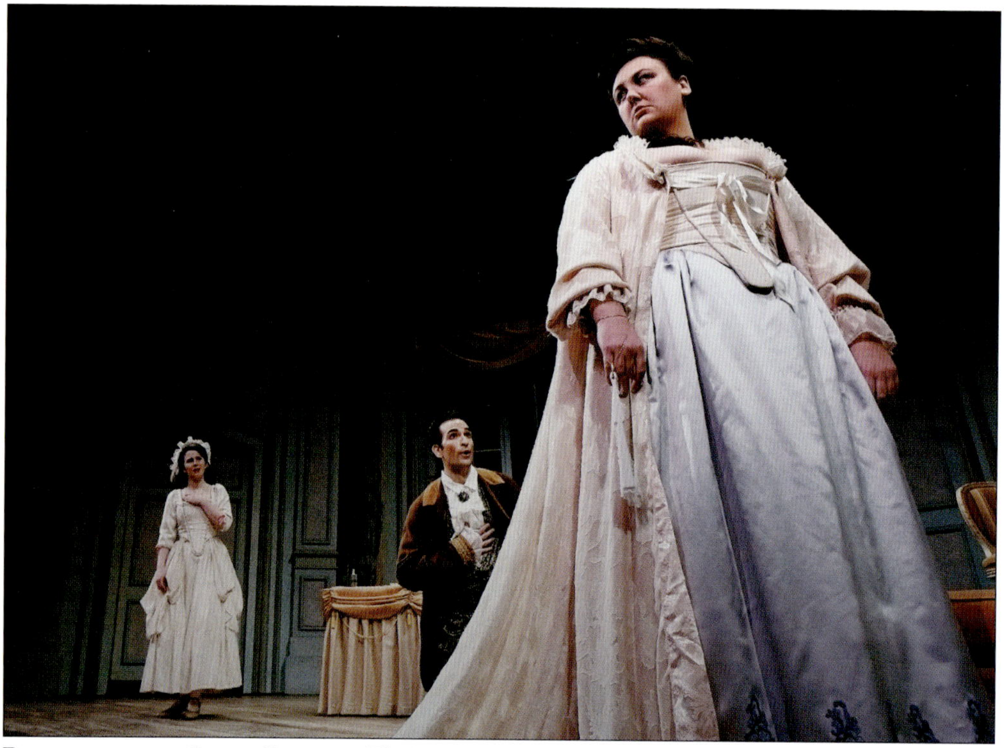

Prepping for an Opera Opening. The Tri-Cities Opera was founded in Binghamton in 1949 by Peyton Hibbit and Carmen Savoca. In 1992, New York governor Mario Cuomo praised the work of Hibbit and Savoca, awarding them a citation for forming the company and developing it into an "acclaimed cultural institution." The opera company stages multiple full-scale operas every year, with many of them taking place at Binghamton's Forum Theatre. The two photographs from this page capture scenes during dress rehearsals from *The Marriage of Figaro*, which was performed in May 2015. (Both, courtesy of MR and Tri-Cities Opera.)

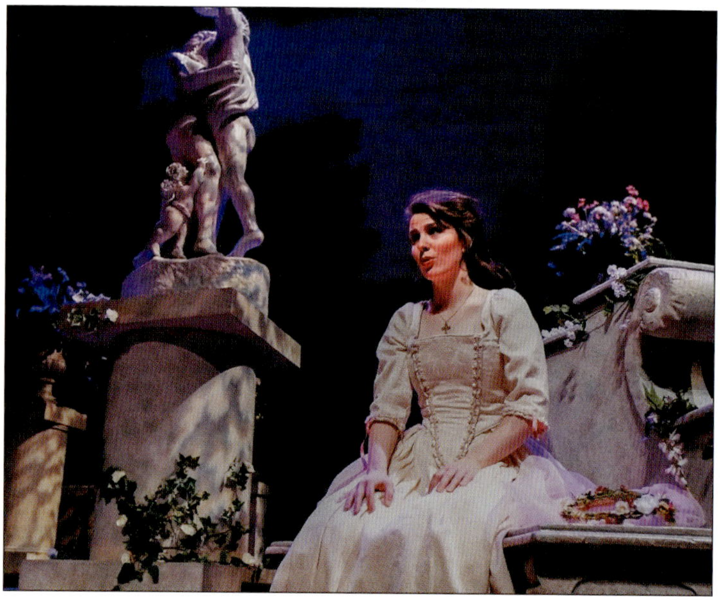

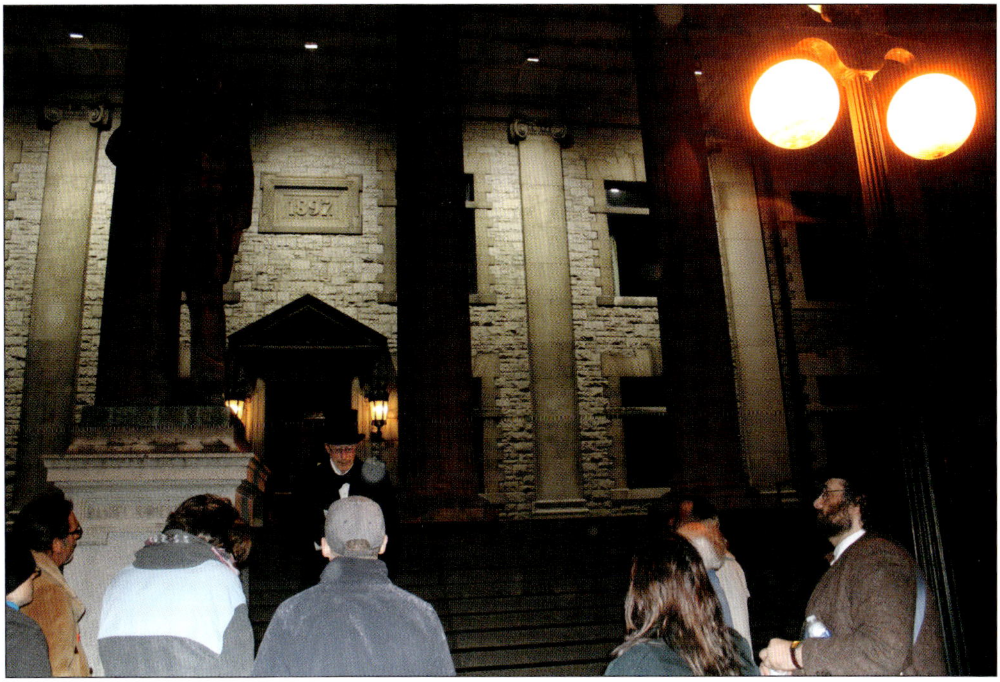

Spirits from the Past. Rick Pescatore portrays statesman Daniel Dickinson, as seen in this photograph shot in front of the Binghamton courthouse during the 2014 *Spirits of Binghamton's Past Downtown Walking Tour.* Each year, as Halloween approaches, the Preservation Association of the Southern Tier (PAST) hosts the walking tour featuring ghosts from Binghamton's history.

A Little Flower from the Big City. Here, Tony Lo Bianco portrays New York City mayor Fiorello H. La Guardia in his one-man show *The Little Flower* in Binghamton on October 21, 2014. The show was sponsored by the Goodwill Theatre Performing Arts Complex and Professional Training Academy in Johnson City. La Guardia was a three-term mayor of New York City from 1934 to 1945 and greatly enjoyed communicating with his constituents by radio. Lo Bianco appears in more than 100 films and has a starring role in the *The French Connection*, which won five Academy Awards. (Courtesy of GT and Tony Lo Bianco.)

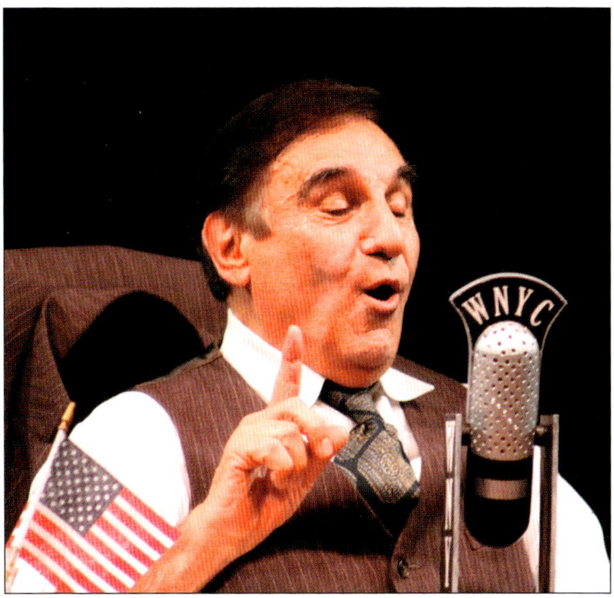

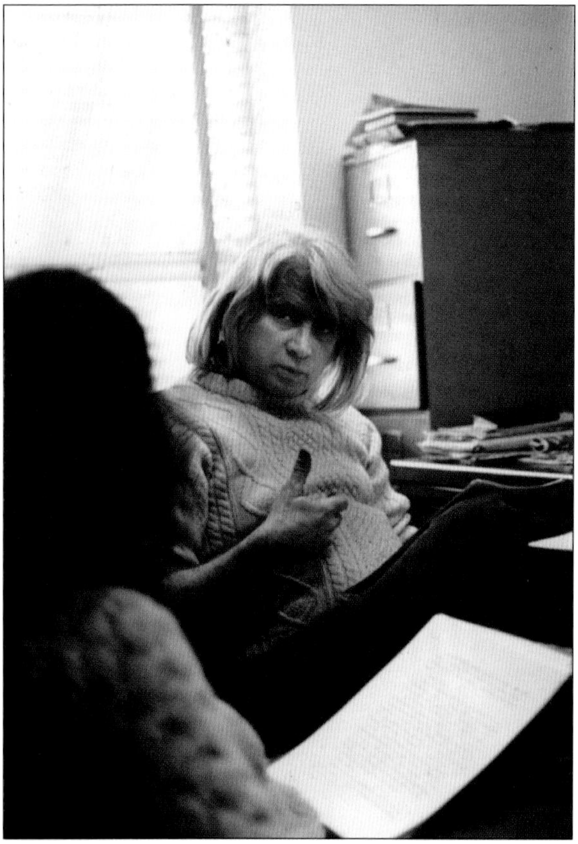

BATAVIA TO BINGHAMTON. In the photograph at left, novelist and professor John Gardner, born in Batavia, New York, provides instruction for one of his students at Binghamton University, where Gardner was teaching fiction writing at the time of his death in a motorcycle accident on September 14, 1982. His 1976 novel *October Light* won the National Book Critics Circle Award. The picture below captures a scene from the stage version of *October Light* that was performed on the campus of Binghamton University. In the center of the photograph is local actor, singer, and member of Binghamton's Walk of Fame Claus Evans. "I love the adventure that acting is," Evans told pressconnect.com in 2016. "As you learn your lines, you try to learn the story, to know the story is very important, because that defines in part the type of character you play." (Both, courtesy of BU, Special Collections.)

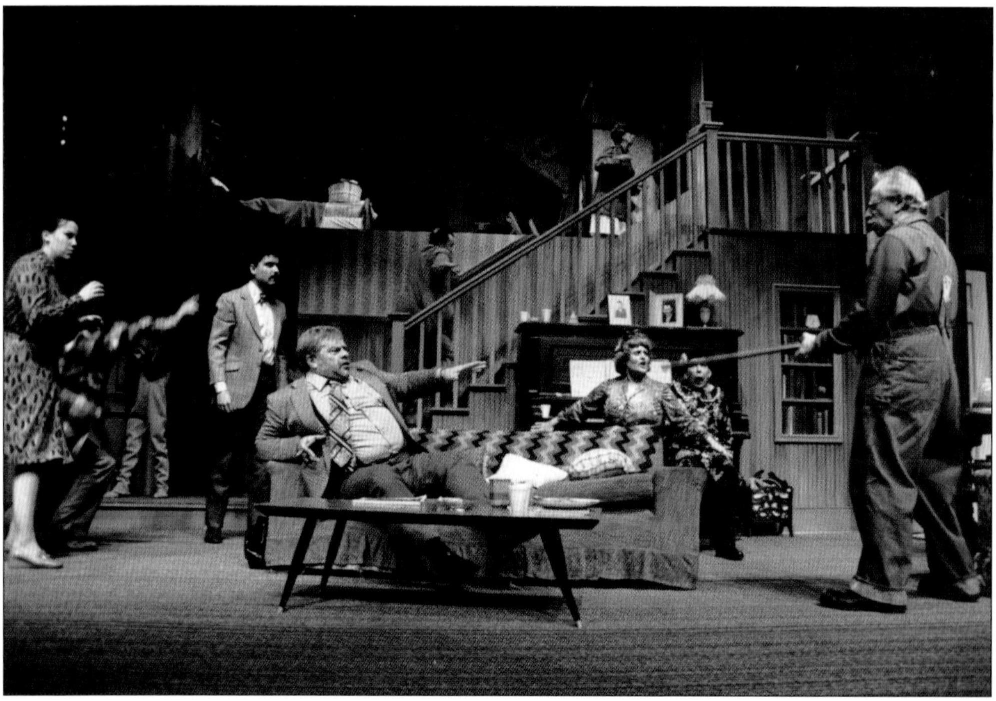

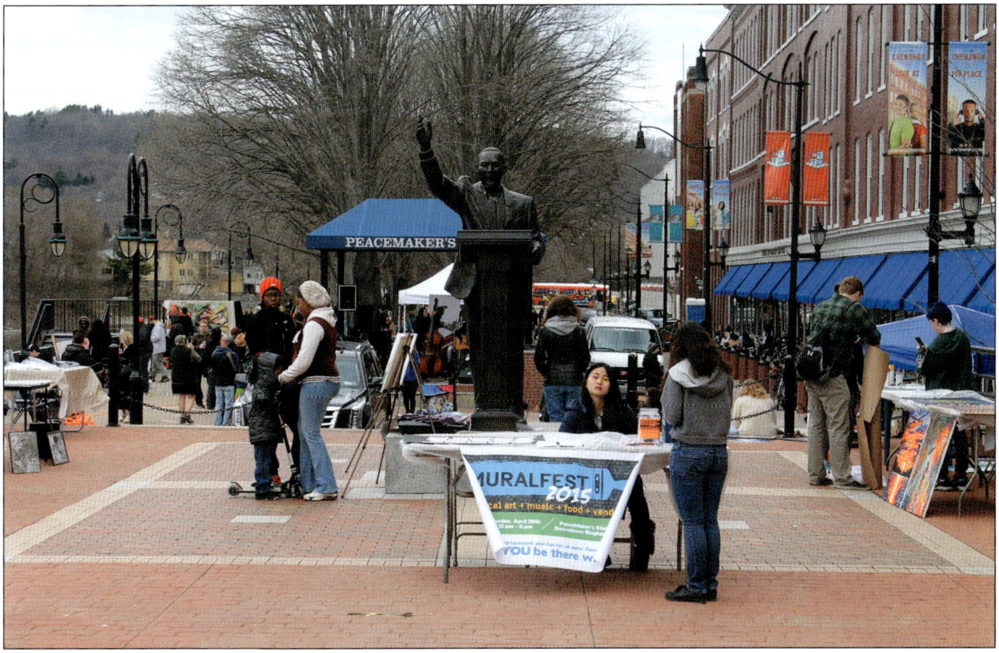

BINGHAMTON'S MURAL FEST. Hundreds of people gathered along Binghamton's Riverwalk Promenade during Mural Fest 2015, as artists painted scenes on large wooden surfaces that would later be installed throughout the city. The picture above shows the main entrance to the event, which has been held along the banks of the Chenango River. The image below shows the artists at work. "This kind of art just gives you hope for the city," said Peg Johnston, one of the event's organizers, in an interview with Shannon Hazlitt of the *Binghamton Press & Sun Bulletin* in 2015.

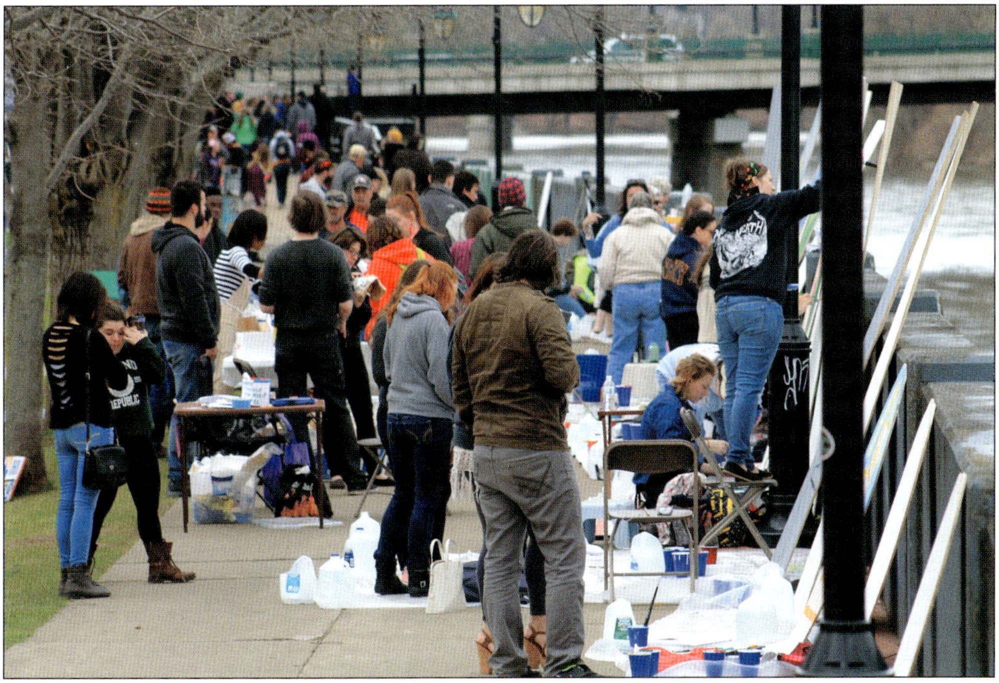

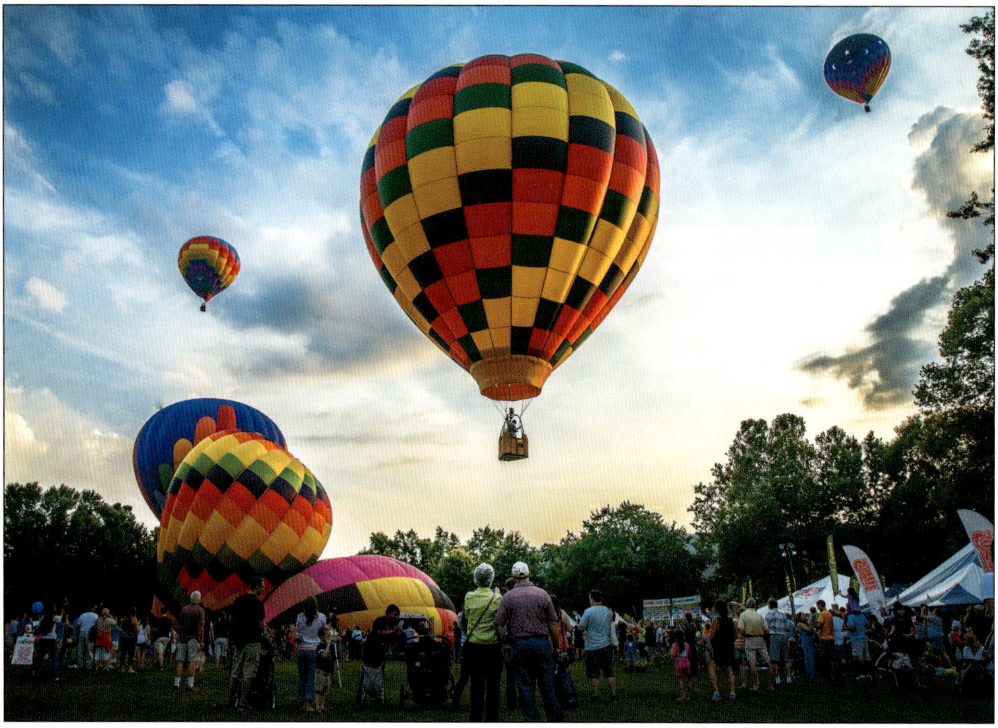

Crowds and Color Dominate the Day. In 1983, a few families got together and "discussed" who had the best spiedie recipe in Binghamton. To put an end to their friendly rivalry, they held the first Spiedie Fest cooking contests in 1983 and 1984. After a successful contest in 1984, a small committee formed and the cooking contest grew into the Spiedie Fest and Balloon Rally. Since then, hot-air balloons of all sizes and shapes have filled the Binghamton skies during the fest. The rally has always been held at Binghamton's Otsiningo Park, except for a few years when it was held at the Tri-Cities Airport, located near the En-Joie Golf Club. (Above, courtesy of BU; below, courtesy of SF.)

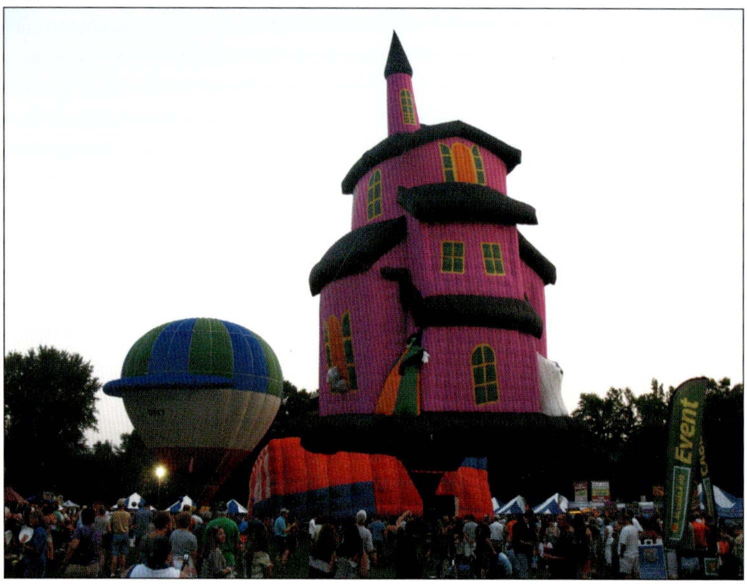

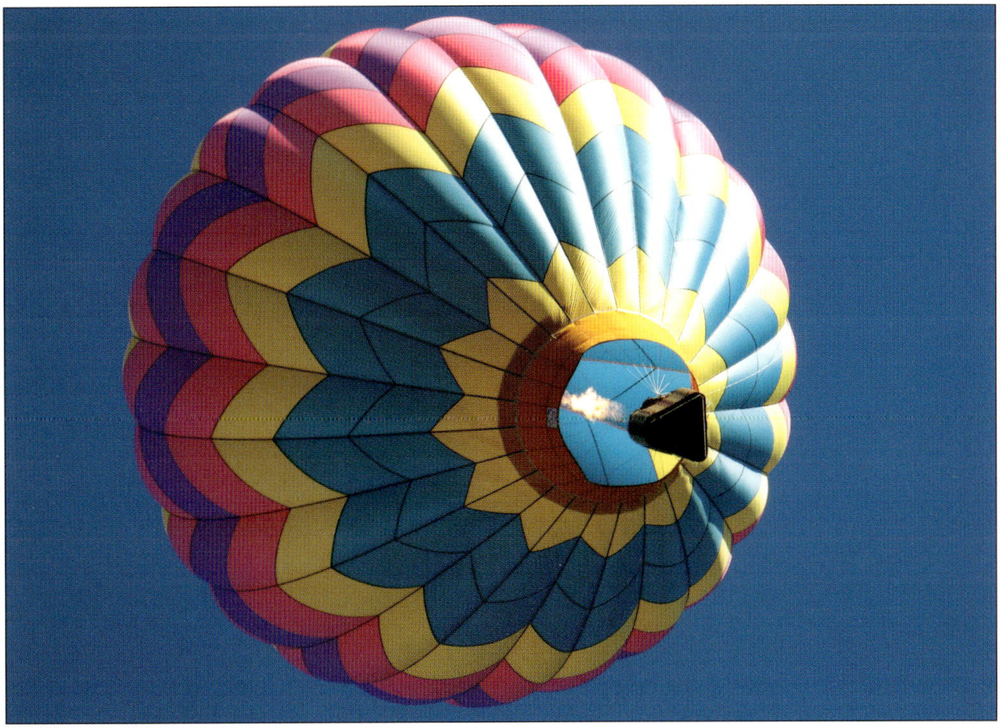

Balloons and Bikes in Binghamton. In the above shot, the flame that generates the heat to provide lift for the balloons is visible. The annual balloon rally is always held on the first full weekend in August. Since its inception, the Spiedie Fest and Balloon Rally has donated over $1 million dollars to local charities. As with the Dick's Sporting Goods Open, the event is largely run by community volunteers, ensuring local charities benefit from the proceeds. The event draws between 90,000 and 100,000 visitors over its three-day weekend. Besides the balloons and cooking contest, food and craft booths fill the park, along with a small array of carnival rides. The event has also become a favorite destination for area motorcyclists, as demonstrated in the row of motorcycles in the below photograph. (Both, courtesy of SF.)

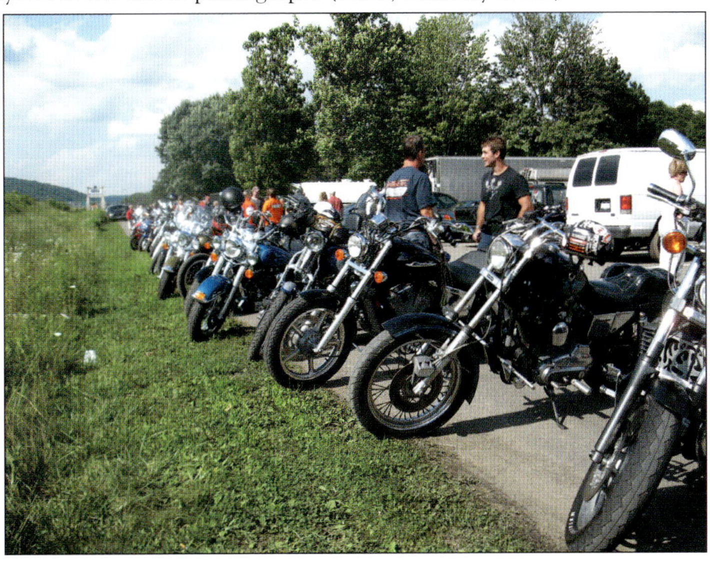

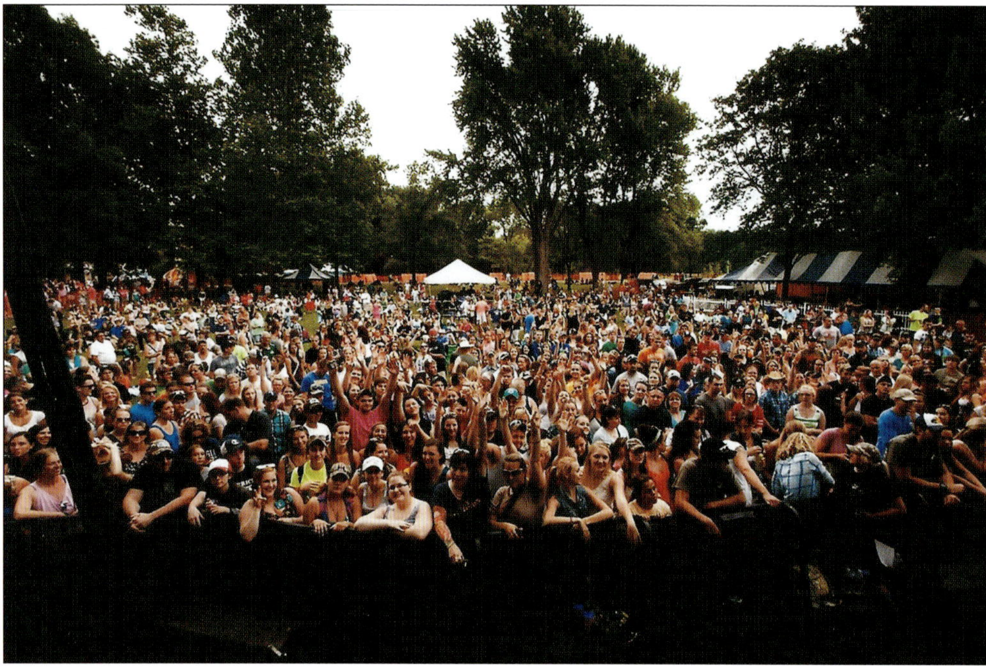

Crowds on Terra Firma and in the Skies. Musical entertainment is now a staple of the Spiedie Fest and Balloon Rally, with such musical artists as Miranda Cosgrove, Rick Springfield, and Joan Jett headlining the entertainment over the years. The photograph above shows the view from the outdoor stage, as thousands fill the concert area. The three-day event allows spectators to get close-up views of the hot-air balloons before they take to the skies, as shown in the photograph below. (Above, courtesy of MR and SF; below, courtesy of SF.)

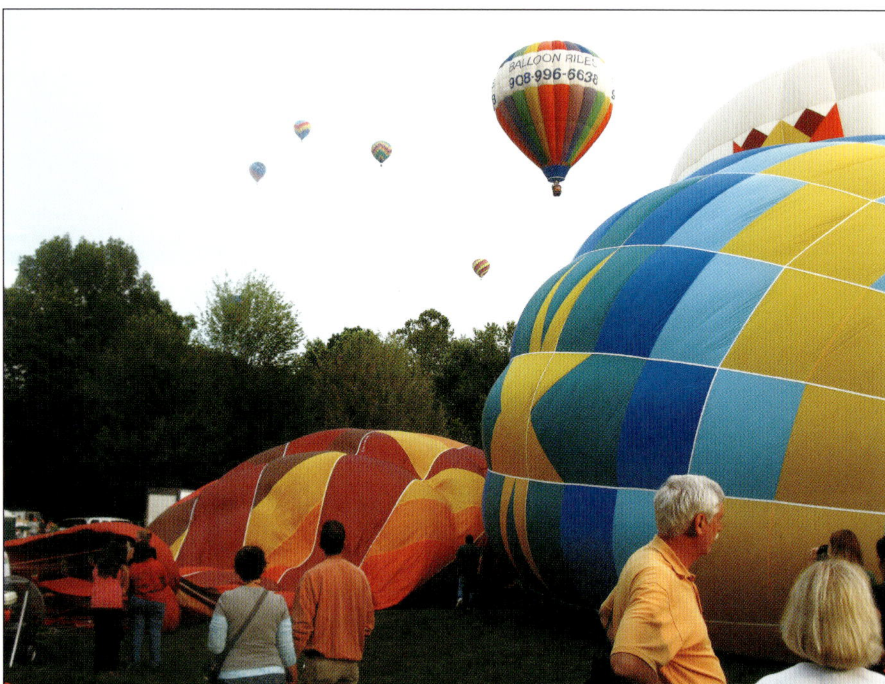

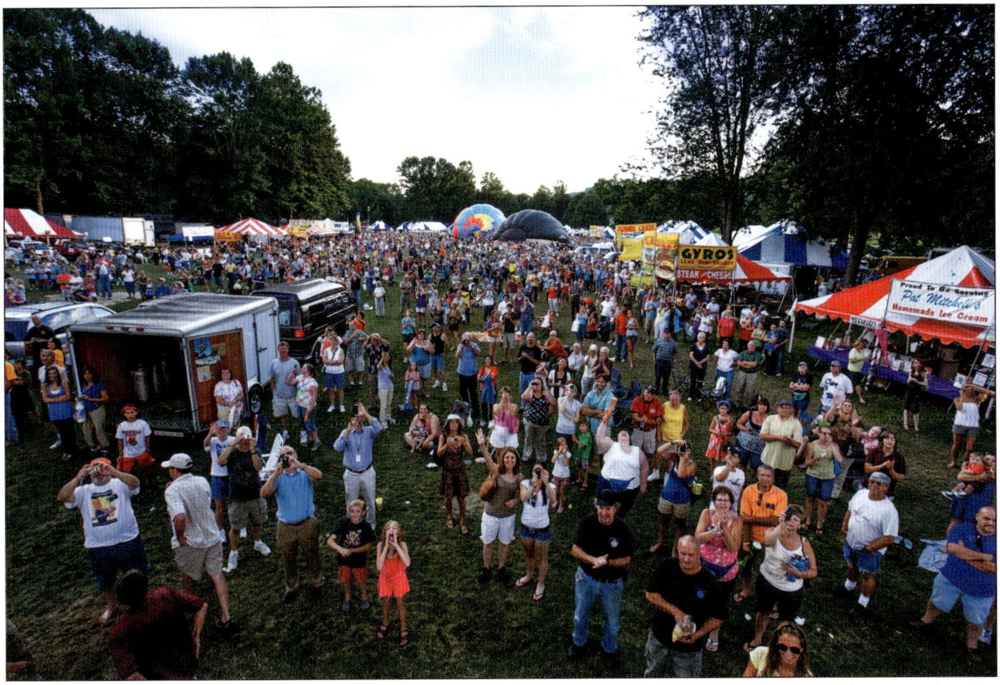

Views from Above. In the above image, photographer Michael Ricciardi shoots the crowd as he heads into the skies. The woman waving in the center of the photograph is his wife, Deborah, while his daughter, Vicky, turns the tables on him and snaps a shot of him. The photograph below captures Otsiningo Park at its colorful best. The highways in the upper right background are the north and south lanes for Interstate 81. (Both, courtesy of MR.)

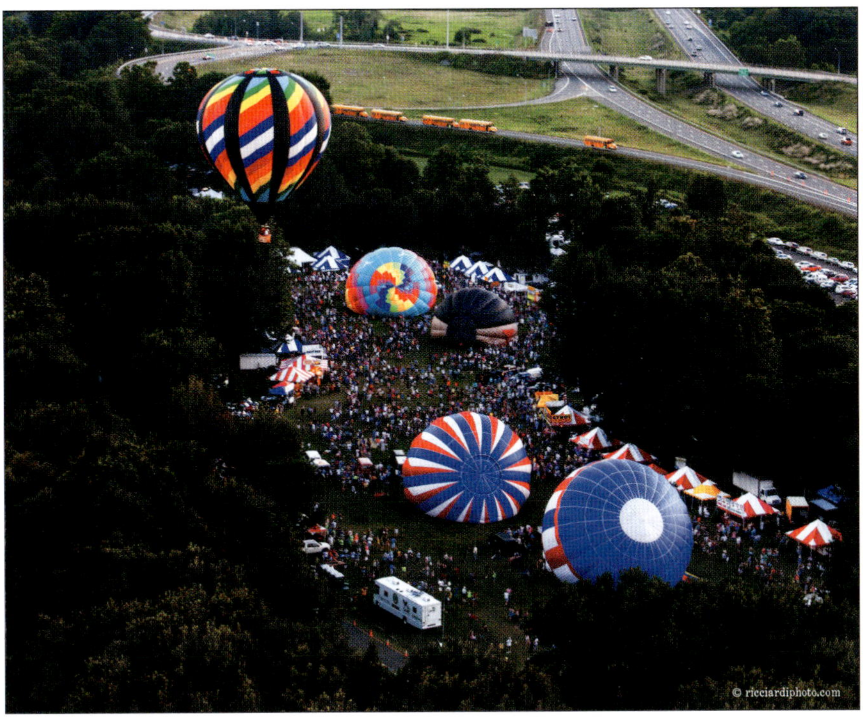

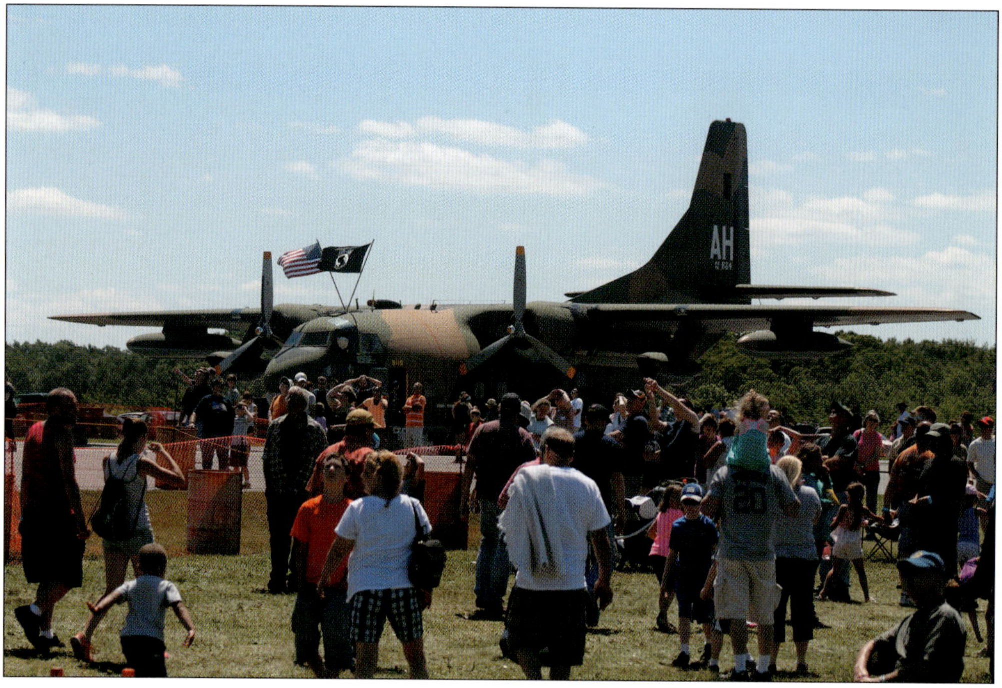

SUN AND BLUE SKIES ON THE FOURTH OF JULY. The Greater Binghamton Airport has periodically hosted air shows that have drawn thousands of area denizens to enjoy tours of World War II planes, as well as see aerobatics and parachutists. In the above picture, spectators flock to tour a cargo transport plane, while the image below shows planes flying in close formation. Both of these pictures are from the show that was held on July 4 and 5 in 2014.

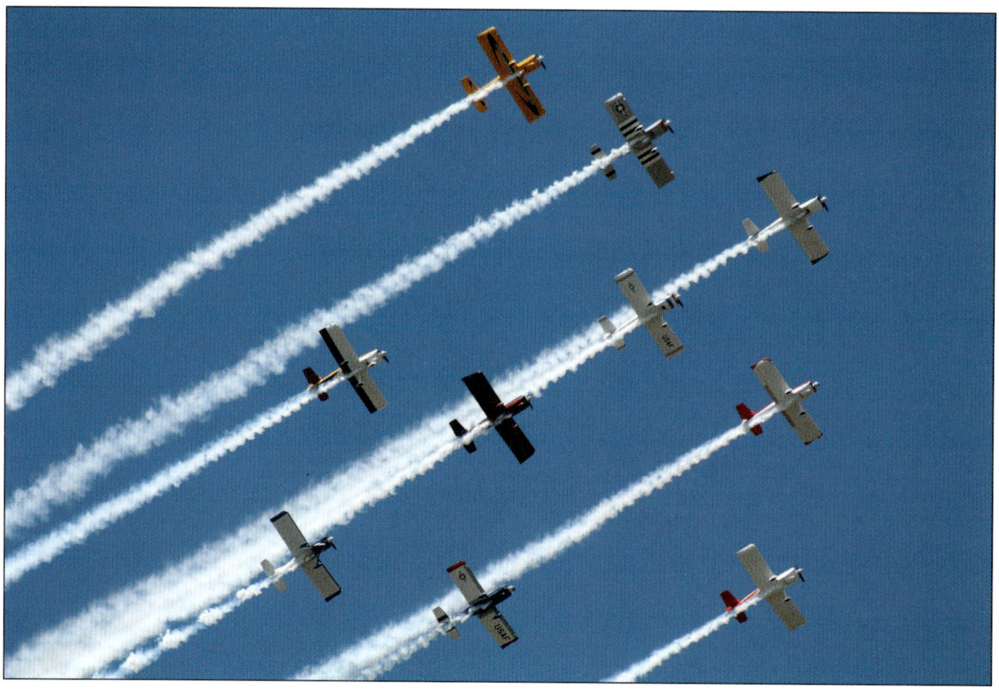

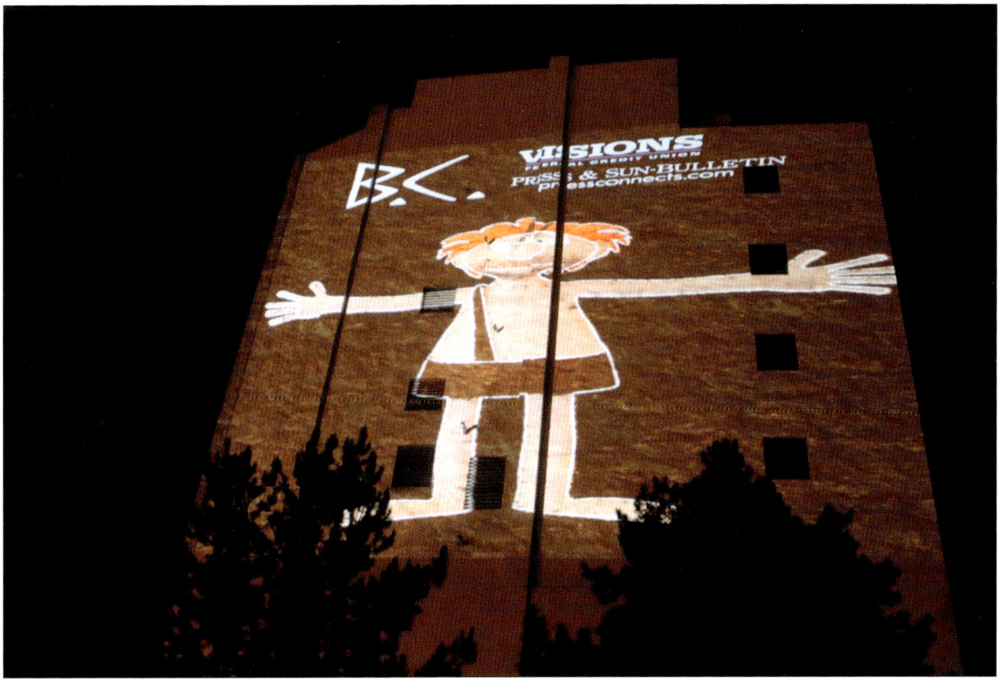

LUMA Festival Lights Up the Streets. During Labor Day weekend in September 2015, Binghamton held its first-ever projection arts festival as part of First Friday activities. Over 20,000 people filled Binghamton's downtown streets to see multiple buildings turn into canvases. A caveman from the *B.C.* comic strip welcomes all visitors in the above photograph, while the below image captures a scene more suited for October than Labor Day. The "projection screen" below is the historic building that houses Atomic Tom's Art Gallery and Event Space. The festival is one of the many ways the community welcomes back its college students.

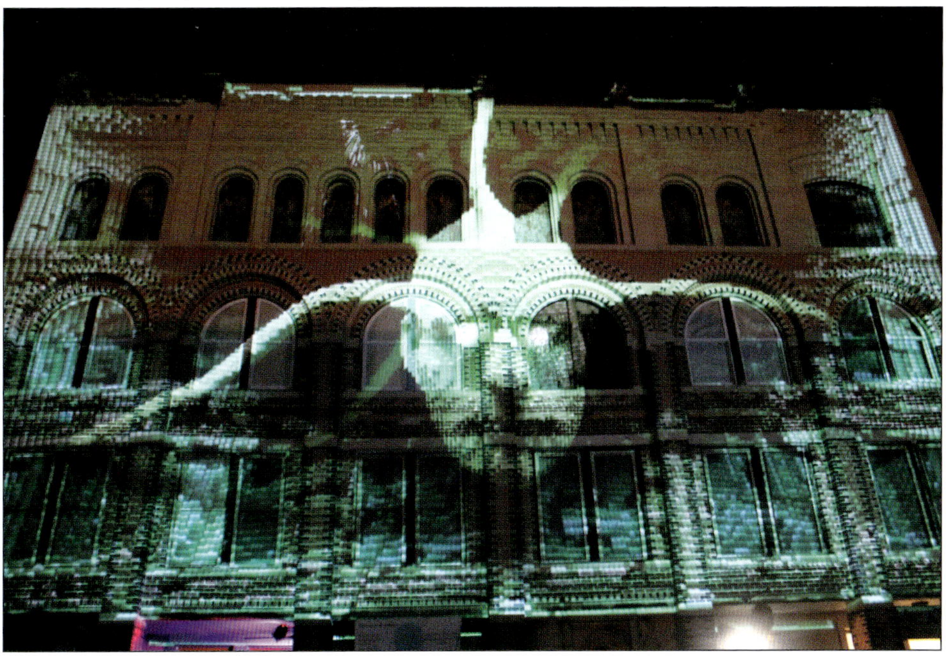

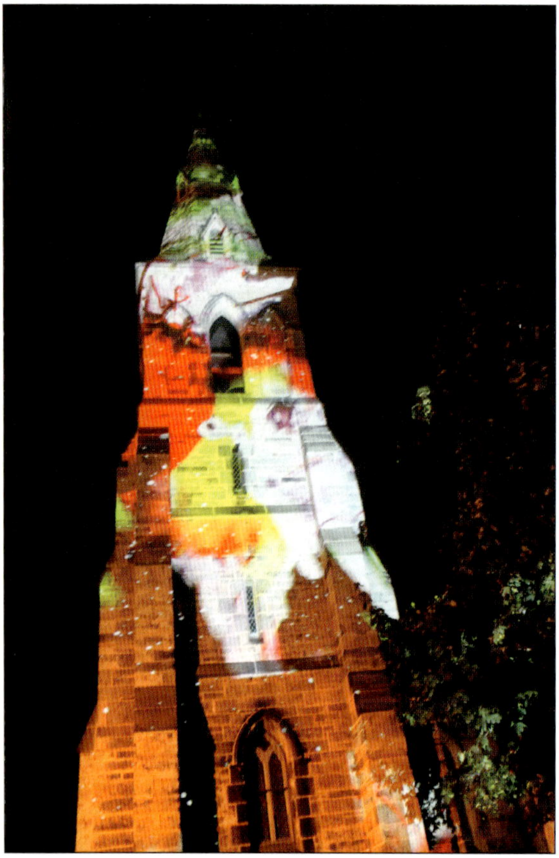

The Bell Tower Beckons RoboWars. The picture at left shows the bell tower at Christ Church, Binghamton's oldest church, during LUMA Festival. The cornerstone for the Episcopal church was laid in 1853, but due to lack of funding, the steeple shown in the this picture was not completed until 1953. The church was designed by architect Richard Upjohn, with noted architect Isaac Perry being called on to design the steeple. The below photograph shows the final scene of *RoboWars*, a video short that used the back of Binghamton's Forum Theater as its canvas.

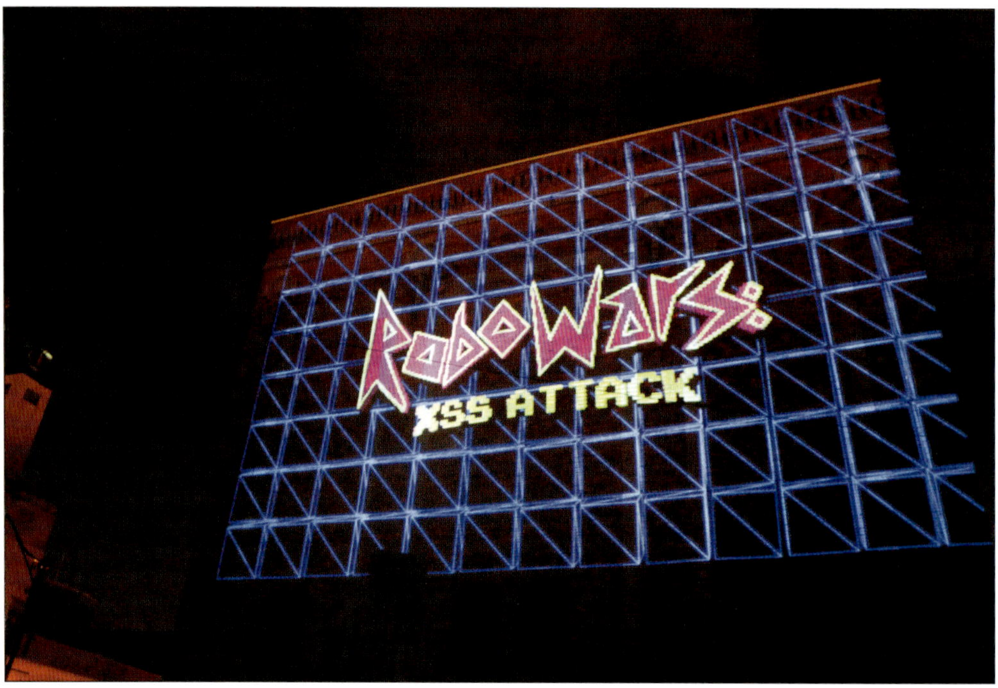

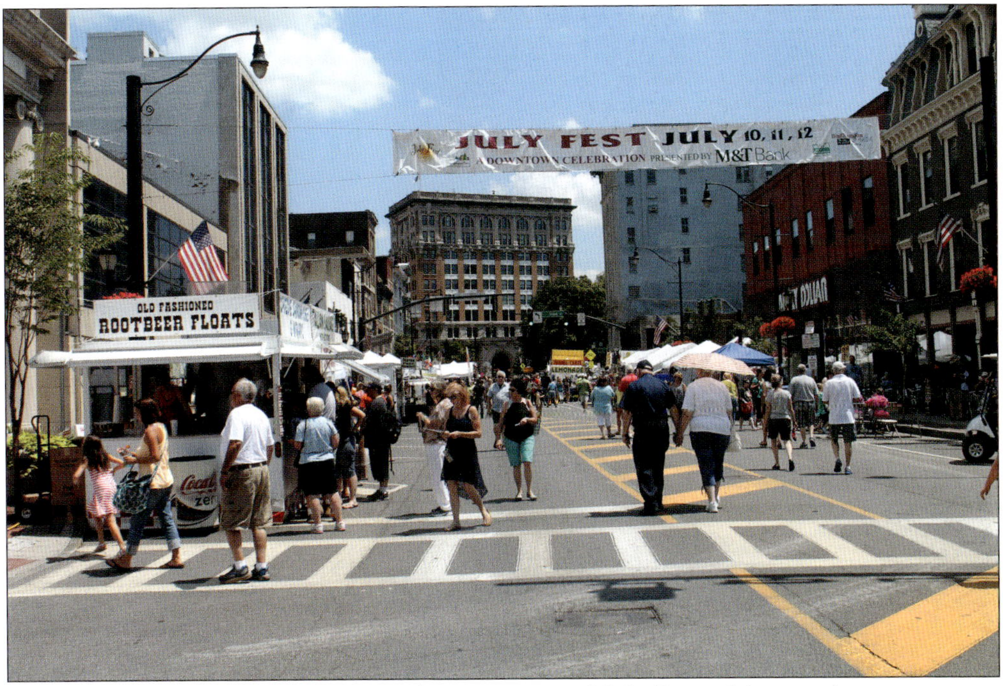

July Fest Brings the Artists. Binghamton's annual July Fest celebration brings artists to Binghamton's streets. For one day, the side streets of the city become an avenue for the artists, while Court Street becomes a pedestrian mall. In the above photograph, the view is looking east along Binghamton's Court Street, with the Security Mutual Insurance Building serving as a sentinel in the background. In the below photograph Paul Uhlman, a retired technical illustrator for IBM, greets visitors as they stroll by his "gallery." After serving IBM for over 30 years, Uhlman now uses his artistic talent to paint landscapes and nature.

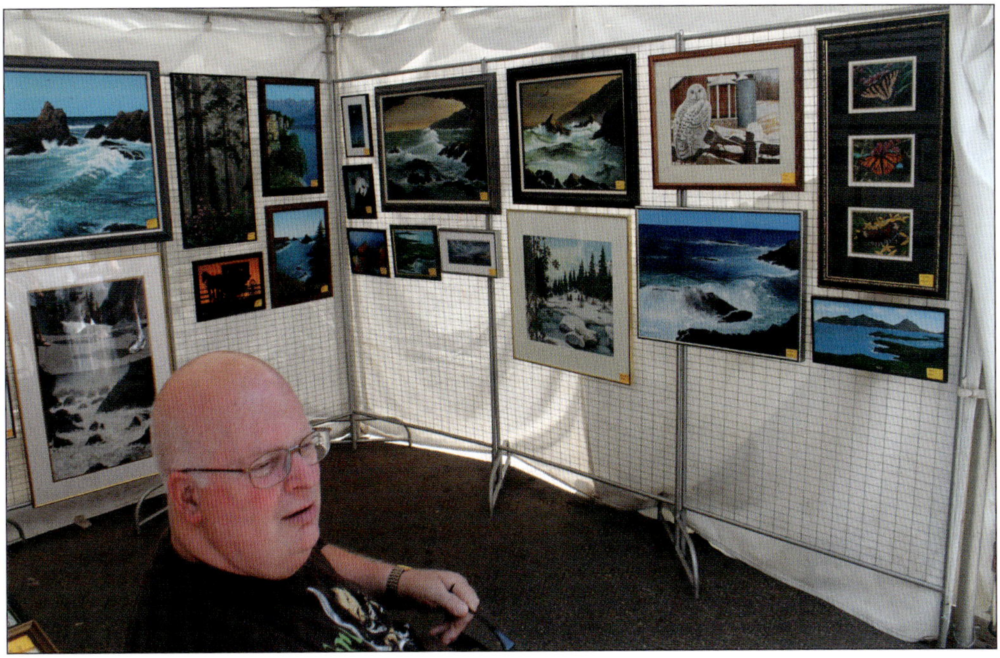

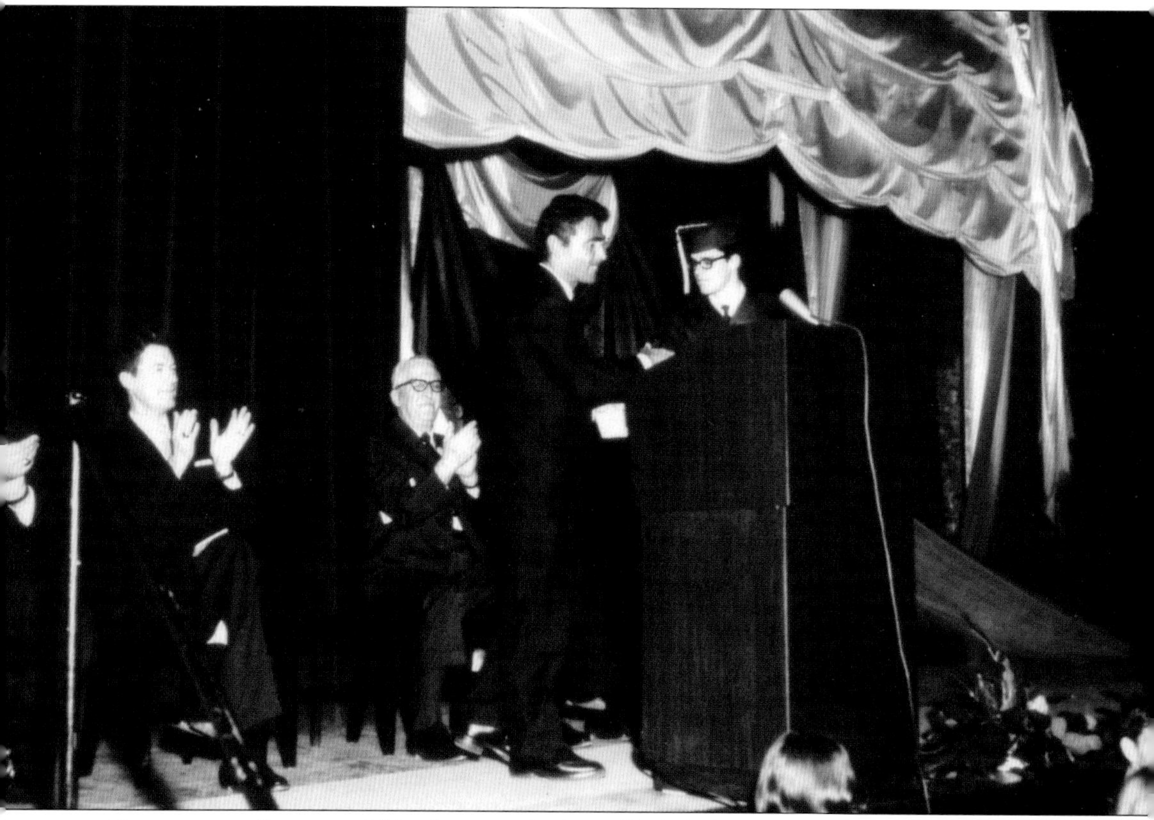

GRADUATION SPEAKER. This photograph shows Rod Serling approaching the podium as the commencement speaker for the class of 1968 at Binghamton Central High School. Some of *The Twilight Zone* episodes that were inspired, at least in part, by Serling's years in Binghamton include "Walking Distance," "Where is Everybody?," "Mirror Image," and "The After Hours." The theme of his speech on this day was "Are you tough enough?," as he described an America at war: "That men die for causes does not necessarily sanctify that cause. And that men are maimed and torn to pieces every 15 to 20 years does not immortalize or deify the act of war." Toward the end of his speech, he advised his listeners: "So in summation—let this be said to you. Be tough enough to wear what you want to wear, wear beards or don't wear beards, enlist or carry placards . . . but always, always, do the things you believe. Don't become monuments, sway with the wind. Change positions, if it is natural and believed. But believe in something and fight for those beliefs. Honor them by your commitment. Further them by your effort." Serling, born on Christmas Day in 1924, passed away from a heart attack in June 1975. (Courtesy of RJA @ BMHA.)

A Jittery Flyer. In the letter that he wrote to his former English teacher, Helen Foley, Serling coordinates part of his visit to Binghamton in January 1968. Note his reference in the middle of the first paragraph to being on an airplane: "flying unnerves me and always has since the war." Serling's reference to being a jittery flyer recalls visions of William Shatner in *The Twilight Zone* episode "Nightmare at 30,000 Feet." In the below c. 1962 photograph, Serling is happy to sign autographs at the Binghamton Regional Airport. (Both, courtesy of RSA @ BMHA.)

ROD SERLING
1490 MONACO DRIVE
PACIFIC PALISADES, CALIFORNIA

January 16, 1968

Miss Helen Foley
Binghamton Central High School
Main Street
Binghamton, New York

Mine Helen,

I'm dictating this letter just prior to a trip to Washington so you'll very likely get it four days after I arrive in Binghamton. But on the chance that my efficient secretary can get it off in due time, it's to let you know that I shall be arriving on Saturday evening, January 27th, on Mohawk flight 394, landing at 8:47 P.M. I really would just as leif not be met since flying unnerves me and always has since the war -- and I'm usually so plumb full of vodka and pills I have to be carried off in a stretcher like an aged guru on his last trip to the elephant graveyard. So what I intend to do is simply go on to the Sheraton -- if, indeed, this is the place you've reserved for me. If it isn't, I'll simply walk around your house with a large placard, announcing to the entire Southern Tier that you stole my watch.

I would much prefer a quiet dinner with you and whoever you choose, Monday evening, than with assorted gentry out of my past who will keep staring at me, taking satisfied note of the lines and crevices in my aging face and cluck sympathetically at the transformation caused by the years. So you be the judge -- make out the list and act accordingly. And needless to say, anything the kids want to do after the speech or before meets with my approval.

I seriously doubt if you can get back to me before I depart here, but if you want to phone me for anything -- the area code is 213 -- the number: GRanite 8-7759. If I don't hear from you, I'll expect a message from you at the Sheraton the night of the 27th.

Warm regards and Peace,

Rod

RS/ml

P.S. I JUST GOT BACK!
R.

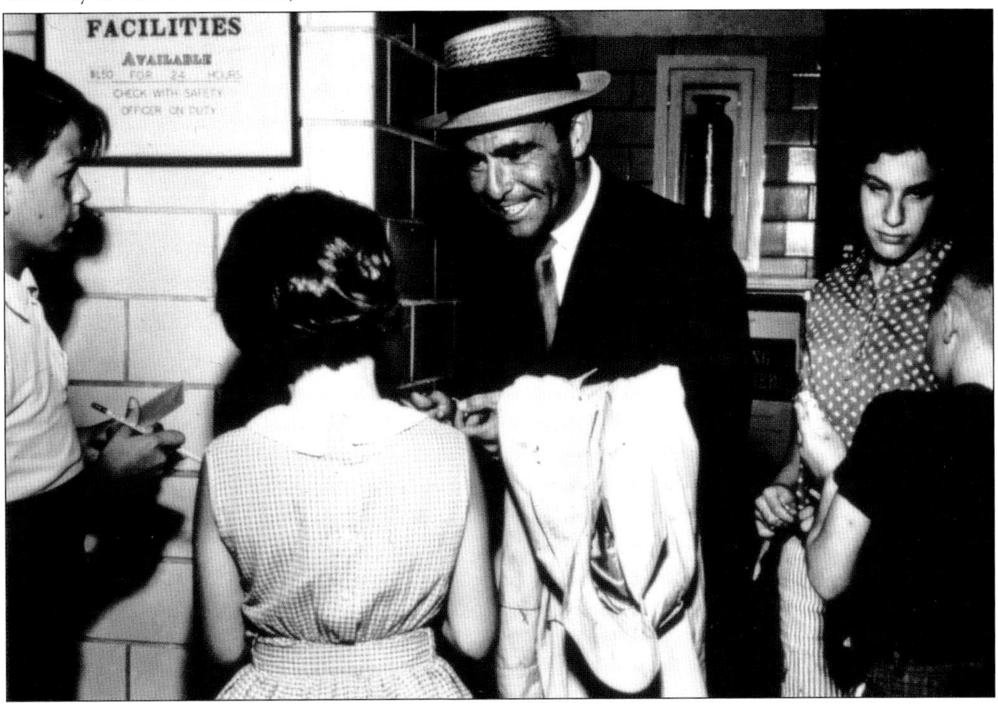

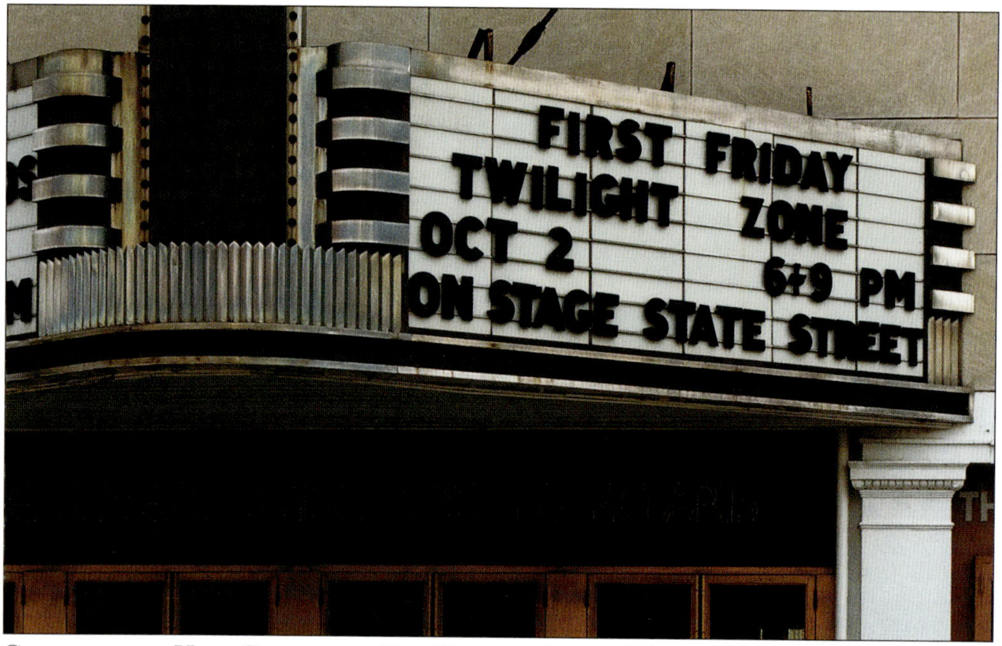

Celebrating a Half Century of *The Twilight Zone*. "Where is Everybody?" was the first episode of *The Twilight Zone* television series. It was shown on October 2, 1959, and 50 years later, Binghamton remembered this significant milestone with a four-day festival recognizing the series and its hometown creator, Rod Serling. The festival included live dramatizations of two episodes, "Mirror Image" and "Walking Distance." The above picture shows the marquee of the Forum Theatre, which broadcast the live dramatizations of these episodes shot at Binghamton's WSKG television studio. In the below photograph, a Binghamton city bus features an advertisement for the festival. The woman waiting to get off the bus is actress Heidi Weeks, who re-created the role of Millicent Barnes in the live dramatization of "Mirror Image." Her expression shows Millicent's confusion in arriving in Binghamton 50 years after her misadventure in "Mirror Image." (Both, courtesy of MR.)

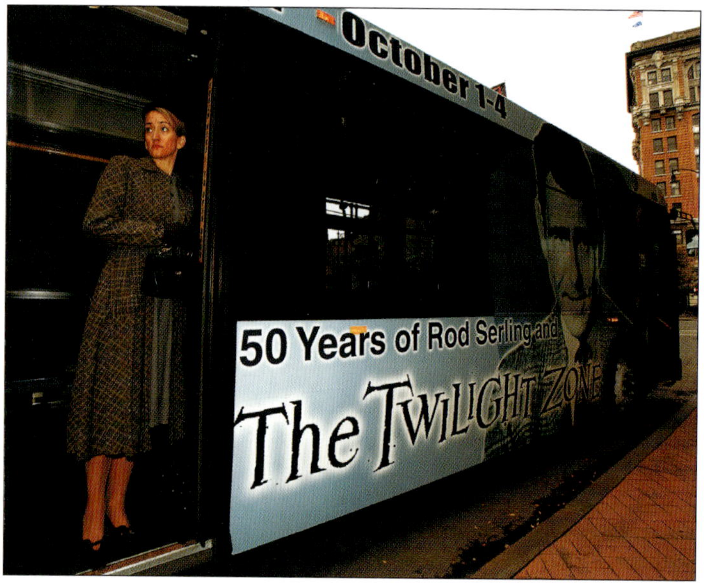

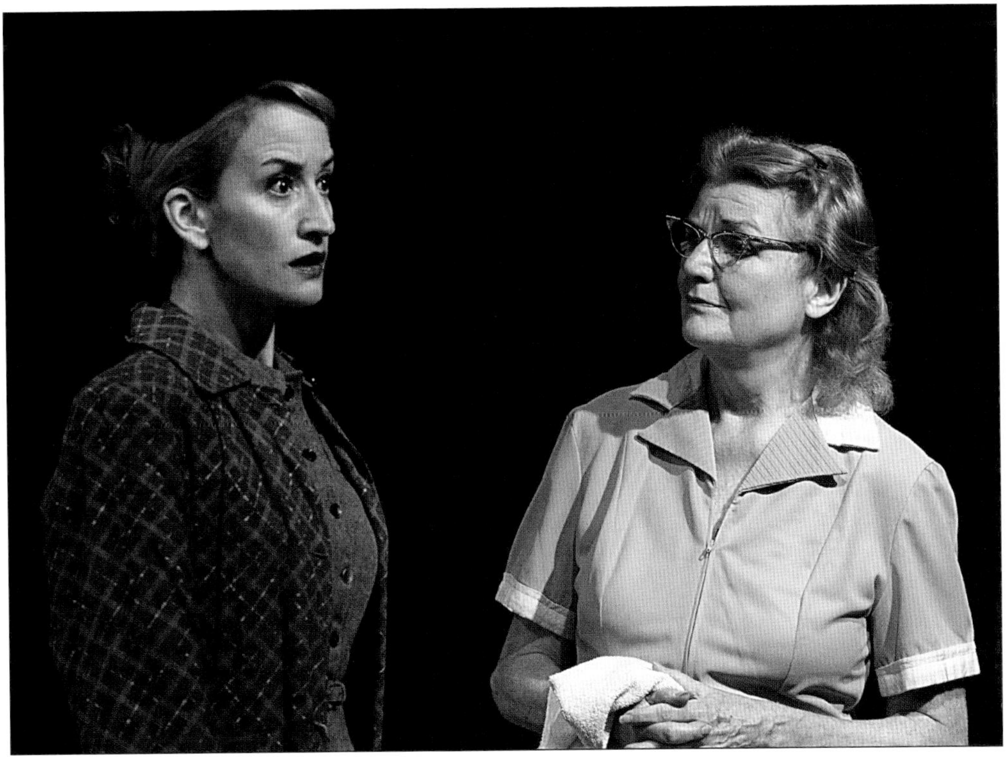

Binghamton Presence. In "Mirror Image," Millicent Barnes has a strange encounter in an Ithaca bus station, meeting her doppelgänger as well as a traveler from Binghamton. The above photograph from the dress rehearsal captures Millicent Barnes's shock as a cleaning lady (portrayed by Judy McMahon) informs her she has been seen in the bus station earlier that evening. The below photograph captures local actor Bob Deluca during a dress rehearsal as he portrays Rod Serling. That is a reel-to-reel tape recorder on Deluca's left; Serling's preferred mode of writing was to narrate into a dictating machine (Dictabelt recorder). In the below image, the character of Serling holds up a photograph of himself and of his father during World War II. Serling's dad passed away while Serling was serving in the Army in the Pacific. In "Walking Distance," Martin Sloan gets to say the good-bye to his father that Serling never did. (Both, courtesy of MR.)

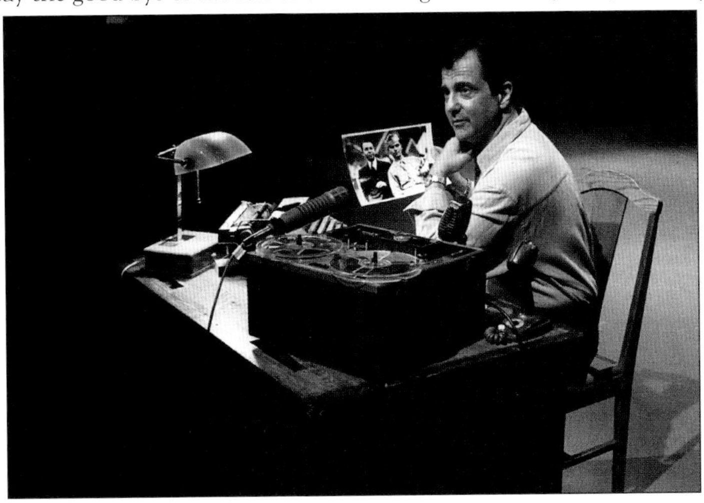

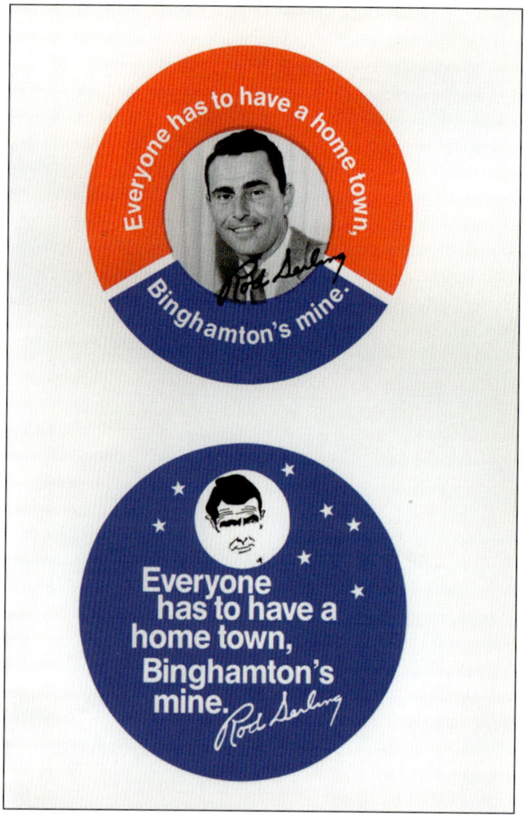

SERLING'S PRESENCE STILL FELT. Rod Serling's presence in Binghamton is kept alive through such formal organizations as the Rod Serling Memorial Foundation and the Rod Serling Archives at the Bundy Museum of History of Art. The photograph to the left shows the design sheet for commemorative buttons produced that captured Serling's opening words of *The Twilight Zone* episode "Walking Distance." The below picture shows Serling's middle school English teacher, Helen Foley, posing in front of the marker that still stands outside Binghamton High School. (Left, courtesy of Michael Pipher; below, courtesy of RSA @ BMHA.)

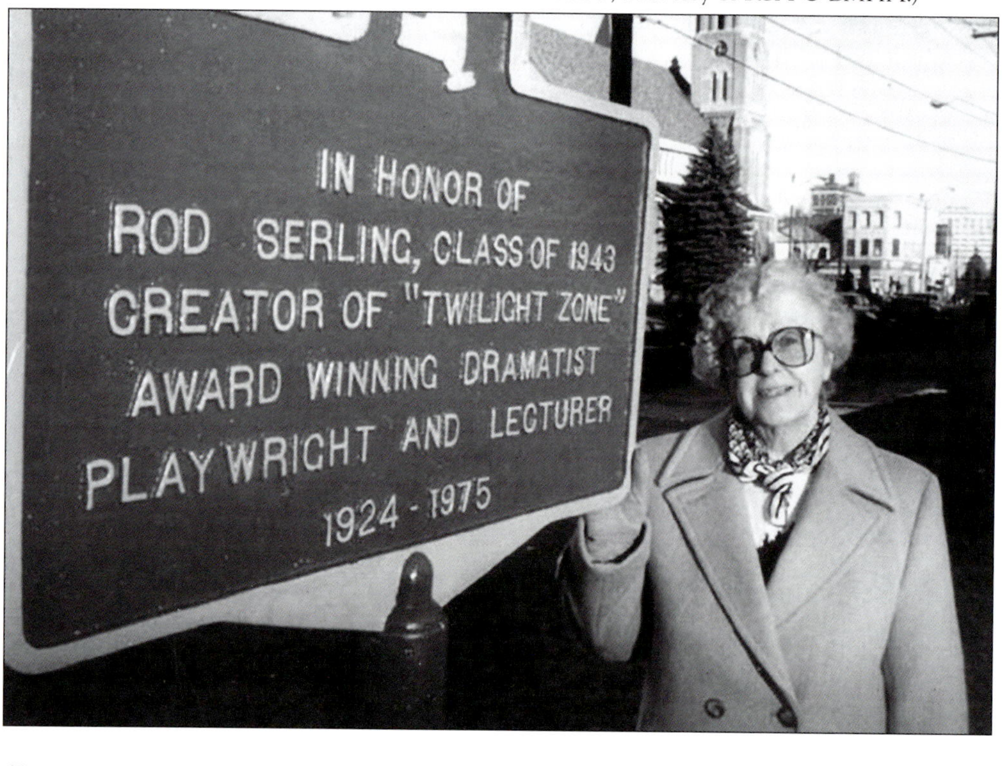

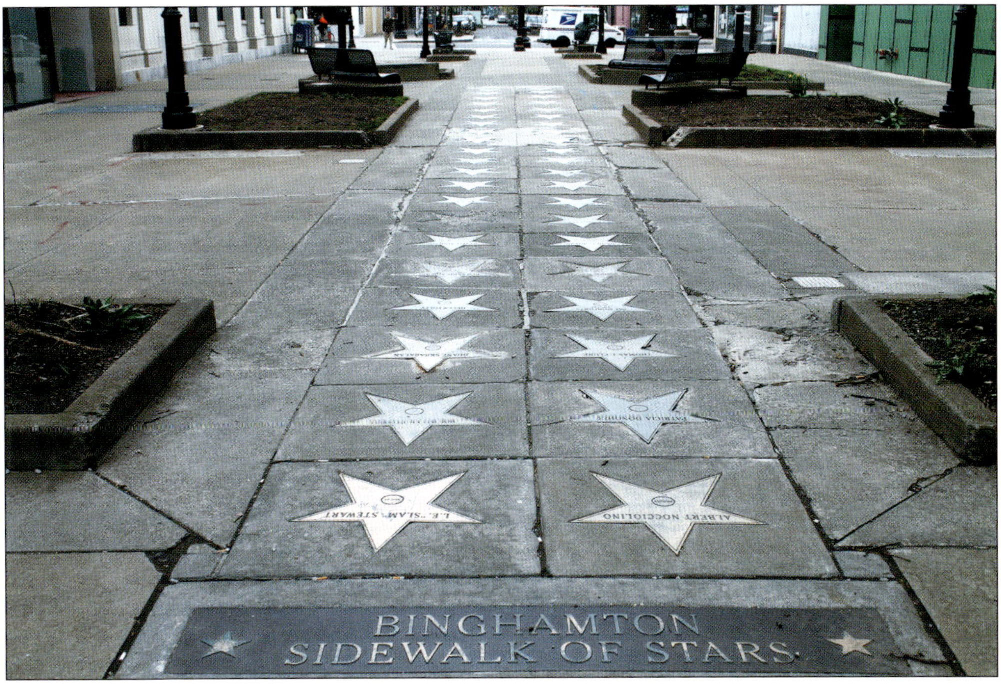

From Walk of Fame to Wall of Fame. Pictured above is the original Walk of Fame (also known as Sidewalk of Starts), with stars and inscriptions lining the entrance to the walkway. Today, the stars in cement have been replaced with gold stars that adorn the walls of Binghamton's downtown Forum Theatre. By moving the display indoors, the city of Binghamton is better able to preserve the stars. Also, the stars are available for viewing by the thousands who visit the Forum each year. As for the site of the original Walk of Fame, the stars are gone, and at present it is a pedestrian walkway, but plans are to put up a parking lot. In the below photograph, Sidewalk of Stars cofounder Michael Pipher (left) poses with actor Anthony George during the December 1992 ceremony for George's star. Before becoming a soap opera star, George starred in the television series *The Untouchables* and *Checkmate.* (Below, courtesy of Michael Pipher.)

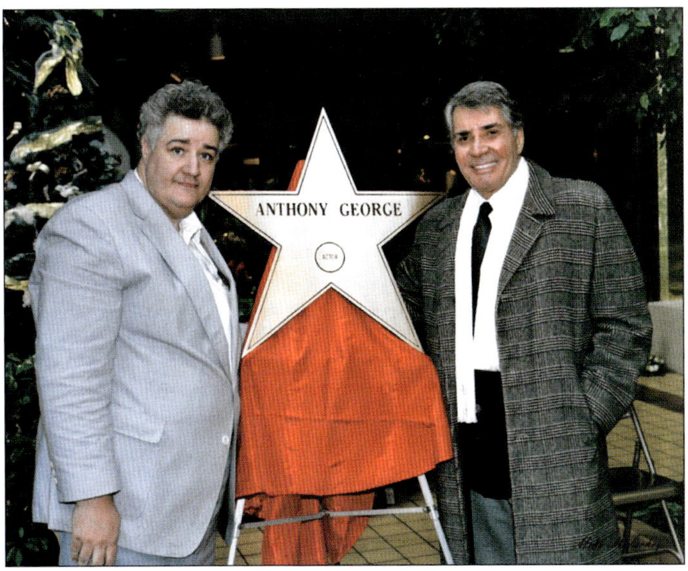

Member	Occupation
Agard, David L.	B.C. Pops
Aswad, Ed	Photographer/Author
Bielenberg, John E.	Producer
Clune, Thomas J	Music Director
Cofini, Santo	Pianist
Colton, Russel	Conductor
Cotter, Ann B.	Director
Covelli, John	Symphony Conductor
Crabb, Alan	Singer
Deacon, Richard	**Actor**
Dellasanta Armondo	Painter
Diorio, Anthony J.	Musician
Donohue, Patricia	Actor
Evans, Claus	Actor
Foley, Helen	Director
Fontaine, Victor	Singer
Foster, Stuart	Singer
Fuster, William "Billy"	Jazz
George, Anthony	Actor
Gorman, Bill	Actor
Green, Stuart	Producer
Grey, Gene	Writer
Hart, Johnny	**Cartoonist**

Member	Occupation
Hibbit, Peyton M.	Opera Conductor
Keller, Robert A	Artist
Kolcun, John	Musician
Kradijan, Naima	Actress
Martin, Keith	Artist
Mincolla, Frank T.	Producer
Montforte, Pat	Musician
Montforte, Tony	Drummer/Teacher
Muratori, Mary Lou	Opera Singer
Nocciolino, Albert	**Producer**
Parker, Bill	Actor
Russo, Sherry	Dancer
Savoca, Carmen S.	Opera Director
Serling, Rod	**Writer**
Shiffrin, Bernard	Conductor
Simpson, Marian	Artist
Skeene, Butch	Vocalist
Skrabalak, Duane	Opera Conductor
Stevens, Val	Singer
Stewart, L.E. "Slam"	Musician
Wallenberg, Fritz	Symphony Conductor
Wright, M. Searle	Organist
Yelverton, Helene	Dance
Zuccolo, Angelo	Director

BINGHAMTON'S STARS. The names in bold underscore in the above image denote those denizens who have achieved a high level of national fame. Richard Deacon was a mainstay of TV in the 1960s, as Mel Cooley in the weekly *The Dick Van Dyke Show*. Anthony George achieved fame as a soap opera star (as Burke Devlin in *Dark Shadows* in 1967, Tony Vincente from 1970 to 1975 in *Search for Tomorrow*, and from 1977 to 1984 as Dr. Will Vernon in *One Life to Live*) after his starring roles in *Checkmate* and *The Untouchables*. Johnny Hart was the cartoonist behind such nationally syndicated comics as *B.C.* and *The Wizard of Id*. Albert Nocciolino grew up in downtown Binghamton and went on to become CEO of an entertainment company that brings Broadway shows to Binghamton. He has been a Broadway producer and has won Tony Awards for his behind-the-scenes work for *Kinky Boots*, *La Cage aux Folles*, *Spamalot*, and *Thoroughly Modern Millie*. Rod Serling was the creator of *The Twilight Zone* and *Night Gallery*, as well as an award-winning writer for television and the movies. Serling and Michel Wilson authored the screenplay of the 1968 film *Planet of the Apes*. As this book went to press, jazz singer Alma Fortez and Margaret "Pokey" Crocker, executive director of the Discovery Center, became members of the Wall of Fame.

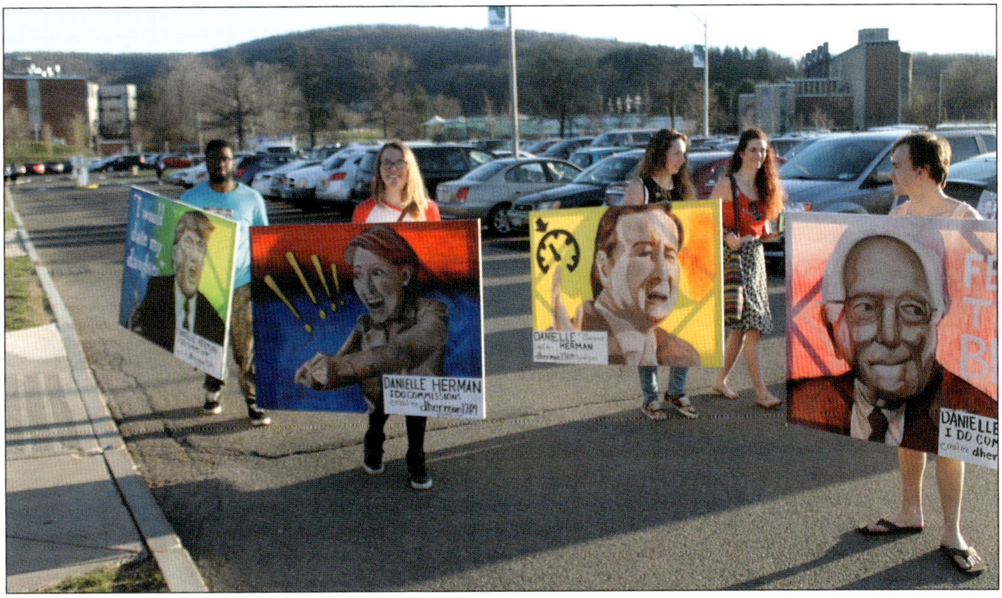

The Crossroads of Binghamton. In the above photograph, entrepreneurs display their creativity as they show samples from a local artist to those waiting in line to hear Bill Clinton speak at Binghamton University in April 2016. In the spring of 2016, in anticipation of the New York State primary, the area also served as a political crossroads of sorts, as Bernie Sanders, Ted Cruz, and Bill Clinton all spoke within the same week. The area has seen its share of inhabitants of the Oval Office. Teddy Roosevelt spoke at the Stone Opera House in 1900, Pres. Franklin D. Roosevelt visited the area in the wake of the 1936 flood and was hosted by his good friend George F. Johnson. Pres. Ronald Reagan gave a speech to over 20,000 people at Endicott's Ty Cobb Field in 1984, and George W. Bush, while governor of Texas, marched in Binghamton's St. Patrick's Day parade in March 2000. Barack Obama held a town hall meeting in 2014. The below photograph shows Bill Clinton stumping for his wife, presidential candidate Hillary Clinton, at Binghamton University in April 2016.

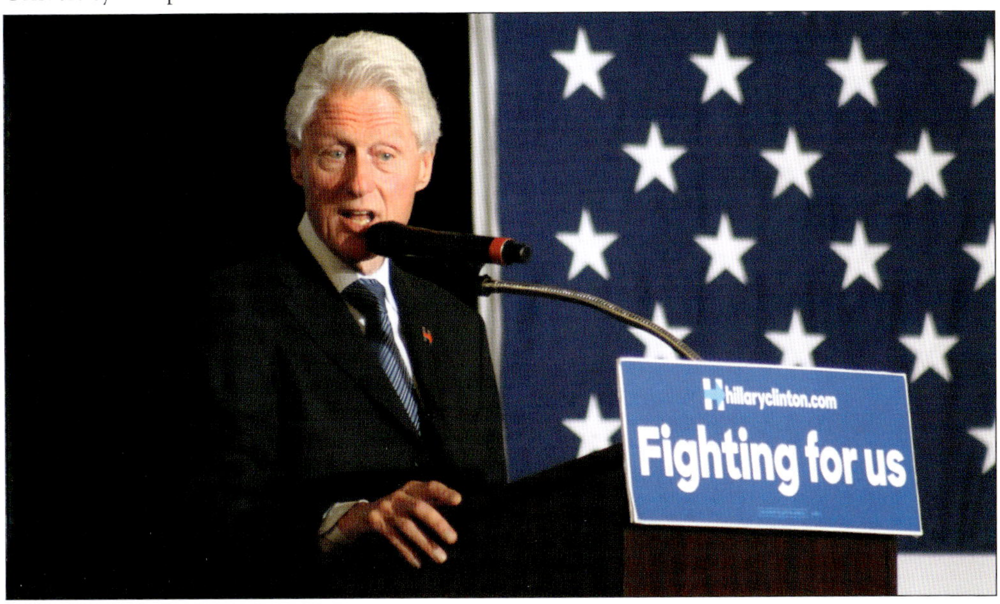

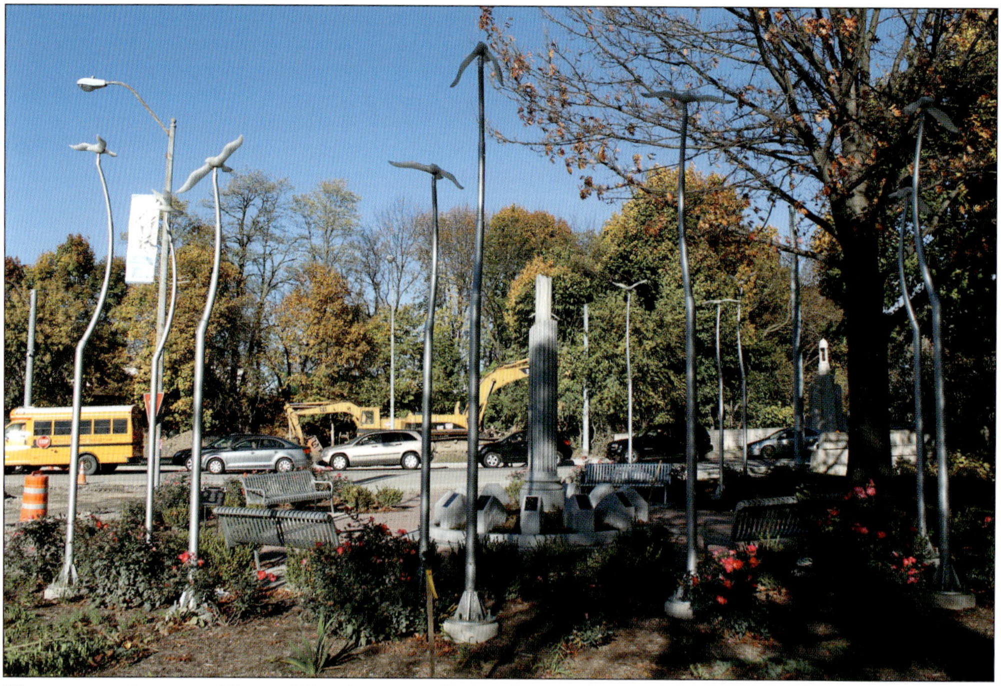

Using the Arts to Heal. The doves in the sculpture above portray the 13 lives that were lost in the American Civic Association shooting on April 3, 2009. At approximately 10:30 a.m., Jiverly Antares Wong (also known as Jiverly Voong) entered the building shown below and started firing, killing thirteen and wounding four others before he shot and killed himself. Pres. Barack Obama recalled this tragic day as part of his address to the nation on January 5, 2016, to announce increased federal gun control laws. The below picture shows the American Civic Association building as it looks today.

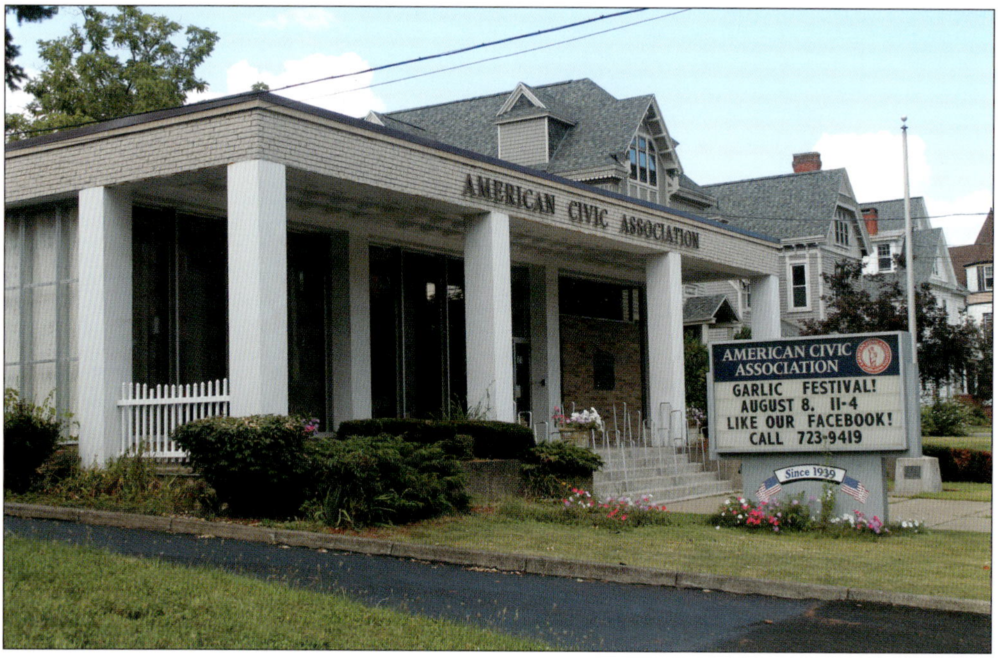

Three

Sports Mecca

Greater Binghamton's sports legacy is a rich one, not only with teams, but also with individuals. The city first hosted professional baseball in 1877; in 1918, local businessman Willis Sharpe Kilmer saw his horse Exterminator win the Kentucky Derby. Jack Sharkey, the heavyweight boxing champion (1932–1933), was born in Binghamton in 1902. The city has hosted professional hockey since 1973, and numerous other sporting events are hosted on an annual basis, including car racing, competitive cycling, golf, harness racing, running, and tennis. The rich histories of baseball and hockey in the area were essential components of Binghamton being selected as the 13th-best minor-league city in America by the *Sports Business Journal* in 2015.

The area hosted its first car racing events in the 1920s and the En-Joie Golf Club opened in 1925. The Endicott-Johnson Corporation opened En-Joie in 1925, as EJ's chairman, George F. Johnson, believed strongly in giving back to the community. Today, this golf course is an annual stop on the PGA Champions Tour. Greater Binghamton has also played a role in the growth of tennis—an annual Masters Tournament was held from 1966 to 1969 at the Highland Racquet and Riding Club, whose site now houses the Binghamton Tennis Center and Binghamton Riding Stables. Since 1994, Binghamton has been a stop on the Association of Tennis Professionals (ATP) Challenger Tour. The Greater Binghamton Area currently hosts two marathons: the Dick's Sporting Goods Marathon and the Herald of Victory Marathon. The Chris Thater Memorial Races and associated events are held over two days in August every year. Gone but not forgotten is the Triple Cities Jets football team, which excelled as an entry in the Empire Football League and related conferences.

The Binghamton area has also been a nurturing ground for amateur athletes. In December 1992, Binghamton started hosting the annual Broome County Stop-DWI Winter Classic, a high school holiday basketball tournament. Though the national division of this tournament was discontinued in 2015, the tournament lives on at a local level. Starting in 2017, Binghamton will host the New York State High School Basketball Championships. Maine-Indwell High School's football team set a New York State record of 62 straight wins over five seasons, finally losing a game in November 2015. And Maine-Endwell's Little League baseball team won the World Series title at Williamsport, Pennsylvania, in August 2016.

This chapter gives a glimpse of these sports before closing with a look at the Greater Binghamton Sports Hall of Fame, which opened its doors in 2014 for both professional and amateur athletes.

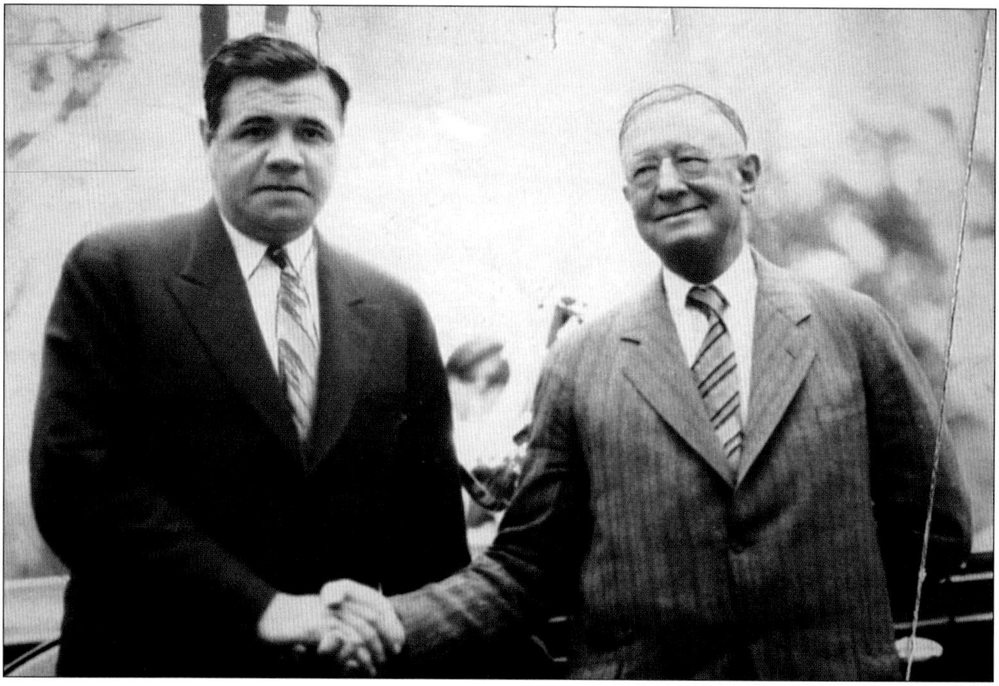

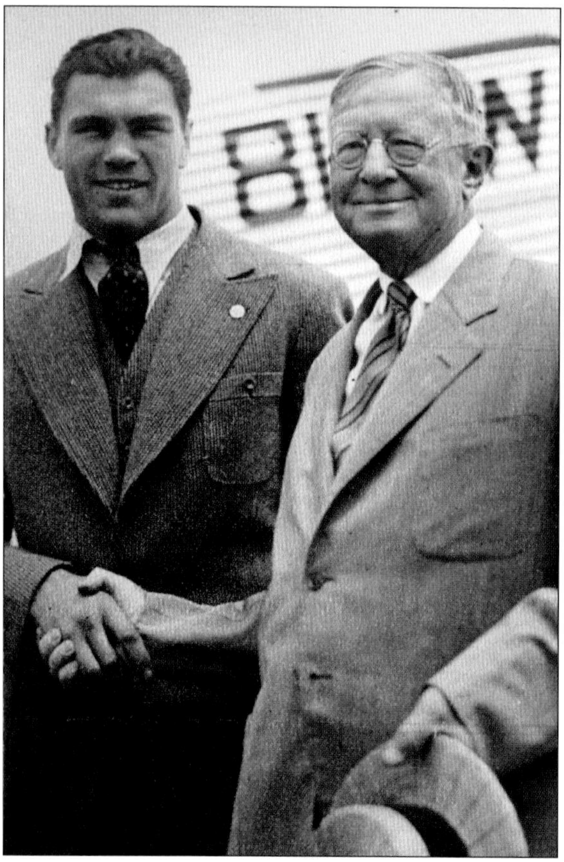

A Roaring Sports World. In the above photograph, George F. Johnson (right) welcomes Babe Ruth to the area on May 16 1929. Ruth was in town with the Yankees to play an exhibition game against Binghamton's Triplets at Johnson Field. Before the game that day, Ruth also visited with fans at Endicott's Ideal Park. "The Babe" went 3-4 against the Triplets and even hit a home run during the Yanks' 4-1 win. The next day, an article under his byline appeared in the *Binghamton Sun*, with Ruth stating, "That's a great bunch of boys you have here in the Triple Cites. They're real, honest-to-goodness American youngsters and I enjoyed the good time I had with them from the time I arrived in Binghamton in the morning until I left at night, more than I know how to express it." In the left photograph, George F. Johnson welcomes Max Schmeling to Endicott, where the German boxer held his training camp for his June 12, 1930, heavyweight championship bout with Binghamton native Jack Sharkey. (Both, courtesy of EVC.)

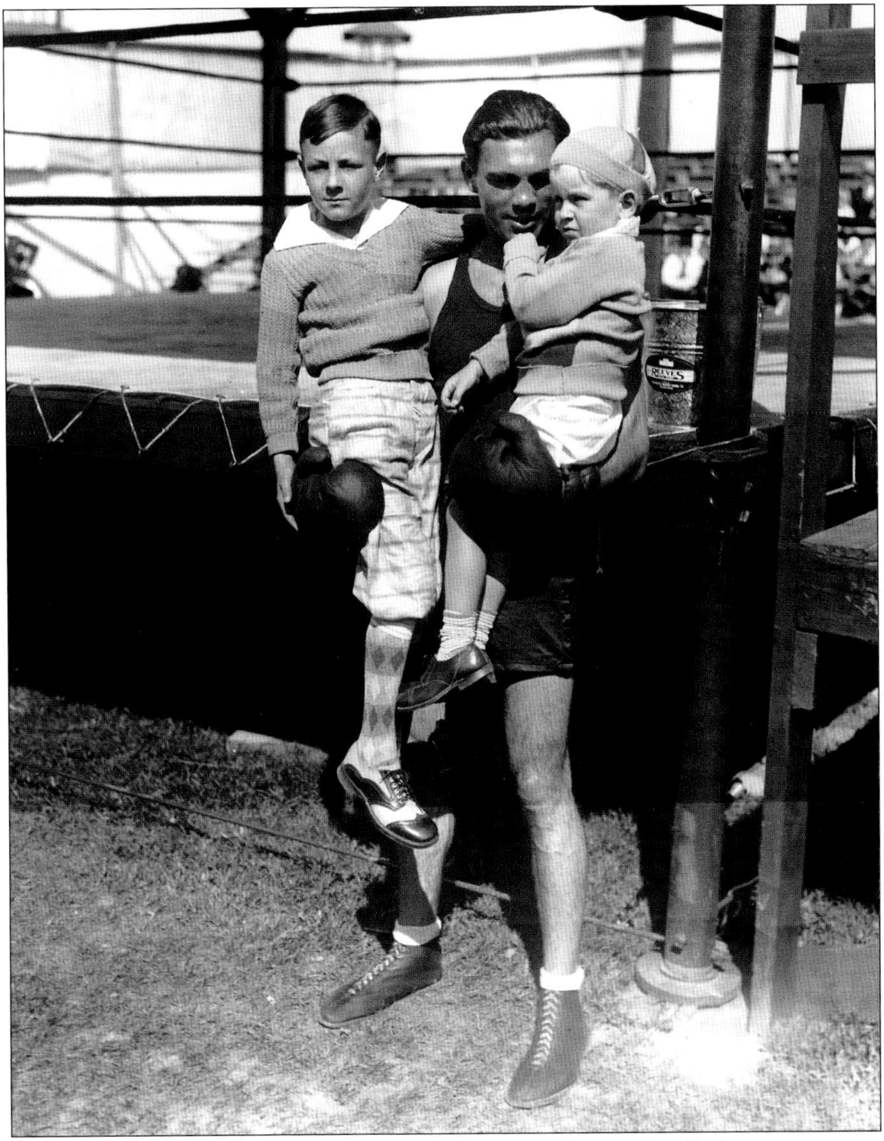

Sharkey's Foe. Here, Schmeling poses with two young fans at his Endicott training camp: John Hastings is on the left, and George B. Sweet on the right. Endicott was the center of the sports world then, as some of the best-known sportswriters of the day visited Endicott to cover Schmeling's training camp, including Grantland Rice and Sid Mercer. The world heavyweight title was vacant at the time, and the winner of the Schmeling-Sharkey match would be awarded the title. Schmeling won the match in the fourth round after Sharkey was disqualified for a low blow that knocked down Schmeling. This is the only time in boxing history that a championship was won on a disqualification! Two years later, though, on June 21, Sharkey took the title from Schmeling in a split decision. Sharkey held the title until June 29, 1933, when he was knocked out in the sixth round by Primo Carnera. Sharkey, born on Binghamton's Clinton Street in 1902, changed his name from Josef Paul Zukauskas in the early stages of his boxing career. After his retirement, Sharkey became close friends with baseball great Ted Williams, as he and Williams were avid fly fishermen. Sharkey was elected to the Greater Binghamton Sports Hall of Fame in 2016. (Photograph by the Associated Press, courtesy of BMHA.)

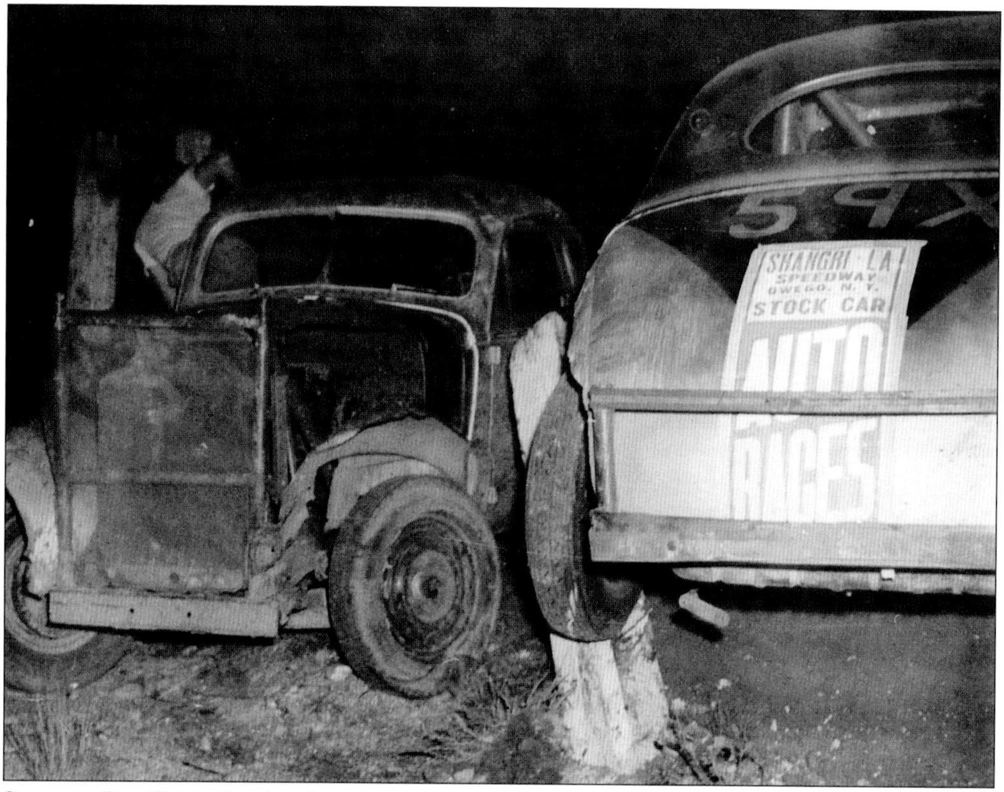

SHANGRI LA. Car racing has been in the area since the 1920s, with the first races occurring at the Stow Flats fairgrounds (now Binghamton Plaza). The above picture shows Irish Joe Donahue climbing out of his car after a 1950 crash at Shangri La Speedway, which was built in 1946 in Owego. The picture below shows Shangri La a few years later. Note the multiple tracks—the top one was a half mile, the second was for the women (the powder-puff circuit), and the bottom track was for microds. Shangri La was an asphalt track built by Bill Owen, who named his raceway despite protests from Owego native Margaret Hastings (Atkinson). A corporal in the Women's Army Corps (WAC), Hastings felt Owen was capitalizing on her military plane crash into the jungles of New Guinea on May 13, 1945. The crash occurred while the group she was with toured New Guinea's "Shangri La" section. Owen countered by saying *Lost Horizon* was one of his favorite books—he had even named his hunting lodge Shangri La. (Above, courtesy of JD; below, courtesy of GG from OHS.)

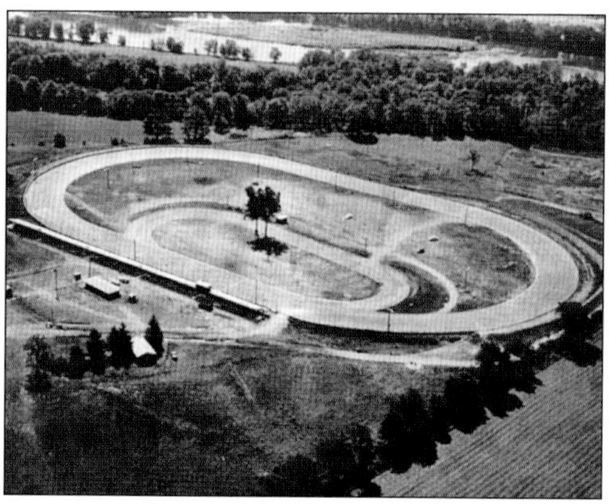

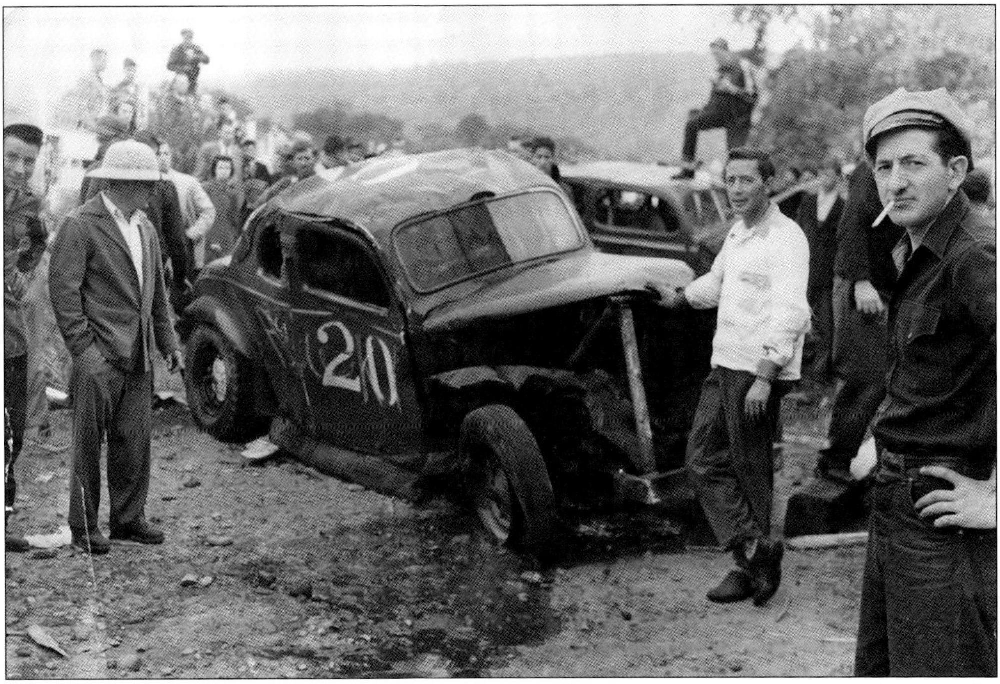

DOUBLE THE FUN. As veterans returned home from World War II, interest in racing grew dramatically, resulting in the opening of a dirt oval in 1951. This other track was located approximately 25 miles west, in Kirkwood, and went by a more mundane name—Five Mile Point Speedway, which was built by Irving Heath. In the above photograph, Wes Craven, a local driver, stands in front of his car that he wrecked in the second turn during a 1950 race. In the picture below, a crowd surrounds the injured. In 1950, the Southern Tier Stock Car Club was formed to organize, promote, and conduct local stock car races, often partnering with local organizations. The club became the sanctioning body for schedules at Five Mile Point and Shangri La. These tracks made the area an idyllic destination for big cars, midgets, and stock cars throughout the second half of the 20th century. (Both, courtesy of KHS.)

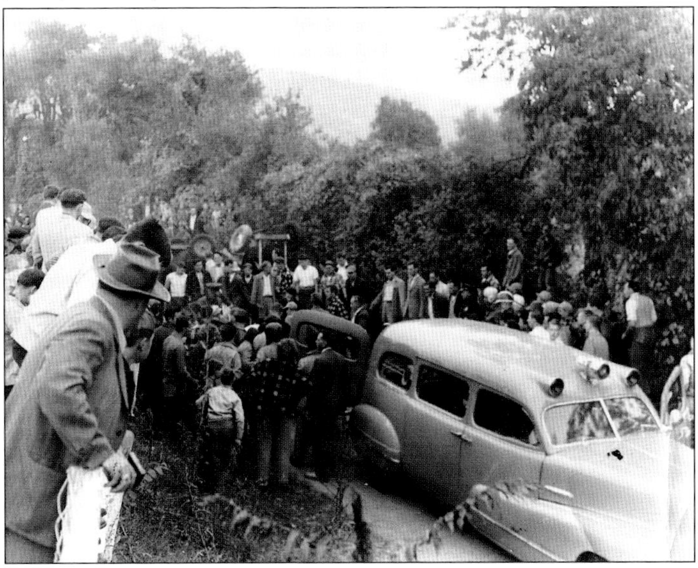

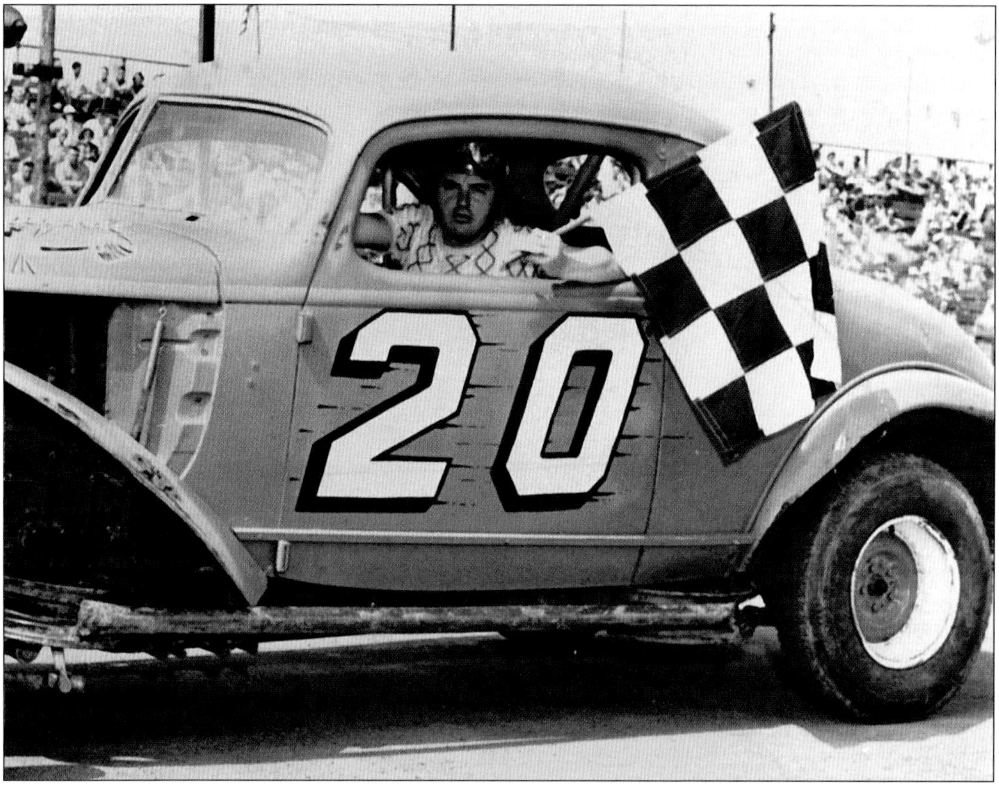

No Sale. The above photograph shows Irish Joe Donahue holding the winner's flag at Shangri La in the early 1950s, with the grandstand full of spectators. In 1963, Irish Joe had a visit from a young driver from Nazareth, Pennsylvania, who came up to buy a Hudson motor that Joe was pulling from his car. The young Pennsylvanian brought his wife, Dee Ann, and infant child, Michael, along for the visit. Even though Irish Joe and his visitor could not agree on a price for the motor, Joe and his wife, Grace, treated the young family to a light dinner before they headed back to Pennsylvania. The surname of that young family was Andretti, and it was Mario who went away disappointed he could not get Joe to come down on his price. (Courtesy of JD.)

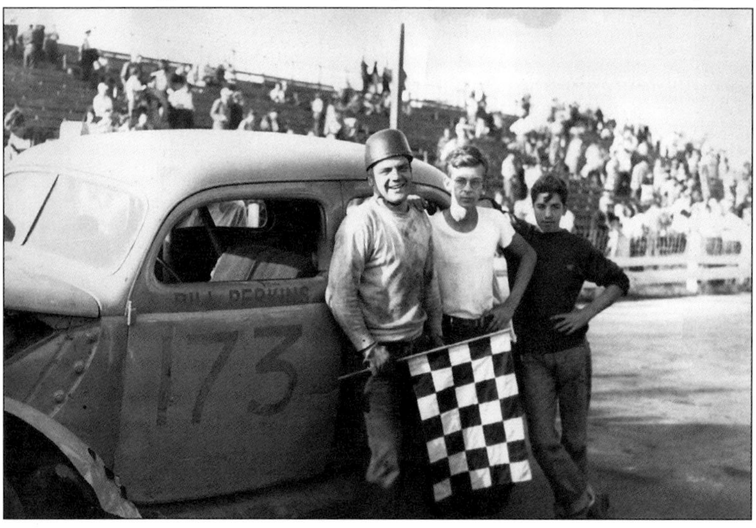

Friendly Foes. Bucky Dew (left) poses with Bill Perkins (center) after beating him at Shangri La. Dew and Perkins were friendly rivals throughout the 1950s and 1960s. The person at right is unidentified. (Courtesy of KHS.)

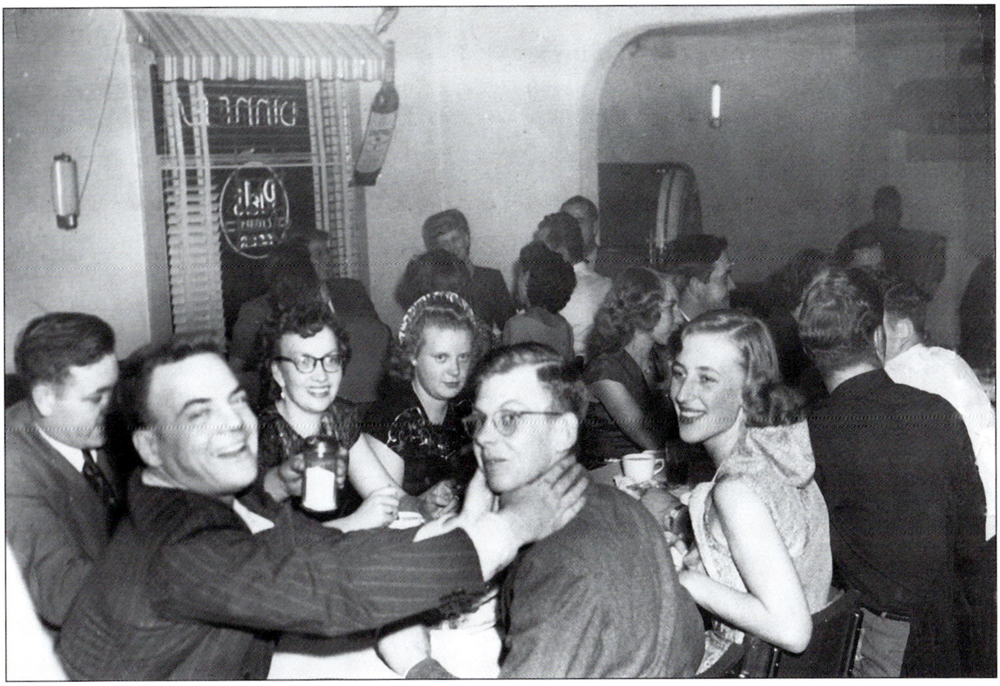

Smiles Off and On the Track. The above c. 1950 photograph captures Bucky Dew in a light moment as he pretends to strangle Bill Perkins at a celebratory dinner at a local restaurant. The below photograph shows driver Joe Donahue Jr. with representatives from race sponsor Don's Automotive Mall, after he beat Ken Schrader (who competed on the NASCAR circuit from 1981 to 2013) in a 1990 thirty-lap race at Five Mile Point. Schrader congratulated Joe Jr. before he even got out of his car; he told Joe Jr., "You had too much for me tonight." Schrader told the *Binghamton Press & Sun-Bulletin* he had hoped to win the race. "I didn't come to play," he exhorted. That night, Joe Jr. won with the Grisworld Family Modified No. 16X, sponsored by Gary's U Pull It. Pictured below from left to right are Greg Beagell, Bonnie Beagell, Schrader, Jenny Colsten, Donahue Jr., and Don Beagell. (Above, courtesy of KHS; below, courtesy of Joe Donahue Jr.)

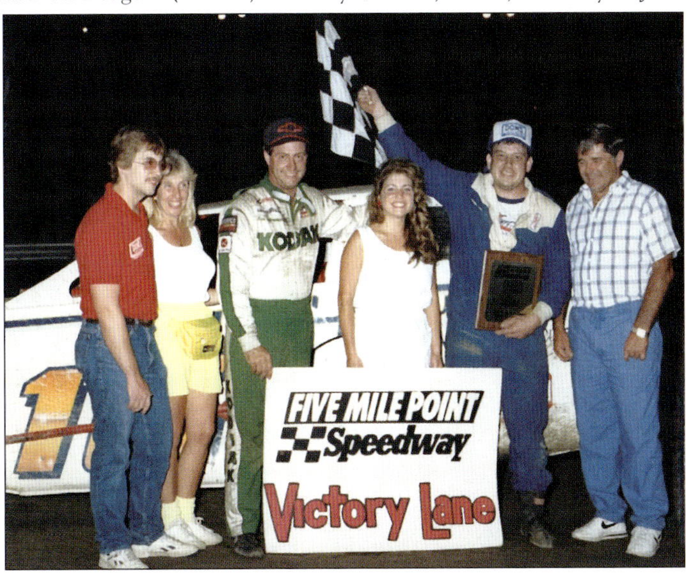

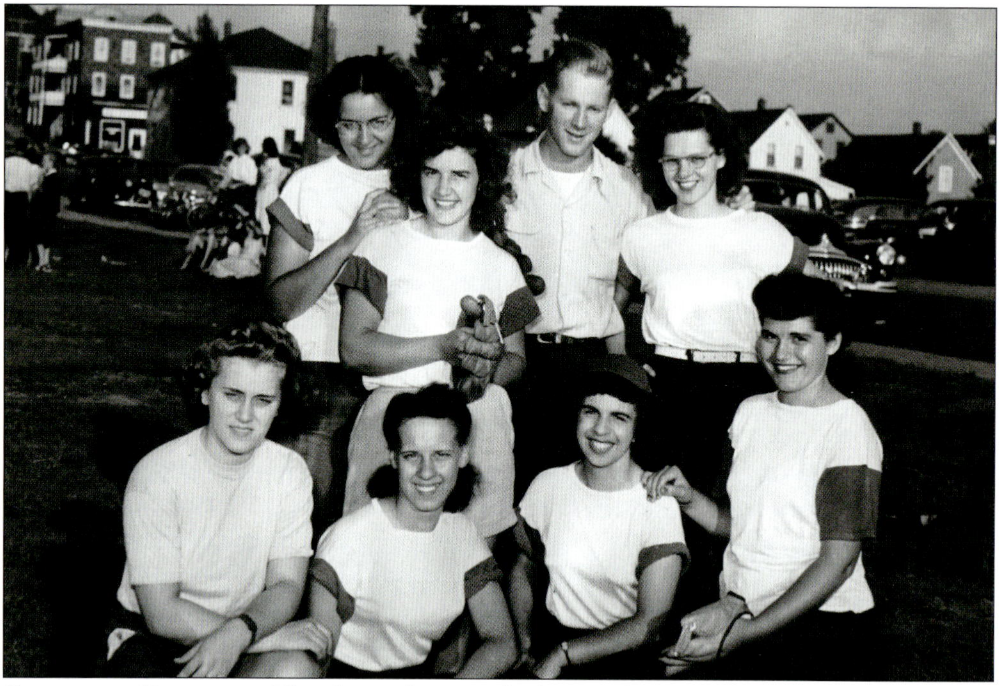

Community Relations. The above photograph shows Whitey Ford in 1949 posing with an Endicott-Johnson factory team at Endicott's Northside Park. Ford starred for the Binghamton Triplets that year, winning 16 games. He played in 11 World Series with the Yankees and was elected to the National Baseball Hall of Fame in 1974. His World Series record was 10-8, with a 2.71 ERA. He was a World Series champion six times. In the photograph are, from left to right, (first row) Ann Saraceno, Evelyn Babucka, Sadie Renda, and Mary Markus; (second row) Rita Jones, Gert Painter Byers, Ford, and Dora Peters. Almost 50 years later, the image below shows manager Rick Sweet chatting with Binghamton's Knothole Gang before a game in 1996. (Above, courtesy of GB; below, courtesy of B-Mets.)

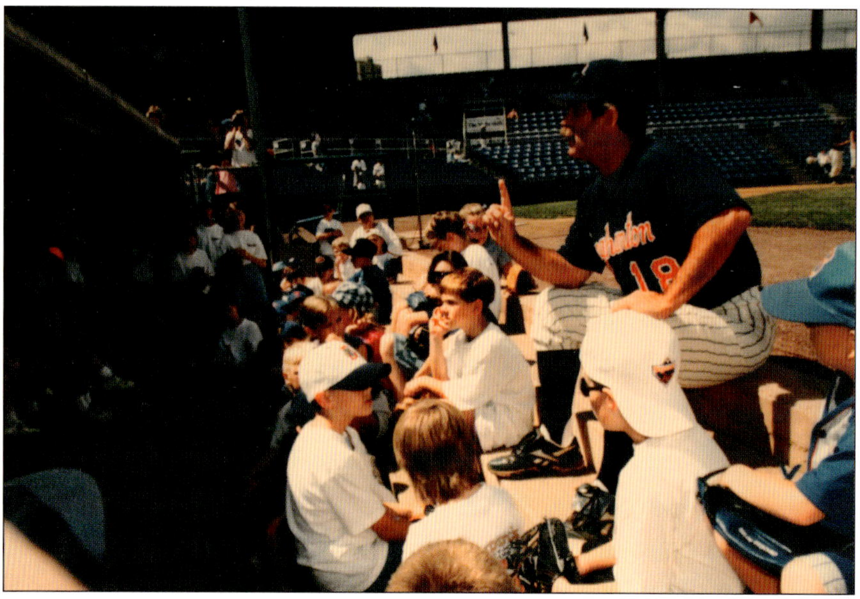

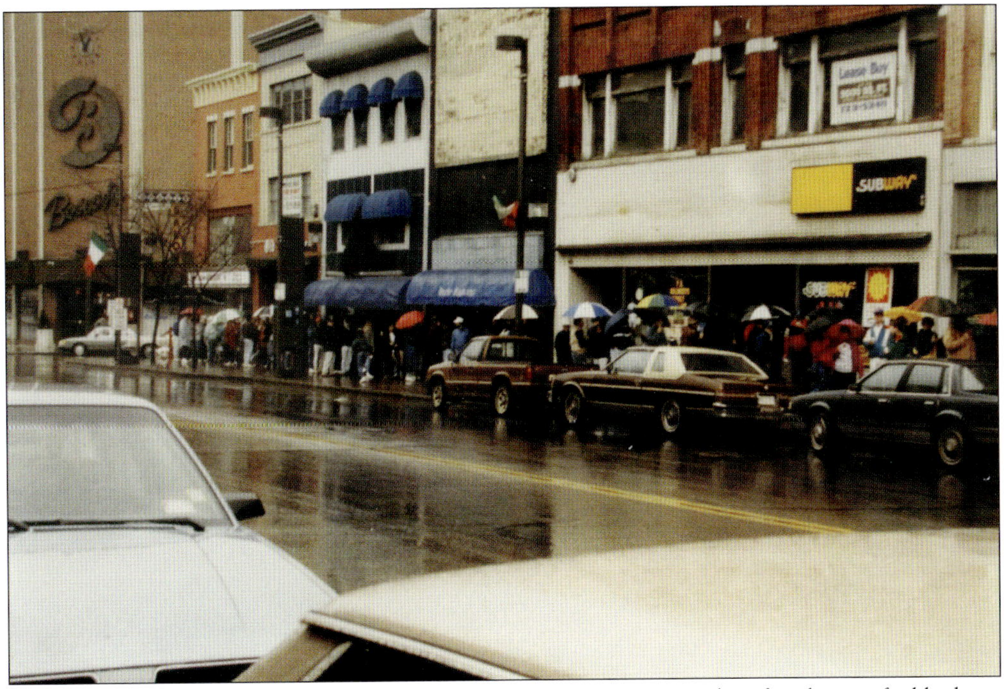

STREETS AND STANDS PACKED. It is March 1992 in the above photograph as fans line up for blocks in downtown Binghamton to purchase tickets for opening day. The area had been without professional baseball since the close of the 1968 season, when future Yankee great Thurman Munson led the Binghamton Triplets in hitting with a .301 average. Interestingly, Munson was the fourth pick in the 1968 baseball draft; the Mets took Tim Foli with the first pick that year and the Dodgers selected Bobby Valentine with the fifth overall pick—all three became prominent players in the history of baseball in New York City. The crowds were still coming out to Binghamton in force a full 10 years later, as shown in the below picture; 6, 953 fans packed the stands for a record-setting crowd on July 15, 2002. (Both, courtesy of B-Mets.)

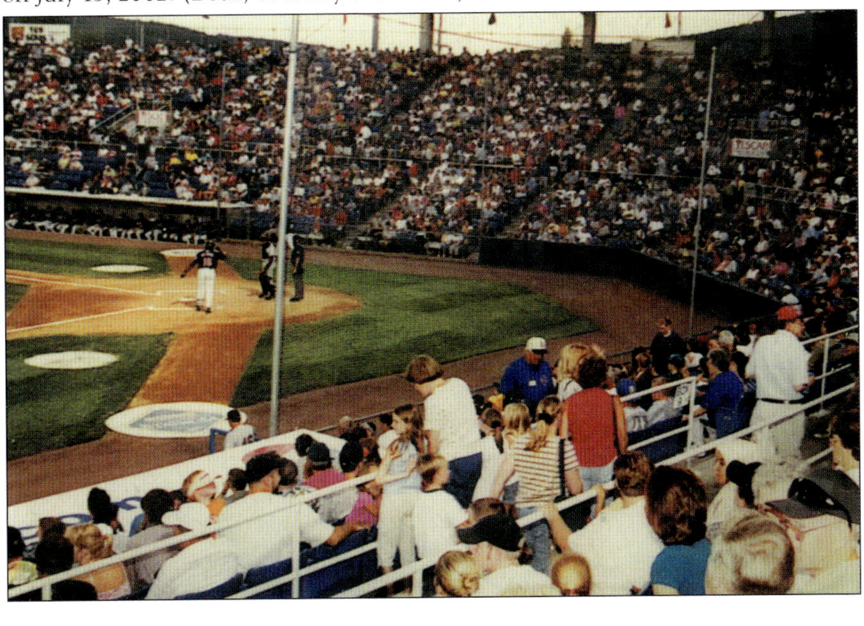

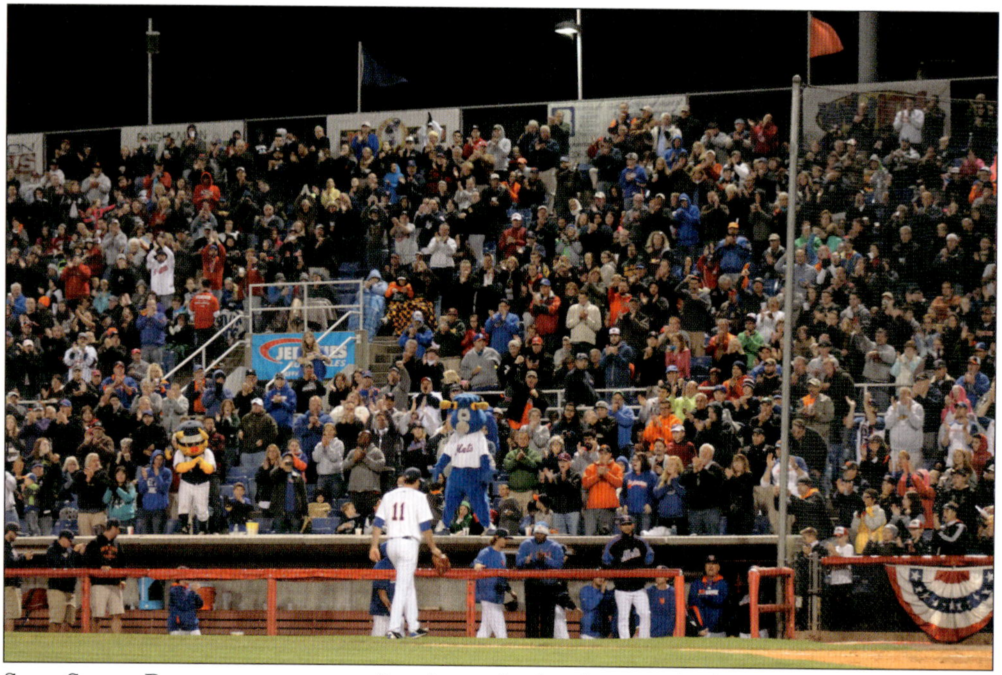

Same Scene, Binghamton or the Big Apple. In the photograph above, Binghamton's Steven Matz walks off the field to cheers of "Ste-ven Matz, Ste-ven Matz!" after carrying a no-hitter into the eighth inning, allowing only one run in 7.2 innings in the B-Mets' 2-1 win over the Richmond Flying Squirrels for the Eastern League Championship on September 12, 2014. In the photograph below, New York Mets pitcher Matz walks off the field to another standing ovation after holding the Kansas City Royals to one run into the sixth inning at Citi Field during the fourth game of the World Series on October 31, 2015.

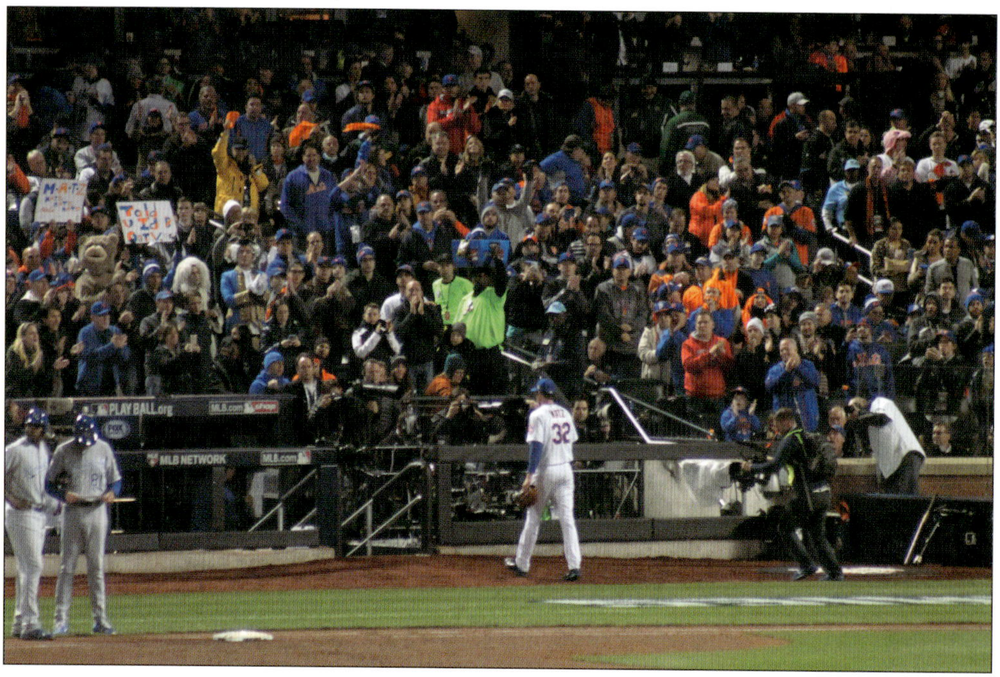

Class	Inductees	Class	Inductees
1993	1. George F. Johnson **2. "Wee Willie" Keeler** 3. Johnny Logan	**2004**	31. Johnny Blanchard 32. Ken Harrelson 33. Frank M. Verdi 34. Jerry Toman
1994	No one selected due to hosting of 1994 AA All-Star Game	**2005**	35. Rob Gardner 36. Bob Grim 37. Jake Pitler
1995	**4. Whitey Ford** 5. "Wild Bill" Hallahan 6. Tommy Holmes 7. Eddie Sawyer	**2006**	38. Bert Campaneris 39. **Vernon "Lefty" Gomez** 40. W.B. Kay **41. Bobby Jones**
1996	8. Ron Luciano 9. John McNamara 10. Steve Souchock	**2007**	**42. Brook Fordyce** 43. Charles Keller III **44. Cory Lidle** 45. George McQuinn
1997	11. Deron Johnson 12. Steve Kraly 13. Thurman Munson	**2008**	**46. Edgardo Alfonzo** 47. Gene Bearden 48. Daniel M. Casey 49. Joe Pepitone
1998	14. John H. Johnson 15. Lee Thomas 16. Bill Virdon 17. James E. Whitney	**2009**	50. Dale Long 51. Danny McDevitt **52. Quilvio Veras**
1999	18. Al Downing 19. Bud Fowler 20. Vic Raschi **21. Steve Swisher**	**2011**	53. Wally Burnette 54. John Fox 55. Harry G. "Judge" Lumley
2000	22. Spud Chandler 23. Eddie Farrell 24. Bobby Richardson 25. Bob Taylor	**2012**	56. Gene Monahan **57. Curtis Pride** 58. Bill "Moose" Skowron
2001	None due to selection of All Decade Team	**2013**	59. Willard Hirshberger 60. Tom Tresh 61. Pete Van Wieren
2002	26. Clete Boyer 27. Ralph Terry	**2014**	62. Ken Gilchrist
2003	28. Fred Norman 29. Pete Suder **30. John Montgomery Ward**	**2015**	63. **Pedro Lopez**

SHRINE ROLL CALL. In 1994, R.C. Reuteman, the first general manager for the Binghamton Mets, established the Binghamton Baseball Shrine, whose members are listed here. The four members who are also members of the National Baseball Hall of Fame are indicated in bold red. Those who played for the Binghamton Mets franchise are in bold orange. The inductees for 2016 were Heath Bell, Nelson Figueroa, and R.C. Reuteman, bringing the membership total to 66.

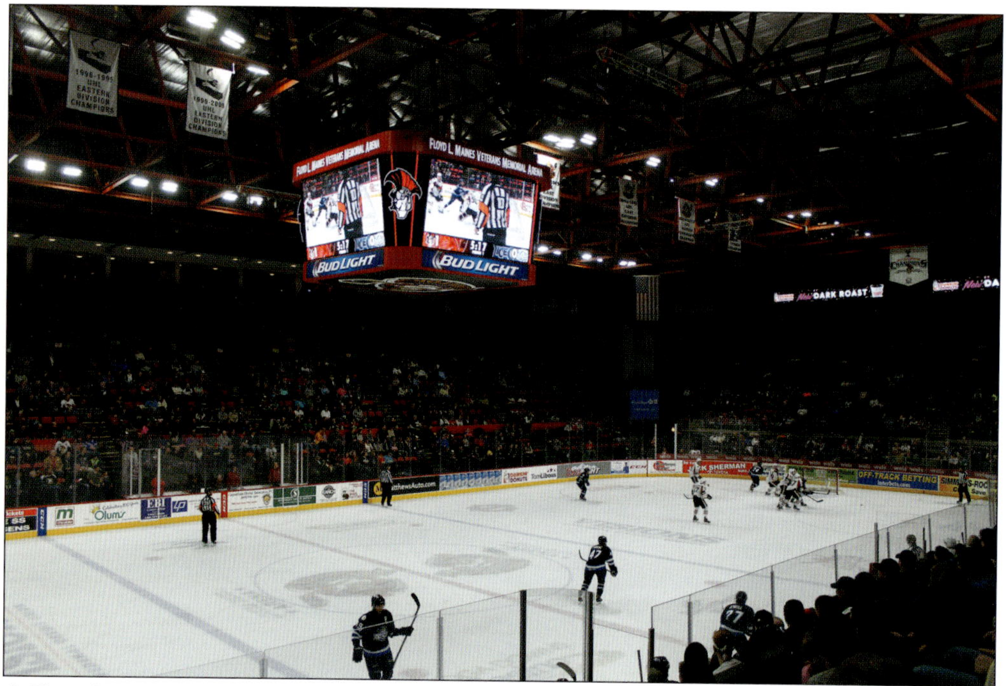

A Face-Lift for the Arena. The Broome Dusters of the North American Hockey League (NAHL) brought professional hockey to Binghamton for the 1973 season. The American Hockey League (AHL), one step below the National Hockey league (NHL), came to the area for the 1977 season in the form of the Binghamton Dusters. From 1997 to 2001, the arena hosted the B.C. Icemen of the Eastern Hockey League. The AHL returned to Binghamton with the Binghamton Senators in 2002, an affiliate of the Ottawa Senators. Below, Binghamton's Andrew Hammond blocks St. John's IceCaps Carl Klingbeck's slap shot in 2014. No. 5, Nick Tuzzolino provides a line of defense for Hammond. Area hockey is extensively covered in the 2005 Arcadia book *Hockey in Broome County*, by Marv Cohen and Michael J. McCann.

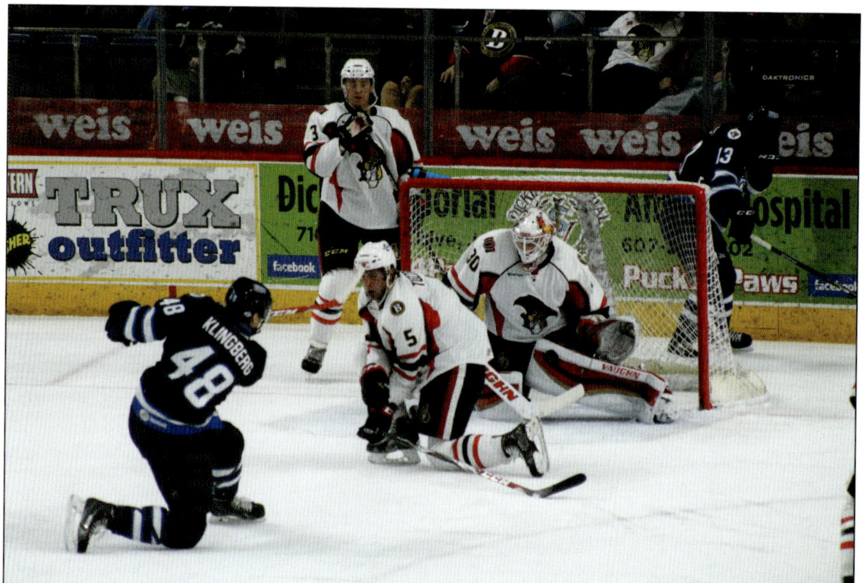

Class	Inductees	Class	Inductees
1998	Ken Holland, Randy MacGregor, Jim Matthews	2008	Doug McKay, Warren Harper
1999	Rod Bloomfield, Jacques Caron, Paul Stewart	2009	Mike Dunham, Glenn Merkosky
2000	Paul Crowley, Paul Fenton, Larry Pleau	2010	Daniel Lacroix, Tom Mitchell
2001	Craig Duncanson, Pierre Laganiere, Brad Shaw	2011	Chris Grenville, Corey Hirsh, John Paddock
2002	Chris Cichocki, Peter Sidorkiewicz, Ross Yates	2012	Mike Busniuk, Chris Ferraro, Peter Ferraro
2003	Roger Neel, Peter Fiorentino	2013	Bob Carr, Al Hill
2004	Peter Laviolette, Jon Smith, Bob Sullivan	2014	Denis Hamel
2005	Don Briggs, Dallas Gaume, Brad Jones	2015	Rob Zamuner, Scott Allegrino, Bob Mopert
2006	Ken Gernander, Dave Staffen	2016	Jean-Yves Roy, Richard Greiner, Justin Plamondon
2007	Gary Jaquith, Brian McReynolds		

HOCKEY TOWN, USA. Area support of hockey resulted in *Hockey News* giving the city the moniker of "Hockey Town, USA" in the early days of professional hockey in Binghamton. This table lists the 48 members of Binghamton's Hockey Hall of Fame. Among those with deep Greater Binghamton roots are Bob Carr, a local businessman who has been a part owner of the franchise since 1985; US Olympian Mike Dunham, who was born in neighboring Johnson City in 1972 and played in the NHL for 11 years before becoming a coach for the New York Islanders; Randy MacGregor, who played in Binghamton for both the Dusters and Whalers before settling in neighboring Vestal, where he coached youth hockey after his playing days were over; Jim Mathews, who was the owner and president of the Broome Dusters; and Roger Neel, a local radio broadcaster who was the longtime radio voice of the franchise.

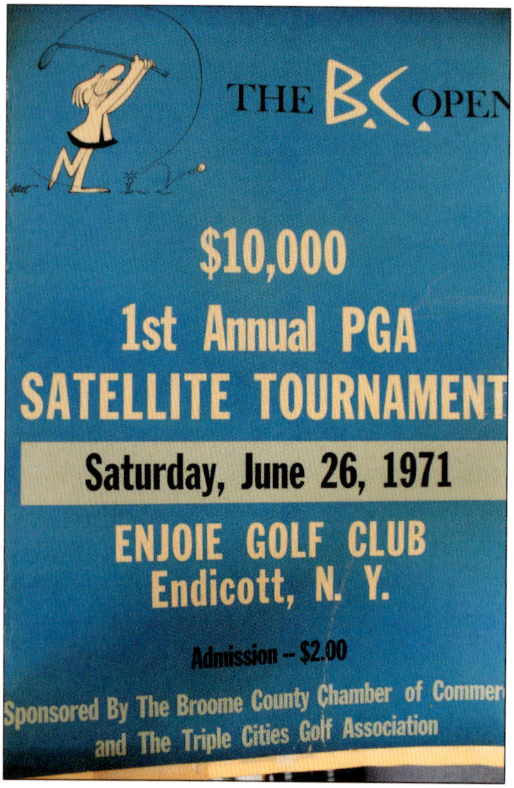

From the Rink to the Links. The "test run" for Endicott to sponsor a golf tournament was a single-round satellite tournament held in June 1971. At left is one of the original posters that advertised this event. In the below photograph, Lee Trevino (second from left) poses for a picture with Endicott cartoonist Johnny Hart and his family at an early B.C. Open. (Both, courtesy of Alex Alexander collection, BCHS.)

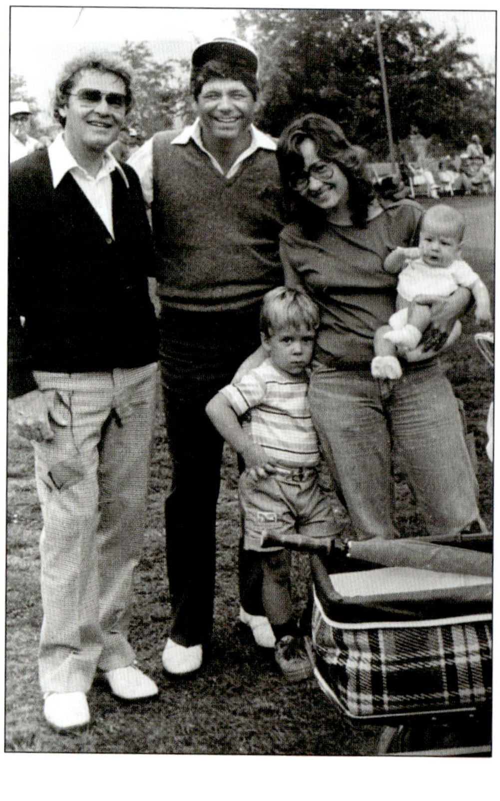

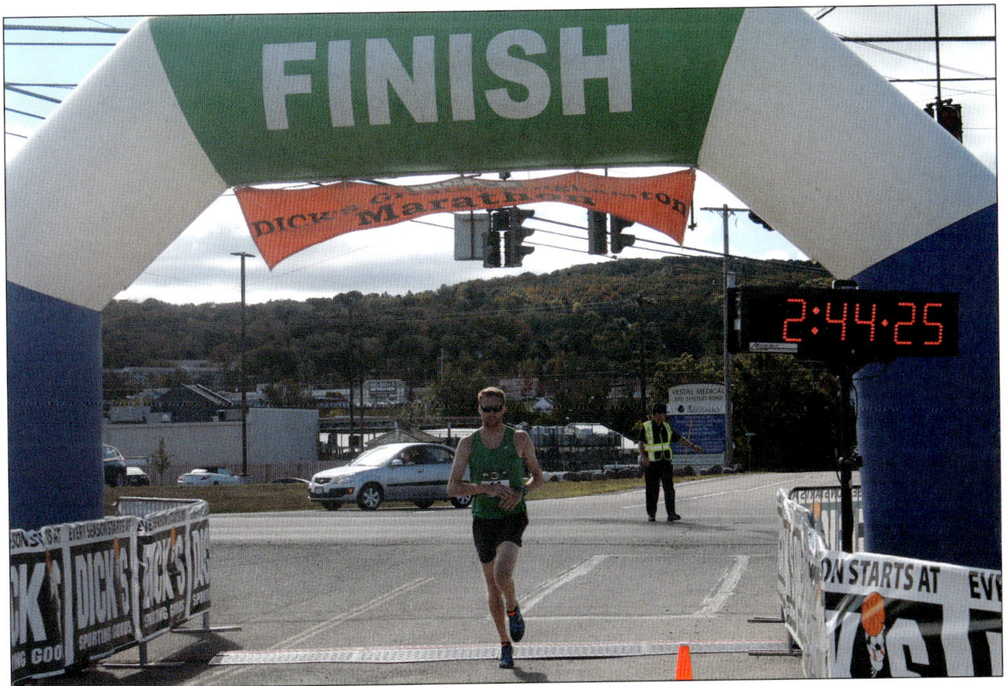

A Finish and a Start. Front and center in the above photograph is Binghamton's Jeffrey Martinez, who crosses the finish line on September 20, 2015, with an official time of 2:44:25. Martinez, 24, averaged 6 minutes and 17 seconds per mile to win the first-ever marathon in the Greater Binghamton area, the Dick's Sporting Goods Marathon. Martinez beat the runner-up, Jon Levesky, by 8 minutes and 56 seconds. The below photograph captures the start of the first-ever Herald of Victory Marathon, which had its starting line outside NYSEG Stadium on May 29, 2016. Mark Villwock, from Liverpool, New York, won the race in 3:22:50, in 85-degree weather. That is indeed a truck above the runner in the yellow cap; the DiRienzo Bakery and Deli, which has been in business for over 100 years, is in the background and uses a delivery truck mounted on a 20-foot-high utility pole as its Binghamton beacon.

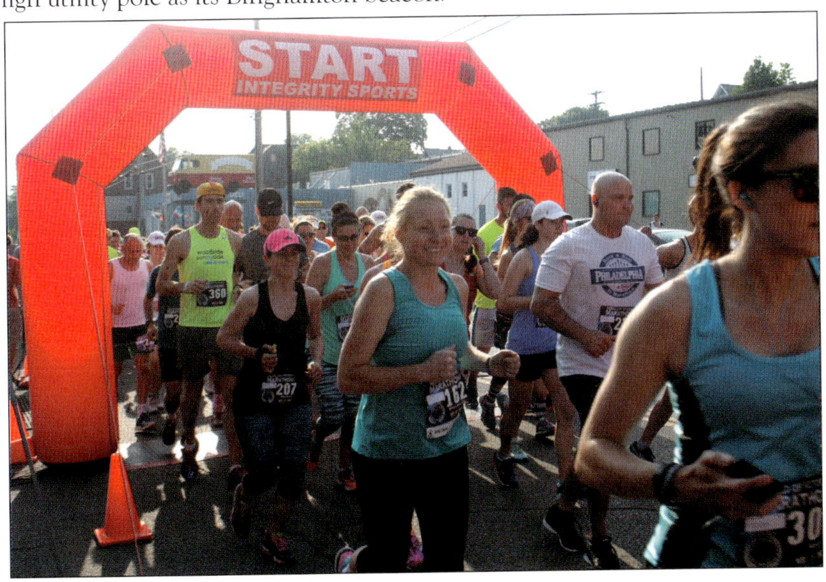

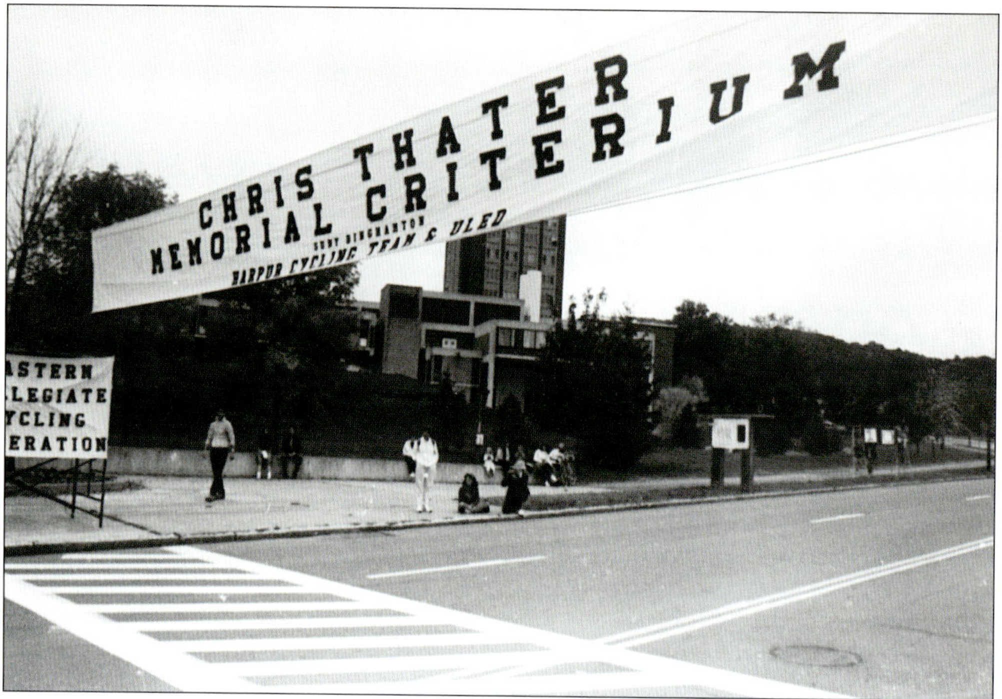

Still Going Strong. The above picture shows the inaugural Chris Thater cycling race, which was held on the Binghamton University campus in 1984. Shortly after its start, the races dropped "criterium" from the name. The races honor the memory of Chris Thater, who was killed by a drunk driver in Broome County in 1983. Thater was a bicycling enthusiast and a graduate of the university. His good friend and former roommate James May established the racing event as part of his duties as Broome County's Stop-DWI coordinator. Today, besides the cycling events, a five-kilometer road race is part of the action, as well as a CrossFit competition. Binghamton University hosted the event until 1987; from 1988 to 1990, downtown Binghamton held the event; from 1991 through 2013, Recreation Park was the venue; and the races returned to downtown Binghamton in 2013. Below, participants in the 5K race run in Recreation Park. (Both, courtesy of KVZ and CTR.)

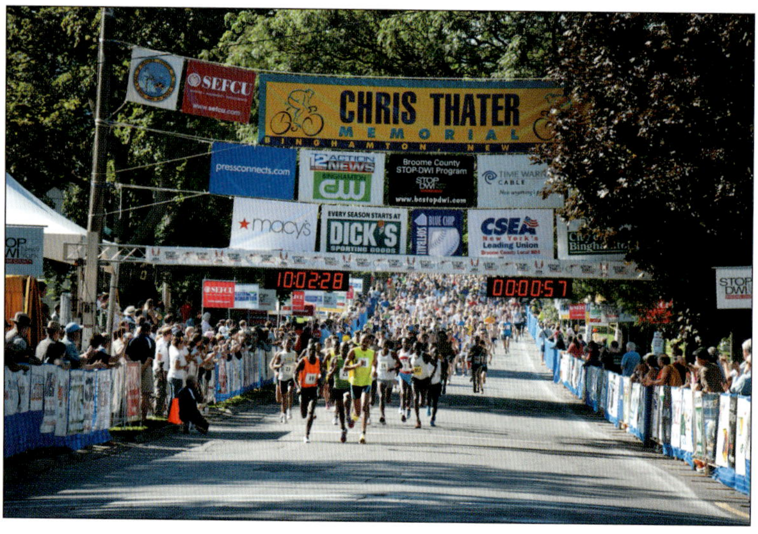

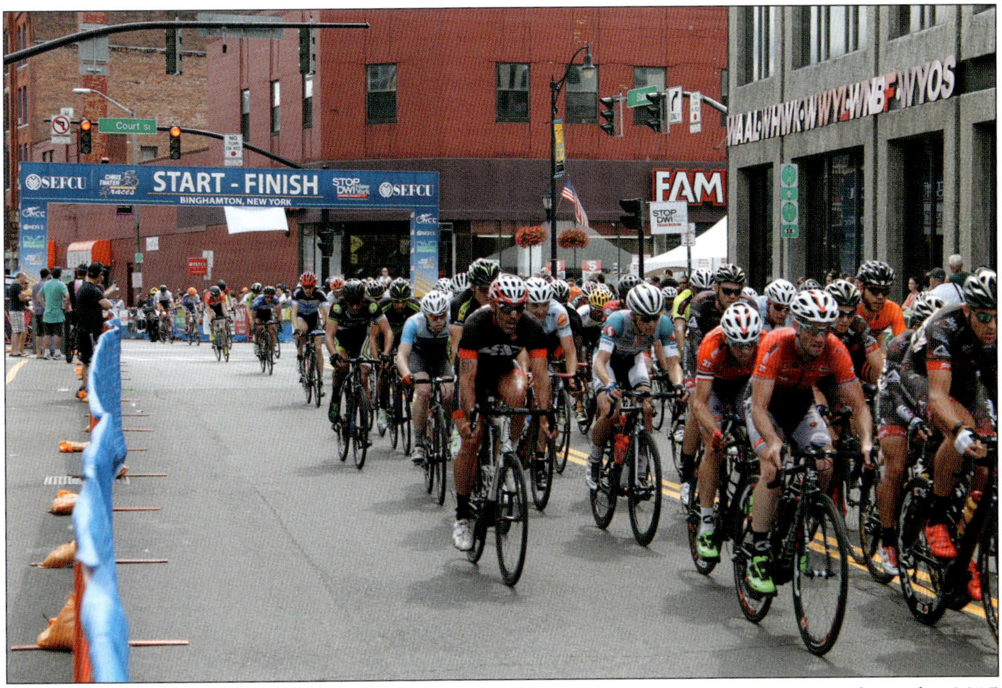

Day and Night, Cyclists Fill the Streets. The two pictures on this page are from the 2015 event. The competition covers two days, with over 20 events filling the calendar. Pro races for women and men are the highlight of both days of competition. Other events include junior cycling (both boys and girls, ages 9–15), master events for both men and women, and fun rides for those aged 6–9. The event relies on its sponsors, volunteers, and Broome County staff and has never charged admission.

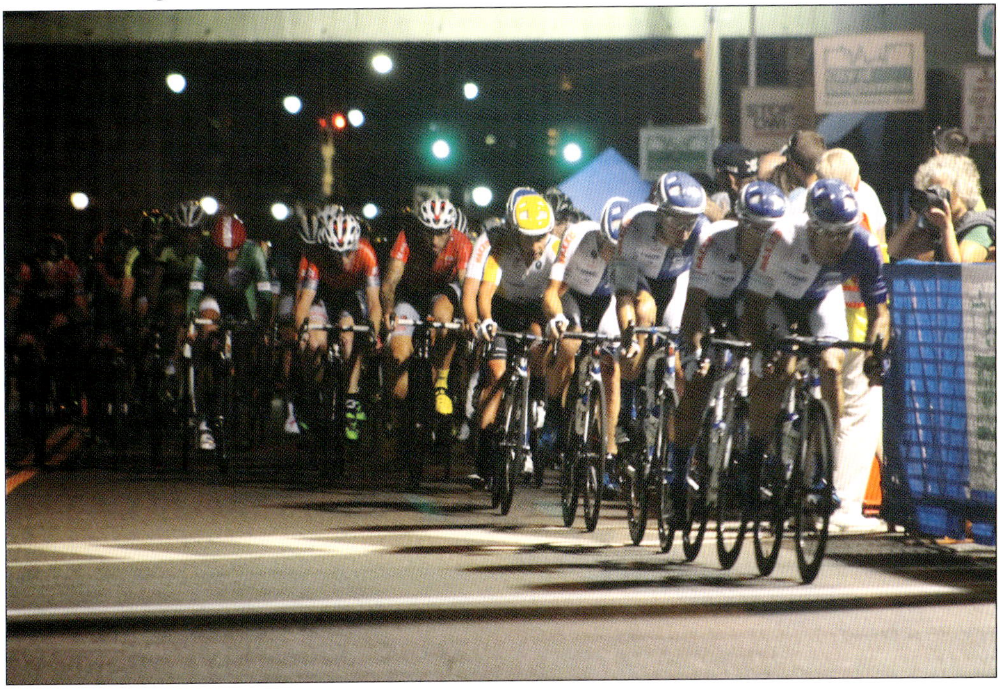

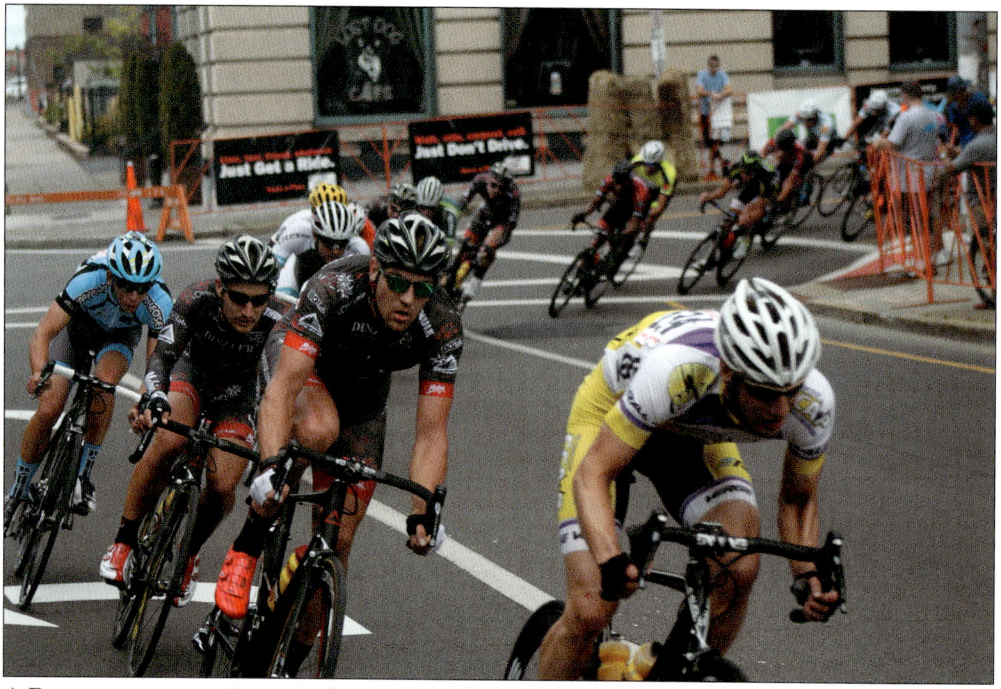

A Reflection and a Turn. In the photograph above, 2015 racers turn a curve in front of the Lost Dog Café, whose logo can be seen in the building's first window on the left. Note the reflection of the street in the sunglasses of the second-place rider. The café now resides in a building that was a noted cigar factory at the turn of the century. In the picture below, the cyclists turn onto State Street, in front of the restaurant Burger Mondays. Behind them, State Street is closed off, providing a viewing place for spectators. Lining State Street is the city's impressive collection of art galleries. The cyclist in the foreground is the nationally renowned cyclist Mark McCormack, whose three wins are the record for most wins in the professional men's division; his brother Frank won the event twice. (Below, courtesy of KVZ and CTR.)

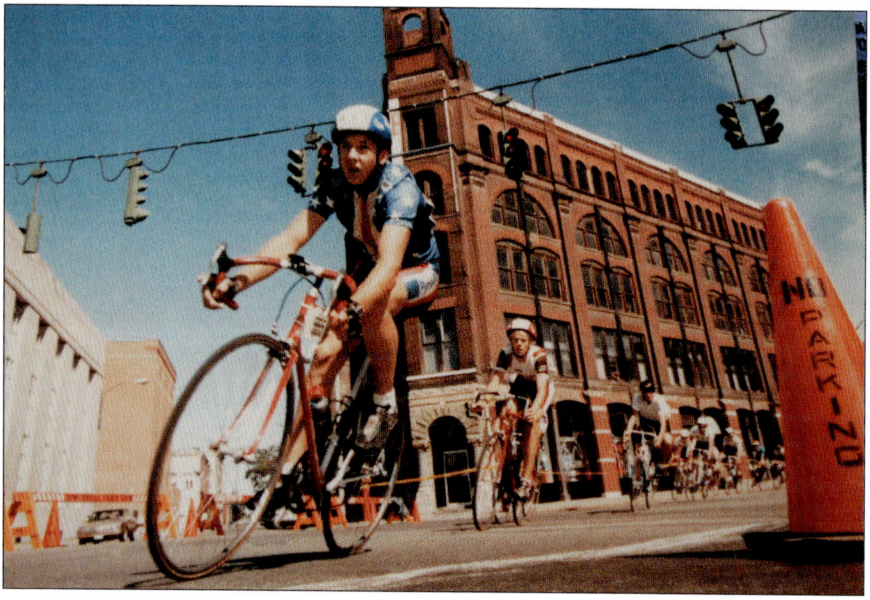

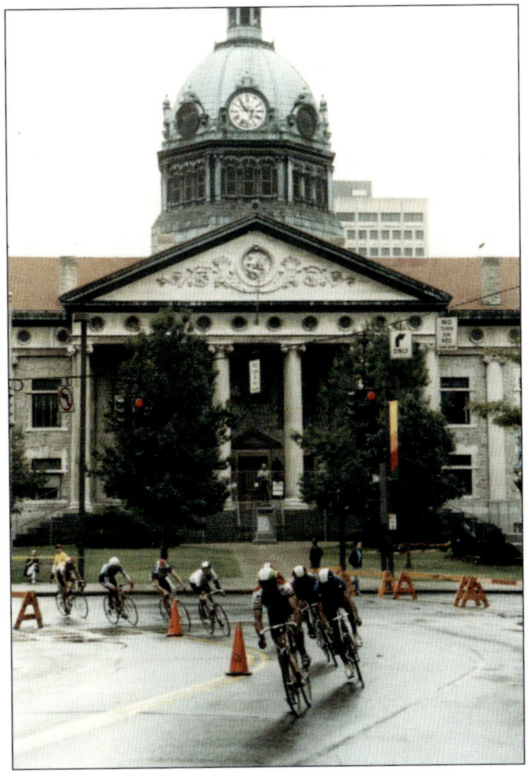

Where's the DeLorean? In the picture at right, Binghamton's courthouse serves as a backdrop as cyclists turn onto Chenango Street. At a quick glance, the courthouse and its clock tower are reminiscent of the one in Hill Valley, which is Marty McFly's hometown in *Back to the Future*, released in 1985. Through the years, Binghamton has periodically been home to cycling events besides the Chris Thater race. In the below photograph, cyclists compete along Binghamton's Exchange Street. (Both, courtesy of KVZ and CTR.)

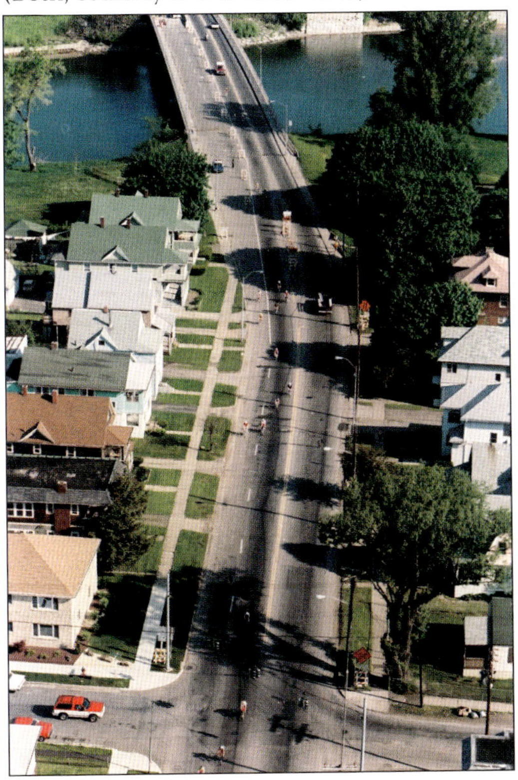

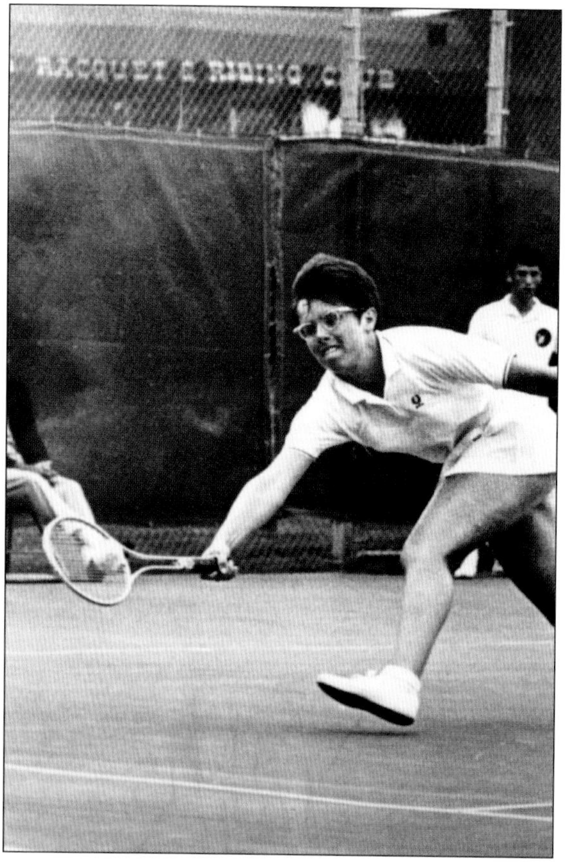

Racquet Royalty. The left photograph shows Billie Jean King in action in the Masters Tournament in 1968 at the Highland Racquet and Riding Club. The first of four consecutive Masters Tournaments was held in 1966 high atop a mountain on the south side of Binghamton. The tournaments were two-day events, with a fashion show serving as the intermission entertainment. Some of the greatest names in tennis competed during the four years of these tournaments, including Pancho Segura, Ken Rosewall, Malcolm "Mal" Anderson, Butch Buchholz, Rod Laver (considered the No. 1 player in the world at the time), and Andrés Gimeno. In 1968 and 1969, women joined the field of competitors. In the below photograph, Fred Stolle and Rod Laver (foreground) participate in a doubles match in 1968. (Both, courtesy of BTC.)

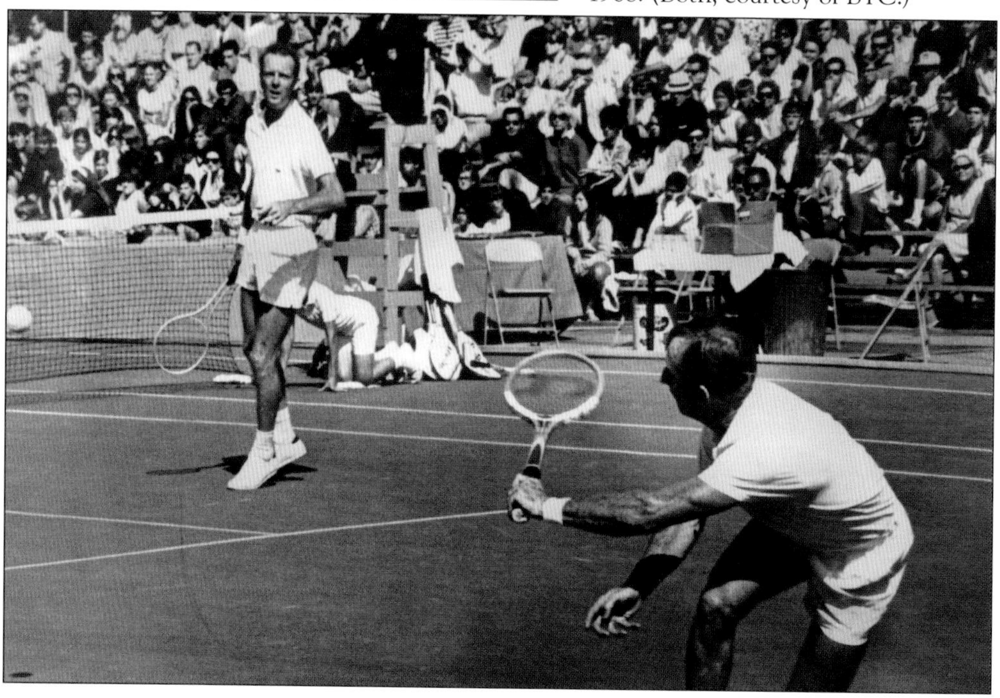

Paes and Matsuoka Pave the Way. In the photograph at right, India's Leander Paes displays his winning form in the 1994 inaugural challenger tour event in Binghamton. Paes is the only tennis player to have competed in six Olympic Games; he won a bronze medal in 1996. In the below image, Shuzoa Matsuoka, then 27, received the winner's check in the 1995 tournament. Matsuoka reached a world ranking of No. 46 in 1992 and reached the quarterfinals at Wimbledon in 1995, before losing to Pete Sampras. He was instrumental in professional tennis changing its rules so that players afflicted with cramps could receive medical attention during a match. At the 1995 US Open, Matsuoka's cramps caused him to default. Michael Starke, owner of the Binghamton Tennis Center and the first tournament director of the challenger event, holds the microphone and is pictured in the left of the photograph. (Both, courtesy of BTC.)

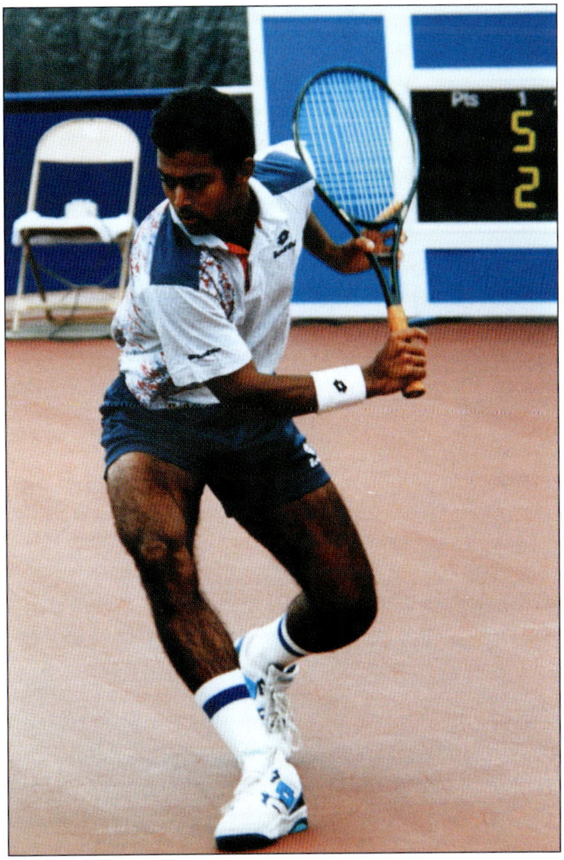

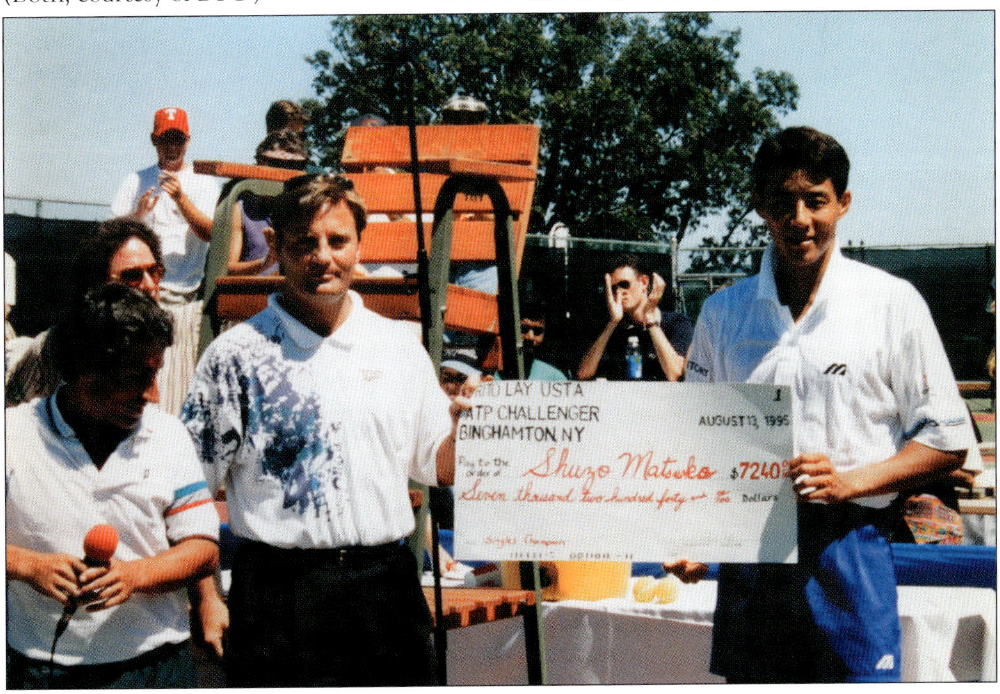

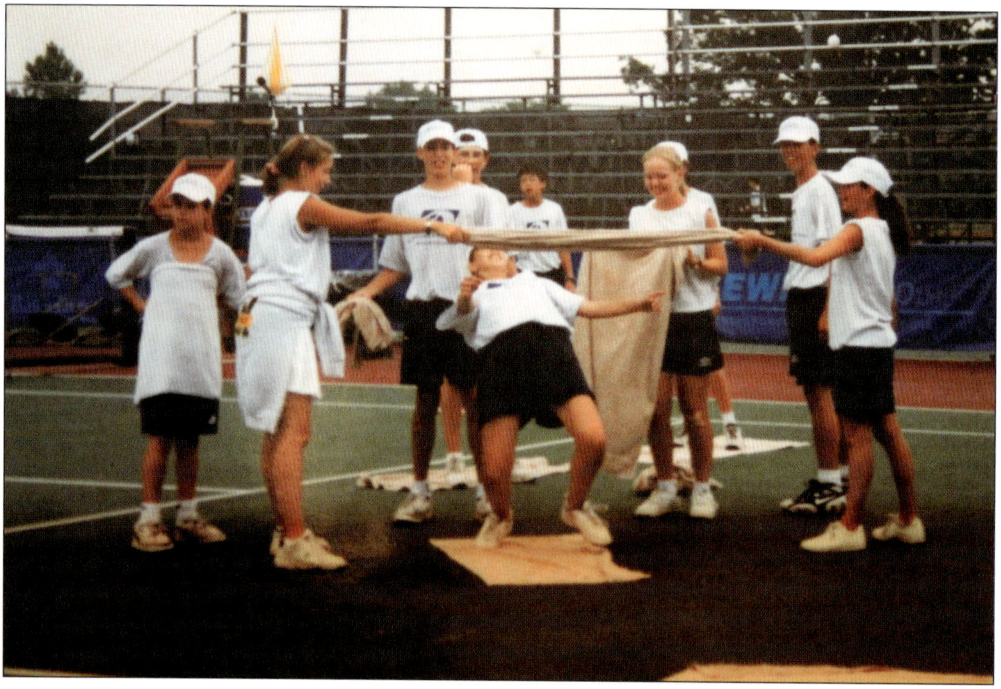

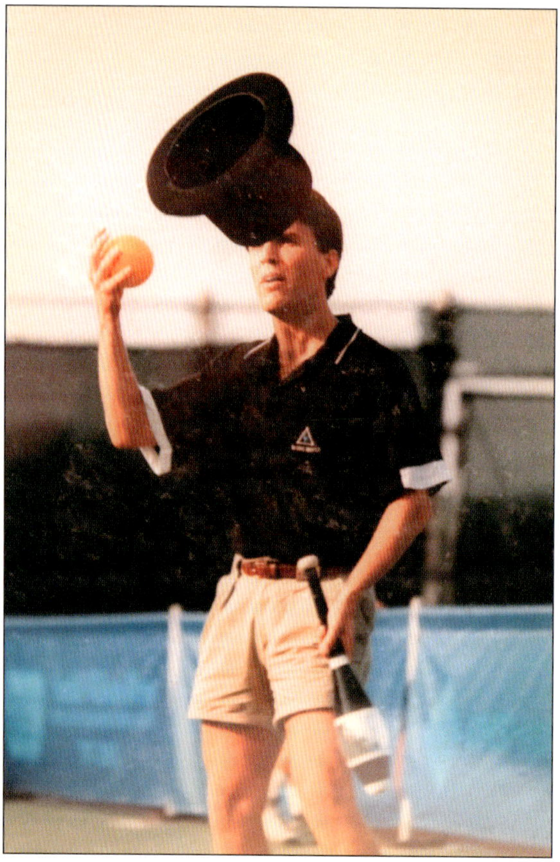

Action off the Court. The ball girls and boys are always the backbone of Binghamton's challenger tournament. Besides tracking down the tennis balls during a match, they all come out to help dry the court after a rain delay. In the above photograph, the ball girls take a break from drying the court to see how nimble they can be. At left, the camera catches juggler Will Stafford providing some between-matches entertainment in the early days of the tournament. The challenger circuit is an international one and typically includes purses of $50,000 and $100,000. Other US cities to host the circuit besides Binghamton include Dallas, Texas; Lahaina, Hawaii; and Tallahassee, Florida. (Both, courtesy of BTC.)

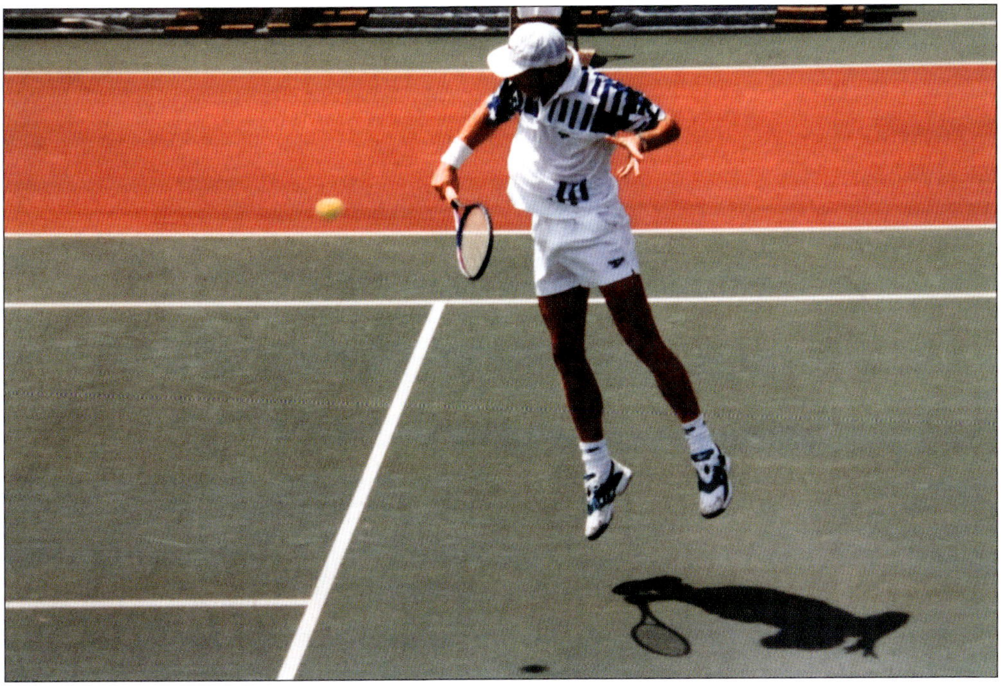

Me and My Shadow. Mark Petchey of Great Britain appears to be dancing with his shadow in the above picture, taken during competition in 1995. Petchey was Andy Murray's coach when Murray first turned professional. In April 2006, they amicably parted ways, with Petchey proving he knew how to recognize talent: "I am very proud of what we have achieved together—getting Andy into the top 50 and winning his first ATP title at the age of 18. I have no doubt that Andy will make the top 10 and be a Grand Slam winner in the future and wish him every success." In the photograph below, the United States' Derrick Rostagno looks like he might also be dancing with his shadow as he returns a shot in 1995. Rostagno was ranked No. 13 in the world in 1991 and finished his career with a winning record against John McEnroe (three matches to two) and Pete Sampras (one match to zero). Rostagno retired from the circuit in 1996 and is now a practicing attorney in Los Angeles. (Both, courtesy of BTC.)

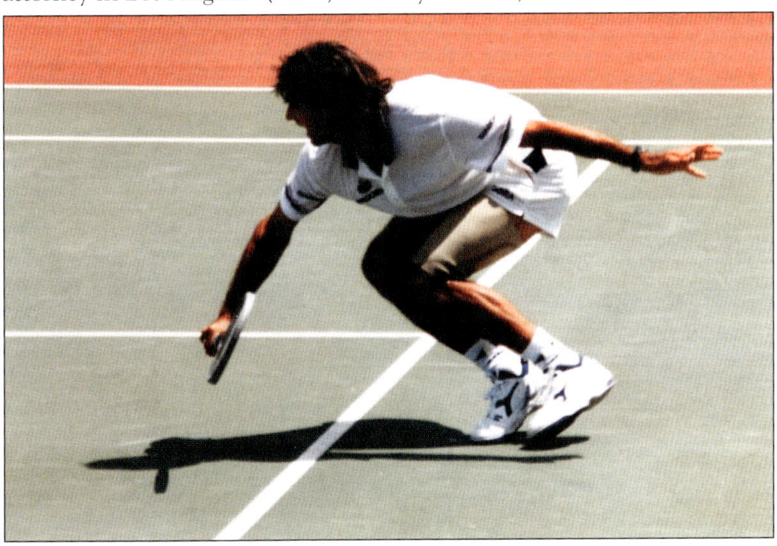

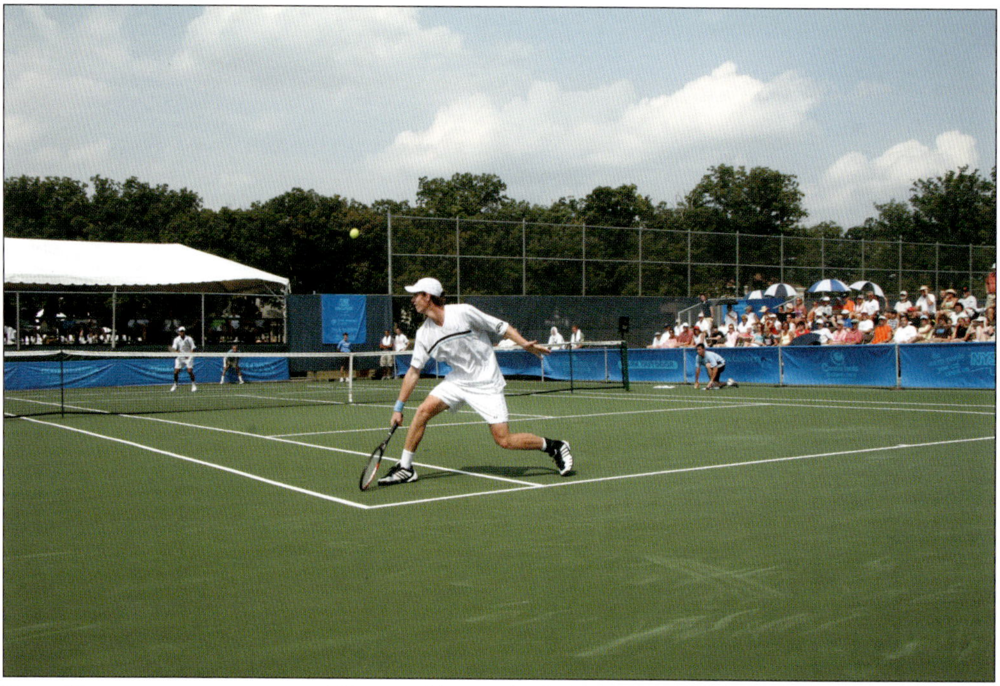

First Binghamton, then the World. Above, Andy Murray returns a backhand on his way to winning the tournament in 2005. He has gone on to crack the top ten of ranked tennis players, being ranked as high as No. 2. Binghamton's United States Tennis Association (USTA)–sponsored event draws top tennis players from all over the world. In 2010, rain moved the finals of tournament indoors to the Binghamton Tennis Center. Kei Nishikori, below, returns a backhand in the finals. Nishikori has cracked the top ten of world tennis players as well, reaching the finals of the US Open in 2014 and achieving a world ranking of No. 4 in 2016. (Both, courtesy of SJA and BTC.)

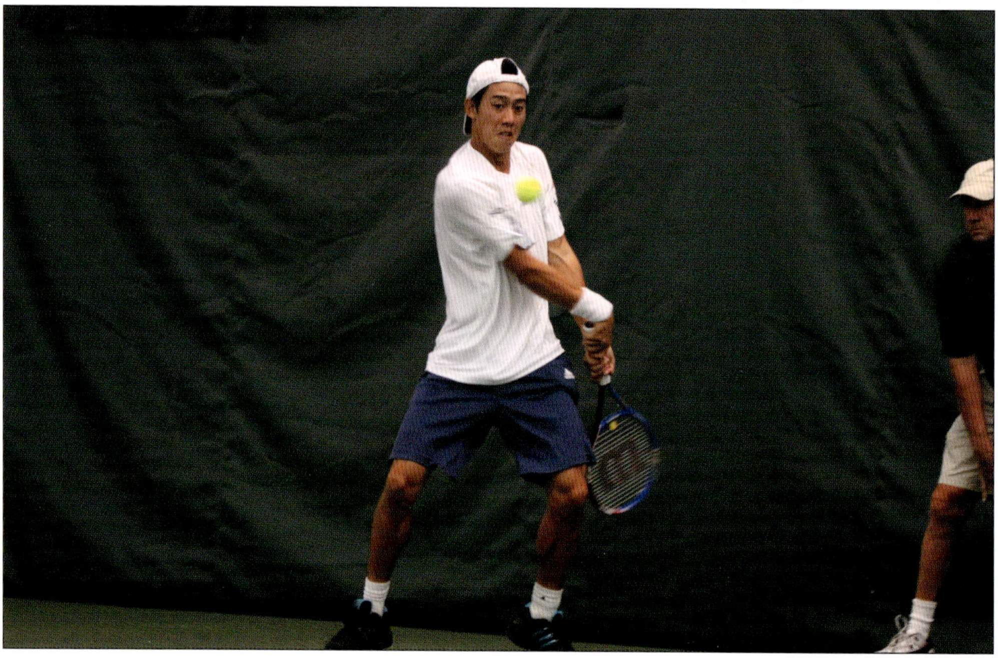

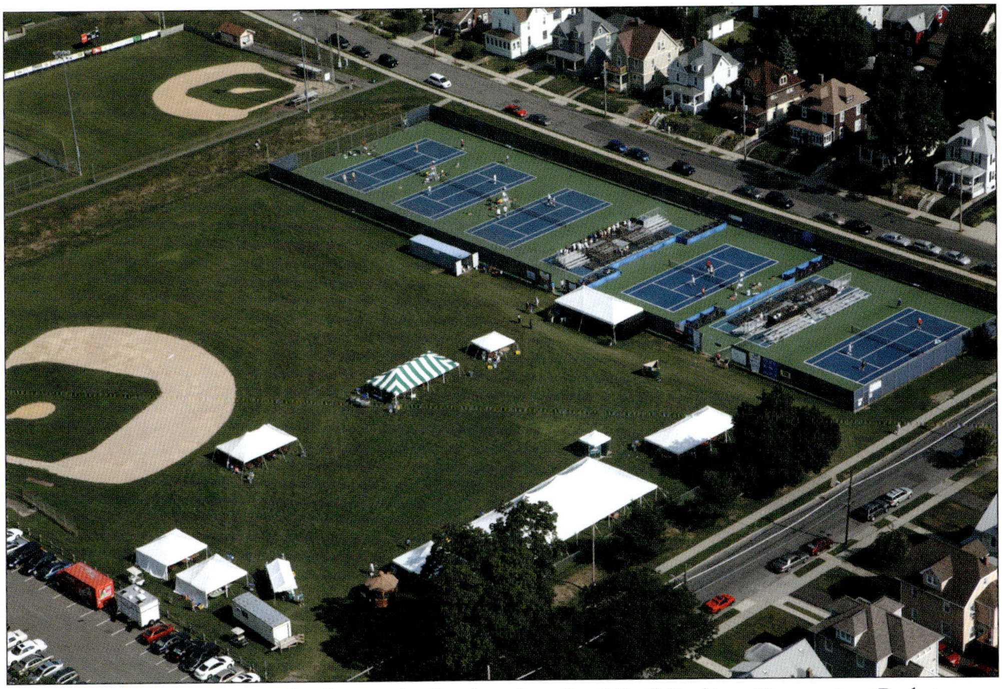

Tennis in the Park. Besides being the boyhood park of Rod Serling, Recreation Park is now home to Binghamton's annual professional tennis tournament, the Levene Gouldin & Thompson Challenger. This aerial shot shows the southeast corner of the park, where the tennis courts are housed. This picture was taken during the qualifying round of the tournament in 2005. The baseball field in the upper-left corner of the photograph is the Little League field named after Binghamton's "Wild Bill" Hallahan, who was a baseball star for the Cardinals in the 1920s and 1930s. Center court for the tournament is the third tennis court from the right. The tents provide vendor spaces, as well as rest areas for officials and staff. The photograph below shows a view from the stands. (Both, courtesy of SJA and BTC.)

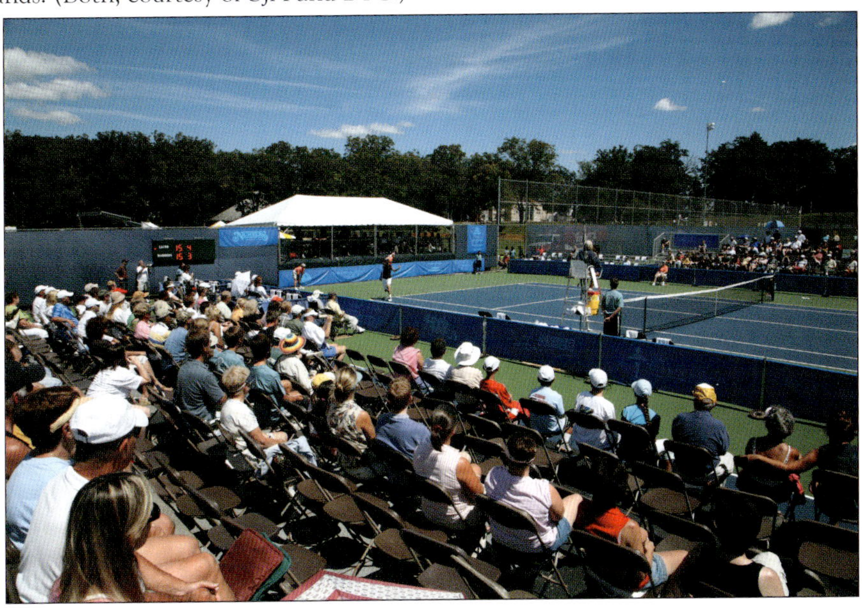

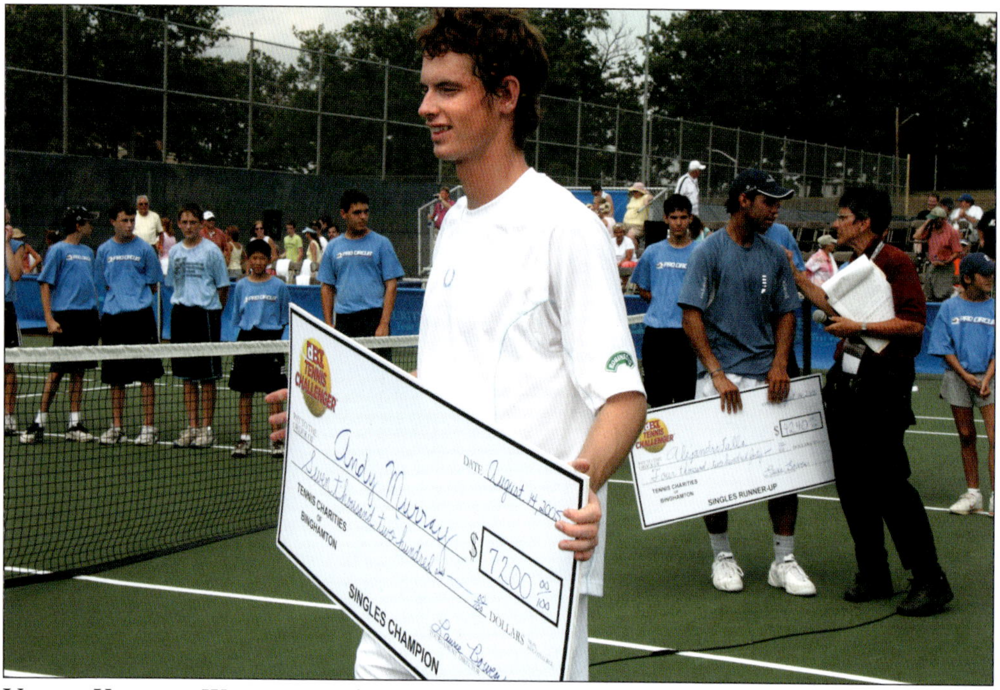

United Kingdom Winners. In the above photograph, Andy Murray returns to the sidelines after receiving his winner's check in 2005. In the background, tournament chairperson Laurie Bowen chats with the runner-up, Colombia's Alejandro Falla. (A look at the check reveals that the winner's purse has actually gone down $40 since 1994.) In the below photograph, Kyle Edmund (left) accepts his winner's share after defeating Bjorn Fratangelo in the 2015 finals. At the end of 2015, Edmund was the No. 3-ranked player in the United Kingdom. Fratangelo was named after tennis great Bjorn Borg and is the only American besides John McEnroe and Tommy Paul to win the boys' tennis title at the French Open; Fratangelo did so in 2011. (Both, courtesy of SJA and BTC.)

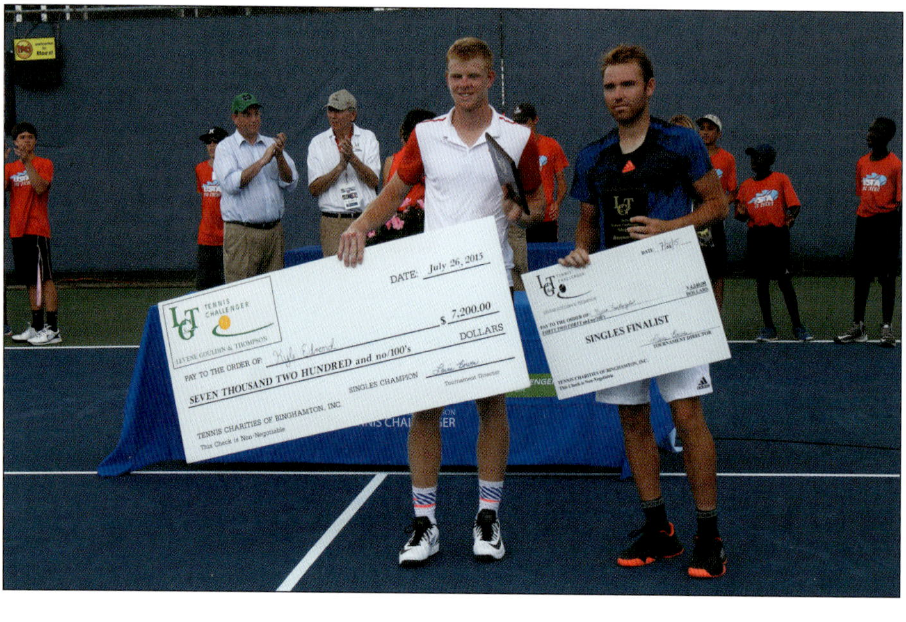

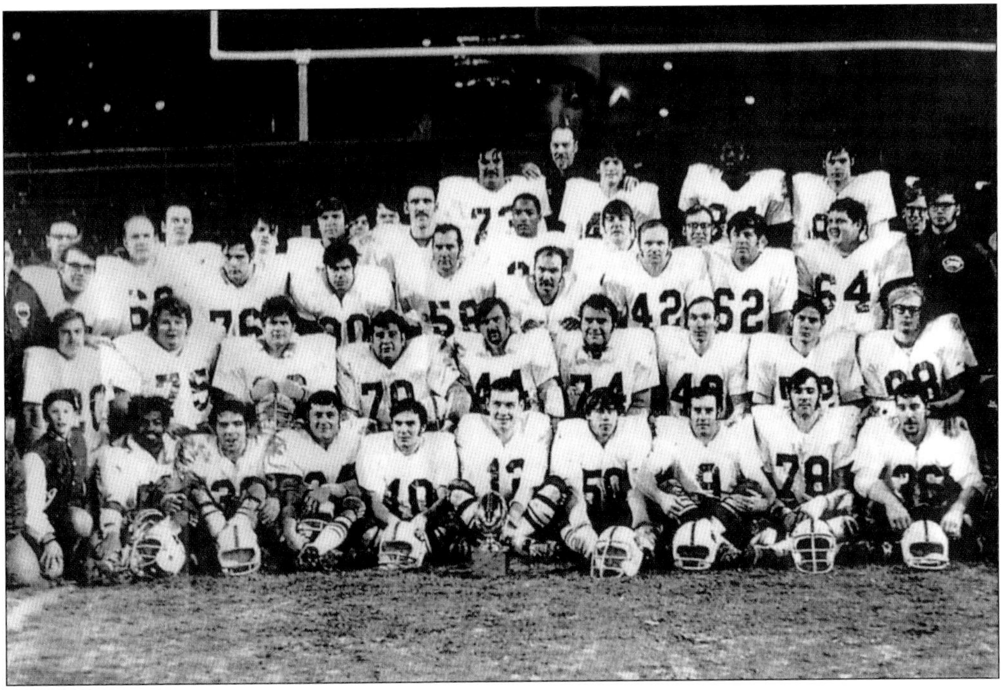

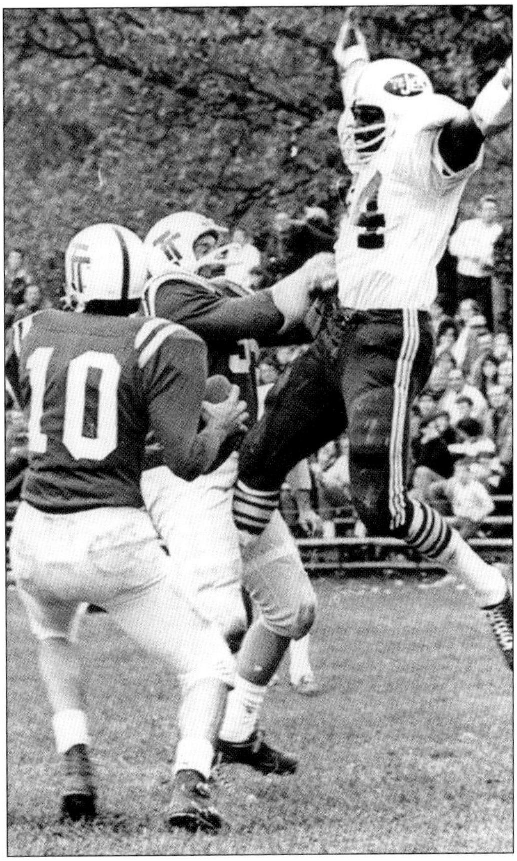

Football in Greater Binghamton. The above photograph captures the undefeated 1972 champions of the Empire Football League—the Triple Cities (TC) Jets. As good as that 1972 team was, the undefeated 1970 team was even better, as it outscored its opponents 692-21. Ray Stanton was the quarterback and franchise founder. In 2015, he told WBNG TV, "In 1970 I went to a league meeting in Oneonta and discovered they needed another franchise. I came back to Binghamton and started the TC Jets." The TC Jets played in Binghamton throughout the 1970s and early 1980s. In the late 1990s, after the team had disbanded for a number of years, Stanton revived the team as the Binghamton Jets and his son was the quarterback. The photograph at right shows defensive lineman Dave Burch (No. 84) harassing a quarterback during the heyday of the Jets in the 1970s. Burch hailed from Richmond, Virginia, and the engineer came to the area to work for IBM. Burch is currently the commissioner of the Empire Football League and president of the American Football Association, an organization devoted to minor-league semipro football. (Both, courtesy of DB.)

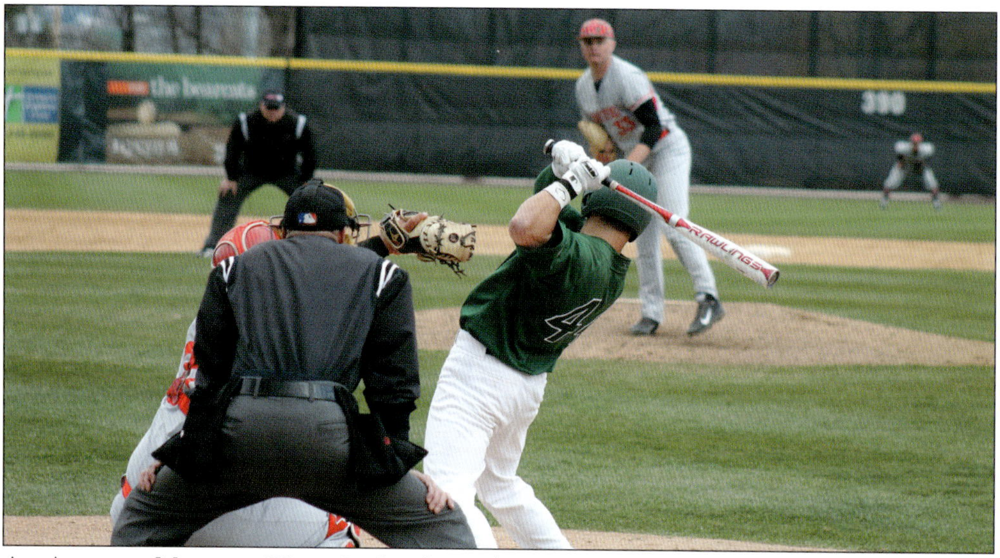

An Amateur Mecca as Well. In the above photograph, Binghamton outfielder Jake Thomas reacts to a high hard one from University of Hartford pitcher Sean Newcomb, who was drafted by the California Angels with the 15th overall pick in the 2014 baseball draft. Thomas was drafted in the 27th round by the Toronto Blue Jays in the 2015 draft. Binghamton University joined the America East Conference in 2001 and competes at the Division 1 level. The below photograph shows the 2016 Maine-Endwell Little League team, which defeated South Korea 2-1 to capture the 2016 Little League World Series on August 28. Maine-Endwell, from the town eight miles west of Binghamton, became the first New York team since 1964 to win the title. The 11-player squad went an incredible 24-0 during the summer and won its five games at Williamsport by scores of 7-2, 3-1, 13-10, 4-2, and 2-1. Besides winning the championship on the field, the team also won the Jack Losch Sportsmanship Award. The 11 members of the team are pictured here, along with the three coaches. They are, from left to right, (front row) Brody Raleigh, Jude Abbadessa, Michael Mancini, Justin Ryan, Conner Rush, and Jordan Owens; (back row) manager Scott Rush, Jack Hopko, Ryan Harlost, Jayden Fanara, James Fellows, coach Joe Hopko, Billy Dundon, and coach Joe Mancini.

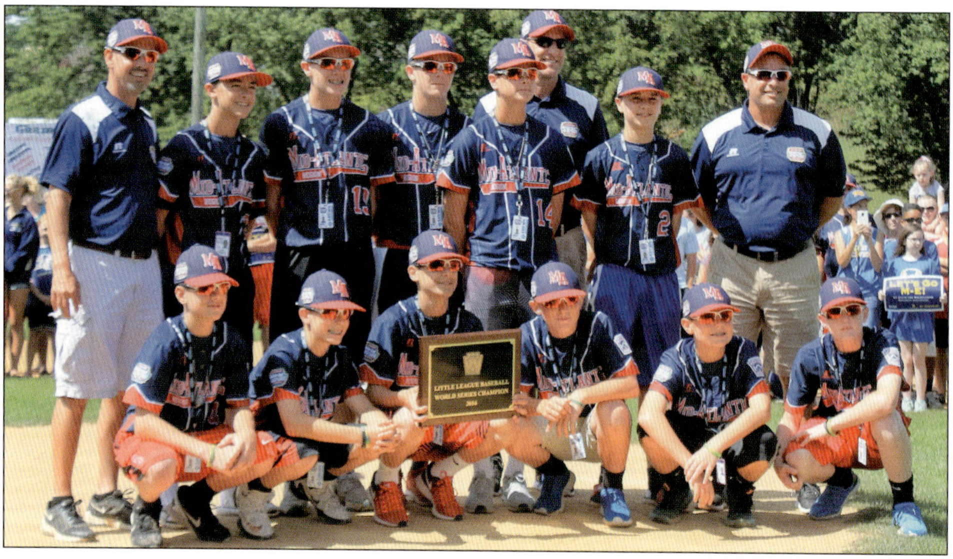

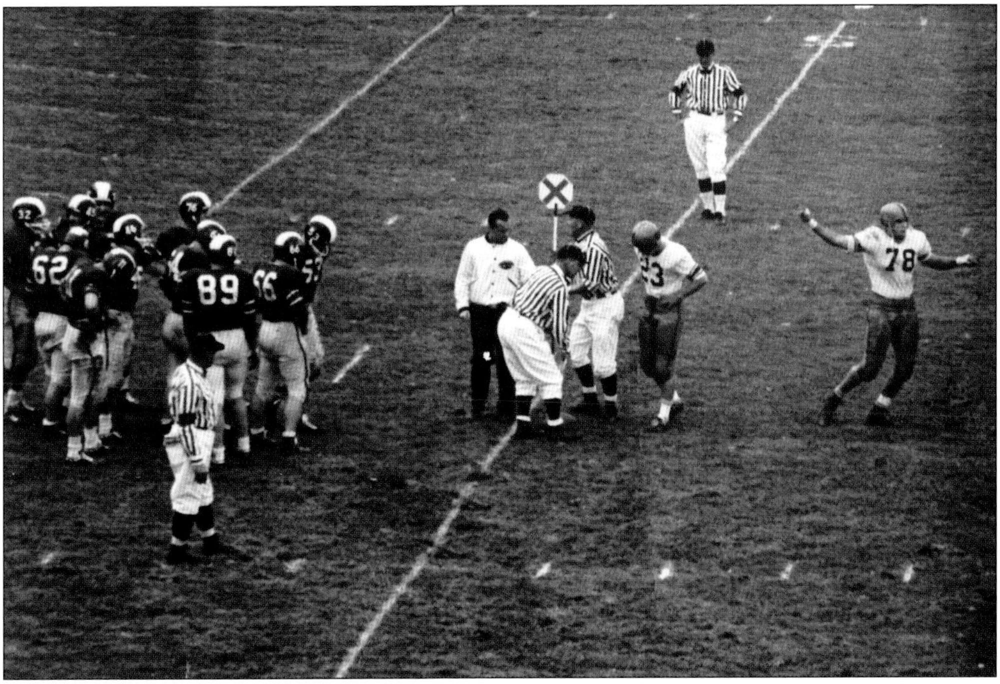

Hometown Heroes. Above, Endicott's Ron Luciano (No. 78), celebrates an apparent first down for Union-Endicott High School around 1955. Luciano went on to star at Syracuse, where he was a teammate of Ernie Davis on the national championship team of 1959. Luciano briefly played professional football before becoming a major-league umpire, baseball broadcaster, and best-selling author. The 2001 Union-Endicott High School baseball team is shown in the below picture. Major-league All-Star reliever Jim Johnson is on the extreme left in the second row; he led the team to the New York Class A championship that year. (Both, courtesy of EVC.)

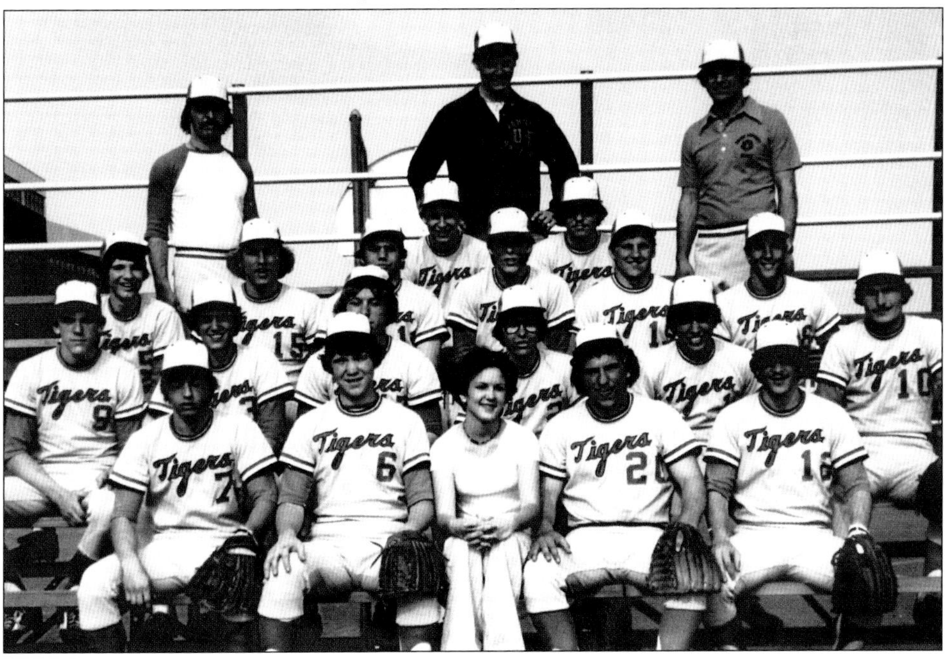

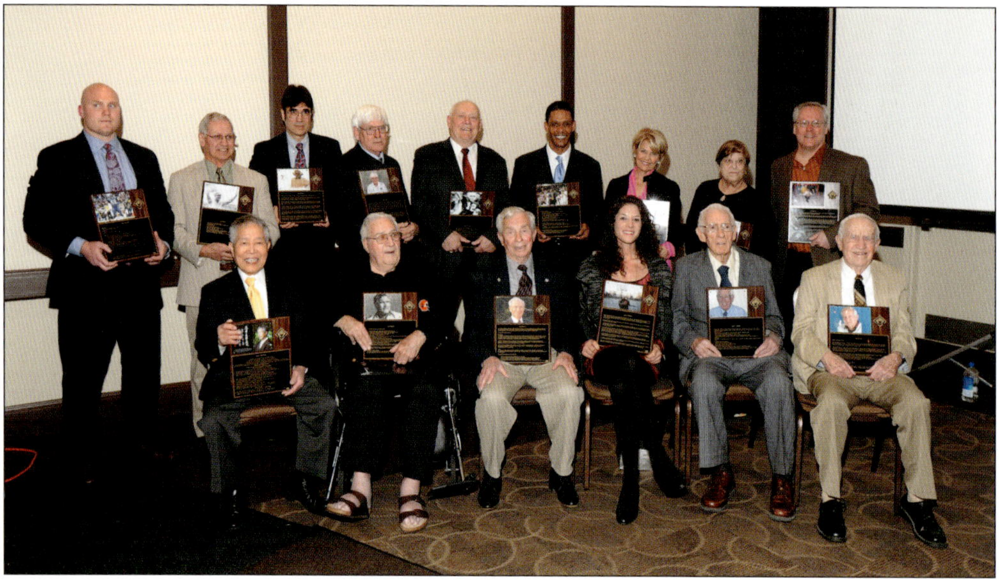

Inaugural Class and Inaugural Speaker. The above picture shows 15 of the 16 members/representatives of the inaugural class of the Greater Binghamton Sports Hall of Fame, which was established in 2015. Pictured from left to right are (first row) Master Hidy Ochiai, Fran Angeline, Jack Halloran, Bess Greenberg, Carl Gaffney, and John Fox; (second row) Isaiah Kacyvenski, Jim Hoover (representing his deceased dad, Dick Hoover), Lou Alexander (representing his deceased dad, Alex Alexander), Bob Campbell, Ray Stanton, King Rice, Sally Baldwin Thomas (for her deceased dad, Dick Baldwin), Dee Jester (for Ron Luciano, her deceased brother), and Jim Mathews Jr. (for his deceased dad, Jim Matthews Sr.). (Note: The deceased Johnny Logan was not represented at the induction.) In the below photograph, Chris Snee, the former All-Pro right guard for the New York Giants, addresses the crowd of 350 as the featured speaker. Note the two Super Bowl rings that Snee wears—one from 2008 and one from 2012. (Both, courtesy of GBSHOF and Tom Ryder.)

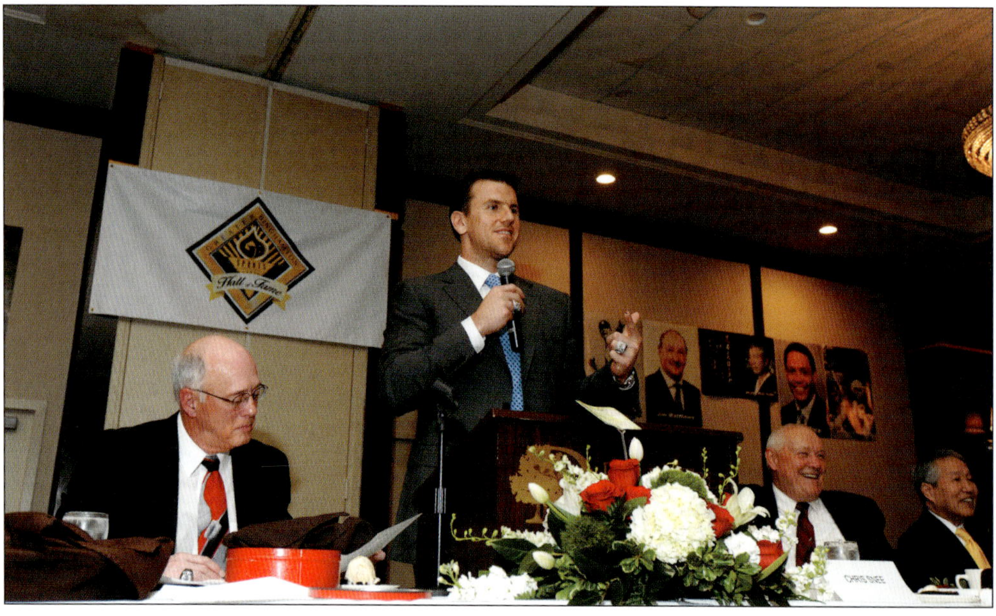

Inductee	Description	Inductee	Description
Alexander, Alex	Community sportsman	**Kraly, Steve**	MLB pitcher; 1953 World Series Champion
Angeline, Fran	High school coach	**Lee, Jim**	College basketball player
Baldwin, Dick	College basketball coach	**Lee, Mike**	College basketball player
Barvinchak, Dick	College football player	**Logan, Johnny**	MLB player
Campbell, Bob	NFL player	**Luciano, Ron**	ML umpire, college football player
Dunham, Mike	NHL goaltender	**Matthews, Jim**	Hockey sports owner
Fox, John	Local sportswriter	**Nickerson, Troy**	College wrestler
Gabor, Billy	Pro basketball player	**Ochiai, Master Hidy**	Martial arts instructor
Gaffney, Carl	Community sports official	**Rice, King**	College basketball player/coach
Greenberg, Bess	College basketball player	**Rolles, Chuck**	College basketball player
Hallahan, Bill	MLB pitcher, WS Champ	**Sharkey, Jack**	Heavyweight boxing champion, 1932
Halloran, Jack	High school coach	**Snee, Chris**	NFL player, Two-time SB Winner
Hoover, Dick	High school coach	**Stanton, Raymond**	Semi-pro football player
Kacyvenski, Isaiah	NFL player	**Sullivan, Shirley**	Amateur golfer

ROLL CALL. The 28 members of the Hall of Fame include three former NFL players (Bob Campbell, Isaiah Kacyvenski, and Chris Snee); two World Series winners (Steve Kraly with the 1953 Yankees and Johnny Logan with the 1957 Milwaukee Braves); and one former umpire and best-selling author (Ron Luciano). Jim and Mike Lee starred for Syracuse shortly before the Carrier Dome was built; King Rice was the point guard for North Carolina during a Final Four appearance in 1991 and was cocaptain along with Rick Fox and Pete Chilcutt, both of whom went on to play in the NBA for a number of years.